the power of retail

BRANDING

Innovative Marketing Strategies for Achieving BrandPower

the power of retail
BRANDING

Innovative Marketing Strategies for Achieving BrandPower

Arthur A. Winters, Peggy Fincher Winters, Carole Paul and the editors of RETAIL AD WORLD

VISUAL REFERENCE PUBLICATIONS, INC., New York, NY

Visual Reference Publications, Inc.
302 Fifth Avenue
New York, NY 10001

Distributors to the trade in the United States and Canada
Watson-Guptill
770 Broadway
New York, NY 10003

Distributors outside the United States and Canada
HarperCollins International
10 E. 53rd Street
New York, NY 10022

Library of Congress Cataloging in Publication Data:
The Power of Retail Branding

Printed in China
ISBN 1-58471-078-0

Book Design: Judy Shepard

TABLE OF CONTENTS

How to use The Power of Retail Branding
The BrandPower Creative Brief 6

Foreward
Retailers as Reinventors of Brand Power 8

A BrandPower Glossary   **174**

Internal Branding   10

DKNY
Signs of Spring 12

Family Britches
Building Relationships 16

Bloomingdale's
Happily Ever After:
The Bloomingdale's Home Planner 20

Mednikow
The Power of Beautiful Branding 26

King of Prussia
Targeting Multiple Markets 30

Macy's East
Star Treatment 38

Aveda
It's a Small World After All 43

Role Branding   46

Crate & Barrel
Reality Check 48

Oakwood Mall
Group Therapy 50

Bootlegger
Going for Edge 54

Saks Fifth Avenue
Lightening Up 58

H. Stern
Gorgeous, Golden and Glowing 62

Pippers America
Thinking Small 65

Fitness Branding   70

Bellevue Square
How to 'Be' 72

Pret a Manger
Fresh Thinking 78

Dufferin Mall
Standing Out Again 84

Mervyn's
In a Perfect World 90

Co-Branding   94

H & M
Art Appreciation 96

Holt Renfrew
A Star is Born 98

Lord & Taylor
Two American Icons Team Up for a
Classic Salute to Dad 100

La Maison Ogilvy
Tradition with a Twist 102

The Gardens of the Palm Beaches
Outclassing the Competition 105

Channel Branding   110

Bebe
Online. On the Money 112

Famous Footwear
Locker Stocker 116

Caché
Out There 119

Ikea
Who are You Calling Crazy? 124

Lloyd Center
More Than Stores 128

Clone Branding   132

Pacsun
That Southern California Thing 134

Joseph Abboud
Visible Changes 137

Timberland
Timberland's Urban Journey 140

Community Home Supply
A Chicago Institution Strengthens its Brand 142

A. Testoni
A New Day 146

Break Through Branding   148

A&P Canada
Fresh Obsessed 150

Nordstrom
Taxi! 156

I.N.C. International Concepts
Inspired Branding 158

The Mall at Millenia
New Center. New Brand 161

Water & Fire
European Style, American Savvy 168

The Power of Retail Branding

The **BrandPower Creative Brief** and the **Brandwidth II Model** are designed to stimulate your analysis of each case.

The **BrandPower Creative Brief** can serve as a checklist of questions to examine how the market situation in each case is described, and how the creative strategies are executed to attain the results indicated in the BrandPower objectives.

The **Brandwidth II Model** identifies the elements of BrandPower and the factors that integrate relationships between them—brand image/shopper image; shopper image/brand channel; brand channel/brand experience; brand experience/brand image.

The Brand Power Creative Brief

MARKETING SITUATION:

- Has the company clearly described the competitive positioning power of its brand(s) in its marketplace? How has it identified the markets in which it is competing? Is there target-audience feedback regarding how its customers perceive *the values of the brand: its attributes; its benefits; its commitments to customer satisfaction?*
- Does the audience feedback indicate customer segment purchasing patterns and usage history?
- Where is the company in multichannel marketing (in-store, catalog, Internet)?

BRANDPOWER OBJECTIVES:

- Are the marketing communications based upon the *objectives of building BrandPower?* Are the objectives primarily marketing? Selling? or both? Objectives should clearly indicate specific goals and what results are expected from one or more of the strategies: Internal Branding, Role Branding, Fitness Branding, Co-Branding, Channel Branding, Clone Branding and Break Through Branding.
- How do these strategies utilize brand associations; brand functional appeals and/or emotional motivations; brand attribute appeals and/or benefit appeals; brand experience appeals; or brand commitment for customer relations? Is there Channel Branding based on a *media mix* that recognizes the customer's media habits?
- Are the BrandPower objectives based on improving: the shopping experience, category dominance, destination preference, merchandise assortment, product differentiation, value-pricing, customized services?

TARGET AUDIENCE:

- Profiles of customers are growing in scope and depth. In addition to basic demographics (age, gender, income, education, location...), consumers and customers are more completely described in psychographics relevant for use in the Role Branding strategy. Updated profiles may include the customer's values, attitudes, lifestyles/lifestages, shopping behaviors, purchasing patterns, special offer preferences, quality/price/value demands, product usage, customized service requests—whatever they *opt-in* to their personal database.
- What evidence is there that the target audiences have been behaviorally profiled for their awareness, trial, acceptance and continued use of the retail brand?

CREATIVE STRATEGY:

- How does the strategy selected empower the consumer experience? Does it create an in-store environment in which *atmospherics* and visual merchandising inform and entertain?
- Does the creative strategy build the brand through competitive differentiation by positioning product attributes or consumer benefits or both?
- Do the messages reflect the personal brand positioning of the consumer, as well as the *image positioning* or *repositioning* of the brand, store or mall?

The Brandwidth II Model

Brand Image

Brand Associations
Brand Promises
Brand Meanings

Brand Positioning
Brand Partnering
I.D./id Connections

Brand Experience ← **BRANDPOWER ELEMENTS** → **Shopper Image**

Brand Culture
In-Store Branding
Brand Services

Lifestyle Wants
Lifestage Needs
Media-Mix Options

Brand Channels

- Are the messages using the target audience's media mix options to surround them with Channel Branding?
- Has the media plan considered Internal Branding for a brand culture that encourages brand loyalty?

MEDIA STRATEGY:

- Is there an integration of marketing communications?
- How does the media strategy reflect campaign objectives?
- How does the media plan match the various media mix preferences of the target audience segments?

BRANDPOWER RESULTS:

- Is there evidence that brand concept managers have monitored the program and evaluated the results as stated in the branding objectives?
- What are the specific outcomes? Are they measurable?
- How has the advertising and marketing communications contributed to the effectiveness of the marketing effort to build BrandPower?

Retailers as Reinventors of Brand Power

Nothing in this country and in this world may ever again be "business as usual." There is a new breed of customers and retail reinventors looking to experiment with the *new and different*. It's only recently that we were contemplating a new age—the information age and a new "e-conomy." Now, with the ups and downs of the markets and consumer confidence, retail marketers must increase the power of the *store*-as-a-brand, the store-*experience* as-a-brand, and the *customer*-as-a-brand. Consumer-centric retailing demands the reinvention of brand strategies that produce innovative store experiences and personalized store services designed to keep loyal customers and attract new ones. The goal is to market *with* consumers not *at* them.

The character of the shopping experience, the information and service performance of the store-as-a-brand, and the emotional expectations of the customer-as-the-brand have been major inspirations for empowering retail brands. An inventive retailer can create a **BrandPower** image around its merchandise assortment plan and through its unique visual merchandising with its own retail brands. It can position itself with **break-through** decisions to increase the relevance of merchandise categories and classifications. It can reposition the store-as-a-brand through its creation of advertising and promotion that communicates its cutting-edge personalized customer interactions.

A retailer can reinvent its brand mission through **co-branding** with sources that help "tell its story"—new designers, manufacturers, charitable causes, sports teams or celebrities who are doing what's different, new and relevant to its target markets. In many cases, co-branding strategies have required retailers to add "what to *make*" to the business of "what to *buy*."

Proactive retailers make an ongoing effort to sense and to be sensitive to what is going on in the lives of their customers.

They sense the changes in the values, attitudes and lifestyles of customers as a result of social, cultural, political and economic trends. They become sensitive to consumer wants and needs that are often more emotional than functional. There are interesting experiments with cross-selling to aspirational desires, and price-point preferences that are now breaking the boundaries of each so-called income class. Retailers recognize that six-figure+ income consumers have been mixing brands and price-points by visiting Neiman-Marcus for luxury products in the morning and shopping with a cart at Wal-Mart in the afternoon. Under his Armani suit, he is now wearing the Hanes briefs his wife bought him in a three-pack.

As the planet of retail competition continues to warm up, consumers may need some intensive care. The retailer may need a **"brandometer"** to assess the customer's temperature, temperament and temper. As visualized in **Brandwidth II Model**, the elements of a brand that create preferences and influence shopping behaviors may provide a new checkup for reviewing how they affect the brand's fitness.

This will be especially true for customers who now must find their security and life comforts from more than shopping and material possessions. Retailers may have to reinterpret the consumer's reasons for shopping—and reinvent their strategies for empowering their brands and their customers-as-brands.

For example, retailers who use **role branding** to offer classic and timeless fashion for "affluent women 35 and older"—may sense that they can now *cross-sell* other lifestage and lifestyle market segments. The program for *cross-marketing* would have to follow through with **channel branding** strategies that offer a broader range of *media mix options* for interactive communications.

Luxury retailers have seen that luxury itself at times can lose some of its appeal

to the rich and wannabe wealthy. People now attend special occasions that once demanded black tie—in a tie-dye. It's a new environment where we see consumers worrying more about the stock in their portfolios than what's in their closet's stock of wardrobe.

The retailer as reinventor will have to identify customer needs more quickly and more accurately. They will create **fitness branding** strategies to reinvent their environments, merchandise assortment systems, and services to respond to those needs. Up to now those needs have been largely based on added value, quality at a price, personal convenience and time-saving. Now this may not be enough. The retailer could create *store fitness appeals* that convince its customers it has gotten into better shape. The concept of quick response has taken on a new dimension throughout the company.

Fifth Avenue in New York City as a shopping street brand has needed its own **brand cloning**. This major shopping street has sported the flagships of a number of the major retailers in the USA and more recently, Europe. It goes through its own cloning by attempting (and not always successfully) to reproduce its "retail genome" from its original brand DNA. Fifth Avenue's ongoing reinvention of new stores is *architectural* BrandPower. It brings new design and treasured tradition together with what is relevant to the customer.

What customers perceive as the quality of life, the value of time, and what they really need personally has significantly changed. Each retailer has to now develop an ongoing dialogue with customers that reflects the store's understanding of what their customers' changing lifestyles now require. Retailers are reviewing, and in some cases, repositioning their *brand promises* so that they are conditioned by these individual changes in values and attitudes.

Here's one important example: There is

nothing consumers now value as much as their time. The retailer who is proactive is inventing **break-through branding** strategies to save its customers' valuable time. This needs a dedication to service systems that deploy wanted information to customers even before it is requested. Some retailers can now deliver information to a customer at anytime—wherever they are. A retailer who supplies delivery information on a special order only when a specific request is made is missing an opportunity. Giving the customer this sort of notification in advance makes the customer happy and gives her control over her own time and schedule. Identifying the store-as-a-brand that delivers more than the customer expects is more important than ever.

In traditional retailing, there have been relatively limited lines of communication for customers with sales people or service representatives. Retail communication networks now rely on in-store media on the selling floor to send messages that reinforce e-mail and voice-mail. Inventive retailers can now provide lines of **channel branding** strategies in their communications that extend well beyond the traditional media that shoppers use to search before, during and after their transactions.

The retailer who wants to invent and reinvent systems that improve customer service must improve its team's skill in anticipating what consumers are facing in their hectic lives. This involves more than attention to fashion and style or a particular product. It involves attention to a customer's own shopper image and her consequent behaviors. It may also demand the retailer's experimentation with new systems that can reveal changes in customer behavior. Some innovative retailers are using the newest PDAs and mobile technologies to learn more from their customers, and then to create new customer services. For example, this could mean establishing mobile two-way communica-

tions to encourage customer requests and comments—while in the store.

However, installing a communications network that covers each place and stage in the customer's shopping process could be too restrictive, as well as too static. But a dynamic wireless network in a store that can provide the two-way communication that anticipates what the customer wants, and responds to what the customer needs, could be appreciated wherever she is in the transaction.

Retail brand builders could think of the different places in a store, and different levels of their emotions, where customers can be at any time. It is valuable to know in what stage of their purchasing decision process they might be. Much of their purchasing decisions are based on a blend of how they identify the retail brand or producer brand (**Brand I.D.**), plus what they perceive about the brand's integrity and character (**Brand id**).

Internal branding strategies are exemplified by hi-tech stores that use a mobile technology designed to complement their chic warehouse design with distinctive category visual merchandising and roving sales associates who are fully informed and wired. Tomorrow's retailers are investing in programs that build the spirit and loyalty of their most important resource—their employees. Every employee is a critical participant in the retailer's BrandPower.

Retail thinkers can no longer rely on basic target-market segment profiling, which assumes that traditional demographics identify a group who all have the same views on anything—who think alike or act alike. The retailer should be inventing ways to help consumers to define themselves. This new approach to self-identity should be the paradigm for the customer's personal profile and shopper image, while adding to the retailer's advanced database.

Retailers are now finding ways to retain their best customers with BrandPower

strategies that offer merchandise and services that may appeal to each of them *for different reasons*. The same attributes and benefits of merchandise can offer many different appeals that focus on the individuality of each customer. This requires an ongoing and in-depth study of current behavior to predict lifestyle trends and shopping actions.

The new state of "business as usual" will require reinventions of retail brand power that deal with external trends in these "times unusual." The case studies that follow are grouped in each of seven parts identified by its *reinvention strategy*. *The Power of Retail Branding* is exemplified by one or a combination of these reinvention strategies in action. The strategies are discussed and interpreted by the retailers who created them.

The authors have developed the **BrandPower Creative Brief** and the **Brandwidth II Model** as "think-tools." They are provided to guide your analyses of the cases in each of the seven *BrandPower Strategies*. The brief is designed to clarify the objectives of the program of brand strategies communicated by the advertising and promotions of the retail marketers in each of the cases. Use the brief to question the effectiveness of their marketing situation analysis, target audience profiling, creative strategy, and BrandPower results. The Brandwidth II Model can be used to evaluate how the retailer has integrated the elements of their BrandPower.

We hope you can use The POWER of RETAIL BRANDING to come up with strategies for powering your brand. It is also intended to help you *empower* **your** *employees*-as-the-brand **and your** *customers*-as-a-brand. **May it serve as a retail branding think-tool to stimulate a process of "***how-to-think***" rather than "***what-to-think***."**

Internal Branding

*Internal Branding is the application of marketing and branding strategies **inside** the company to encourage customer-focused values. A strong "employee-as-the-brand" culture helps communicate a brand integrity message to customers, building belief and trust.*

Some strategies are a matter of choice; **Internal Branding** is a prerequisite to successfully positioning a company to the public it wishes to serve. The old adage "We're only as good as the people in our company," is particularly true in retailing. Retailers have the closest connection to the ultimate consumer. Where there is personal interaction with the customer, the *employees are the brand*.

Shoppers can feel it almost immediately when they enter a store or a mall or see the advertising of a company that has an ongoing Internal Branding program. They sense when the employees have been integrated into the spirit and mission of the company and are motivated to serve their customers and carefully communicate a consistent message.

This customer-focused philosophy and an employee "esprit de corps" don't come easy. They require genuine sincerity of the corporate executives and a sustained program of integrating employees into the branding and marketing thinking, planning and execution.

Research has shown that the more employees feel like part of the company and the better informed they are about its business strategies, the higher their morale. Investing in one's employees leads directly to higher customer satisfaction. The manner in which employees perform will be a direct consequence for how customers perceive the brand's performance.

Selling one's marketing program to the internal teams that have the responsibility to make the company a success requires an on-going program to gain and keep their support. Involvement and understanding of the strategies and programs is a two-way process that is not linear. Feedback loops create more of a network to deliver and receive valuable information. Four basic ele-

ments to good brand relationships include establishing programs for: Informing ALL employees; motivating all teams and departments; empowering each employee; and especially—listening to all employees and customers.

Internal Branding is dependent on communications. Feedback loops incorporating employee intranets, company newsletters, e-mail, voice-mail and even bulletin boards, plus customer research panels, roundtables and mall intercepts are helpful in keeping the information circulating.

The proof is in the integrated marketing communications strategies and programs that exhibit the brand relationships being built from strong Internal Branding:

- **One Message** – While *DKNY* is both a high-profile bridge brand and a retail store, all its photography, image books, magazine and newspaper ads, in-store signage and design is done as one thought. "Everything is done to work together hand in hand. When you conceive a season, it has an advertising component, it has a direct-mail component, it's used in windows and for point-of-sale needs, but it's all conceived and executed as one campaign that can be adjusted to each need." Whether it's DKNY, the brand, or DKNY the store the effect is inseparable. See page 12.

- **We listen** – *Family Britches* listens by reaching out to its customers by phone, asking: "How's that suit you bought a year ago?" They talk to people frequently throughout the year through their direct mail, ads, special events, and their website. "Personal service is difficult to explain and advertise, but we attempt to pique the customer's interest and bring them into

our stores." And we listen—"We are always looking for ways to form that relationship." See page 16.

- **Lifelong relationship –** *Bloomingdale's* objective was to forge a lifelong relationship with its bridal registry customers. It set out to "rebuild and reinvent" this service and involved everyone in the process to go beyond the wedding to help a couple "with life after" the one-day event. See page 20

- **Carrying on a tradition –** *Mednikow* is well known in its market as a venerable, family-owned business that has carried on a tradition of quality, service and integrity since the late 1800s. It caters to regular customers with its white glove service. "Every ad we do is sincere… we've come to be recognized for our believability." In terms of ROI (return on investment), its catalogs go long and deep when it comes to *branding its business* in the eyes and minds of its clients. "We are also branding our own name and image today and for the years ahead." Everyone in the company is invested in projecting and protecting this image. See page 26

- **Customer feedback loop –** *King of Prussia* mall stays on top of its diverse demographic mix of customer segments. It knows what customers are looking for by gathering extensive data from phone research, mall intercepts, as well as by listening to its stores' feedback. "An outside company conducts research for us on an annual basis." Reaching all of the diverse audiences in the market segments they want to target is no small task. Involving all of the stores in the mall is crucial to its success in communicating why King of Prussia is *the* place to shop. See page 30.

- **Brand Icons –** *Macy's* embarked on a major new branding initiative in September of 2002. The program is far-reaching across the entire chain, through all of its communications. The well known "Macy's Star" was expanded into the more impactful graphic symbol that represents everything the store stands for—fashion, magic, wonder, theatre, a total experience. "Macy's already had equity in it, so at this point we just reestablished the star as Macy's icon in a dramatic way." Over time, the "Macy's Star" has become more subtle. "It is ever changing like the store, yet always the same like the brand." See page 38.

- **Our Mission –** "Our mission at *Aveda* is to care for the world we live in, from the products we make to the ways in which we give back to society. At Aveda, we strive to set an example for environmental leadership and responsibility, not just in the world of beauty, but around the world." See page 43.

With the intense level of competition building, **differentiation** is a critical component to a company's success. Sometimes it is not so much what you are saying as it is the way you are saying it and how deeply you mean it. The strongest brand images that have the longest life lines also have the best relationships with their employees, vendors, customers and other stakeholders. Their efforts and actions are believable.

Signs of Spring

WHILE DKNY IS BOTH a high-profile bridge brand and a retail store player, all the photography for its image book, magazine and newspaper ads and signage is done as one thought. Trey Laird, who was with Donna Karan's company for many years, before founding Laird + Partners, explained, "It's all one creative process. Everything is done to work together hand in hand. When you conceive a season, it has an advertising component, it has a direct mail component, it's used in windows and for point of sale needs, but it's all conceived and executed as one campaign that can be adjusted to meet each need. Drive by a store, and you see the same images in a window—each touch point with the brand is to reengage you and press that same button." The bottom line: whether it's DKNY, the brand, or DKNY the store the effect is inseparable. The purpose of the imagery for each is to enhance and strengthen the other.

That strategy, according to Laird is to have consumers react in a certain way emotionally. "When you do it in a way that feels authentic for that brand, it feels even better. It engages the customer," he explained. "It's not successful if they just say 'that's pretty.' You want someone to feel something and then experience something and get what you're trying to say."

While "pretty" is an understatement in terms of the image book and ads for "Signs of Spring," the recent campaign clearly has a lot more going for it. It elicits an emotional connection. Everything from the lush lifestyle photos to the inside front cover's copy with its reference to "California dreamin," has a dreamy, languid mood. As Laird explained, you can be in New York, in fact anywhere, and have that spring-induced, laid back frame of mind." "Signs of Spring" conveyed the mood of the season and illustrated Laird's strategy for branding DKNY consistently.

The dreamy feeling runs throughout the ads which, because they utilize photography from the same shoot as the image book, reflects all the same marvelous mood of the season. Throughout the spring season readers of fashion and lifestyle magazines couldn't

miss "Signs of Spring" in various incarnations, all different. Some were key spreads, some gatefolds, others a singular sensation. Among the numerous publications were *Vanity Fair*, *Vogue*, *Harper's Bazaar*, *W*, *InStyle*, *Jane*, *The New York Times Magazine* and *Sunday Styles*, *Marie Claire*, *Glamour*, *Lucky*, *GQ*, *Esquire* and *Details*.

The cutting-edge image book takes on an additional function—driving traffic into the stores. "Wherever possible we try to make the book interactive," Laird noted. "Driving traffic is such an important part of the retail challenge at a designer level. DKNY bridge is not like a mass chain retailer that's going to offer coupons. You have to come up with a way to give people an incentive in a brand-appropriate way like things that seems like a surprise. Sometimes an incentive can work to your advantage because it makes the experience more personal and more special."

The book has a number of these surprising touches. Inside is a hand-mounted envelope holding an invitation to come to a store the first two weeks of February to get roses (roses are a motif in the book). February? Now *that's* a smart way to get a jump start on spring!

And there's a hand-mounted snapshot that appears a little askew. No accident. Laird: "Everybody wants something personal, especially now when we're in a day and age when things that feel mass produced don't feel right. Donna's clothes have certain details, certain stitches, so we try to put those special touches, like the clothes, into what we do."

One doesn't expect to see an offer from a spa in a fashion catalog, but that's just what Bliss a luxury NYC spa, did. Pasted on one of the pages is a card with an offer for a beauty gift valued at $30 when $100 in purchases were made online. "Lots of people in the fashion world are clients of Bliss," Laird pointed out. "There's a synergy between what goes in DKNY and Bliss. DKNY has always been about a lifestyle, never just about clothes."

A text stock was used throughout the book, because it has a bit of a scrapbook feeling or that of a family album. "We did some tests on different papers. This one has an earthy tactile feel. We didn't want it to feel slick or overproduced," Laird commented.

DKNY

signs of spring

who's in the pink? open to find out

a spring surprise just for you!

DKNY, New York
ADVERTISING AGENCY: Laird & Partners, New York
CREATIVE DIRECTOR: Trey Laird
PHOTOGRAPHER: Mikael Jansson
ART DIRECTOR: Hans Dorsinville
STYLIST: Karl Templer
HAIR: Marc Lopez
MAKE-UP: Mark Carrasquillo
PRODUCTION: Ray DiPietro
MODELS: Milla Jovovich, Aaron Ward

Magazine ads.

Newspaper ads.

Building Relationships

"Although my business takes me
to New York, Paris and Florence,
I buy 90% of my wardrobe in
New Canaan at Family Britches."

Bill Schaefer
William Gray Schaefer Interiors
New Canaan, CT

"I could shop anywhere, but the clothing at Family Britches has the
design, cut and color that's right for me. Their mix of informal sport jackets,
European designers and great personal attention to their clientele makes
shopping a pleasant and convenient experience."

Corneliani sport jacket coordinated with Sea Island cotton shirt from John Smedley of England and suede outercoat trimmed with glazed leather and lined with cashmere and wool.

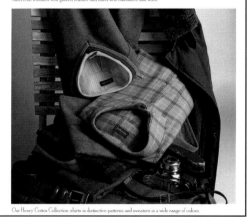

Our Henry Cotton Collection: shirts in distinctive patterns and sweaters in a wide range of colors.

Up close and personal—the 30th anniversary self-mailer had a photography theme, featuring portraits of customers.

FOUNDED IN 1970, Family Britches has grown from a jeans and tops store into a retailer of men's, women's and boys' clothing. Along the way, it has built a loyal following, so loyal in fact that it is the only men's, women's and boys' retailer left in Westchester and Fairfield County.

That's no small feat at a time when, because of competition from shopping centers and larger retailers, many specialty stores have gone out of business. The customers Family Britches attracts can shop just about anywhere. (The majority commutes to Manhattan.) Nevertheless, Family Britches' two stores, in Chappaqua, NY and New Canaan, CT, have managed to endure.

How do they do it? According to Barry Mishkin, one of the two owners, "In our particular niche in the market, people are looking for quality, relationship and service. We're always looking for ways to form that relationship."

The strategy is to reach out to customers in different ways. "People seem to like something a little different," said Mishkin. "We try not to do what every one else does. We try to make it interesting."

This could mean anything from a special event to personal services such as wardrobe consulting or making a special delivery to a customer's home. "People desire personal attention," Mishkin said. "A lot of our customers work a 9 to 5 job,

so we have to be flexible to meet their needs. We'll make a delivery late at night or on a Sunday."

Mishkin stressed repeatedly how crucial it is to find ways to have contact with the customer "even if it's a phone call asking 'how's that suit you bought a year ago?" Sometimes he and his partner, Rick Bungee, will show up at the local train station. "It's a great opportunity for us to meet our customers on their turf without any pressure and it's a fun way get to talk to people."

Family Britches also talks to people frequently throughout the year through direct mail, newspaper advertising (usually to support a trunk show or other event),

"Family Britches makes it a breeze
for me to know what goes with what."

Jerry Mellinger
President & CEO, Forum Computer Services
Mt. Kisco, NY

"I used to dread facing that rack of clothes each morning. I had to sort
out what matched—and what didn't. Family Britches made it easy for me. Their
experts coordinated every aspect of my wardrobe—sport jackets, pants,
shirts, ties, the works. Now I know exactly how to put myself together."

From Ermenegildo Zegna, rough-cut velvet sport jacket combined with cashmere cardigan and brushed cotton shirt.

The Barbour coat and sportswear collection from England.

"Over the years, styles have changed
but one thing hasn't: the impeccable
service at Family Britches."

Mike Curry with wife Meg
Ossining, NY
Vice President, MPE Communications

"I grew up in Ossining and went to Family Britches when they first
opened. My wife Meg and I returned to Westchester in 1991 and I've been
coming to Family Britches ever since. They know what's in my wardrobe
better than I do, so they can help me put together complete outfits. And since
Meg shops here, I can't go wrong when it comes to picking up a gift."

Customer portraits by photographer Jeffrey Shaw of Greenwich.

Washable goatskin shirt from France with vintage jeans and shirts from our sportswear collections.

Casual comfort from North 44.

WIN A FAMILY PORTRAIT

Come to Family Britches to
celebrate our 30th anniversary and
enter your name in a drawing for a
free family portrait by photographer
Jeffrey Shaw.

FAMILY
BRITCHES
MEN • WOMEN • BOYS
70 King St., Chappaqua, NY 914 238-8017
30 Elm St., New Canaan, CT 203 966-0518
www.familybritches.com

**The back cover offered the opportunity to
enter a drawing for a free family portrait.**

special events and a website. They work
with a small ad agency, Foreman &
Resnick, to create interesting campaigns
that reflect the friendly atmosphere of the
stores. "Personal service is difficult to
explain and advertise, but we attempt to
pique the customer's interest and bring
them into our stores," noted Mishkin.

Much of that effort is accomplished
through direct mail—a logical choice since
Family Britches marketing strategy is centered around the personal touch. One such
example is a direct mail piece that com-
memorated the retailer's 30th anniversary.
It featured family-style portraits of actual
Family Britches customers, accompanied
by statements from each describing their

BRITCHES
MEN • WOMEN • BOYS

Dear Xxxxx Xxxxxx,

It's never too early to think about spring—and sprucing up your wardrobe. Come in now to take advantage of these preseason offers:

1. **Custom Shirt Department:** Buy five, get the sixth custom shirt FREE. Whether you want casual business or dress shirts, our wide selection of swatches will make your choices easy. Take advantage of this opportunity to save through March 31. If you'd like to try a custom shirt or two, we'll also waive the four shirt minimum.

2. **Expanded selection of swatches for made-to-measure suits, sport coats and trousers at 10% savings.** Fabrics from Zegna, St. Andrews, Loro Piana, Corneliani and Hickey Freeman have been enhanced by selections from the world's finest mills. Order before March 31 and save 10%—and have your wardrobe choices ready for spring.

3. **Womens Department:** Preview new collections from Max Mara, Zanella and Gran Sasso. The same custom shirt offer applies to ladies, too.

4. **Boys Department:** Come see our new collection of suits, sport coats & trousers made in Italy.

At Family Britches, we're showcasing Italian style this season. We'll have representatives from the following Italian manufacturers in our stores to assist you:

- Paul & Shark Mens Collection: Saturday, March 29.
- Max Mara Womens Collection: Friday-Saturday, March 28-29.
- Corneliani Mens Collection: April 5 in New Canaan, April 19 in Chappaqua.
- Zegna Mens Collection: Saturday, April 12.
- Mens and Womens Collections from Zanella and Gran Sasso.

We look forward to seeing you soon. Thank you for your patronage.

Cordially,

Barry Mishkin   Rick Buggee

70 King Street, Chappaqua, NY 914 238-8017 ❖ 39 Elm Street, New Canaan, CT 203 966-0518
www.familybritches.com

The personalized letter. It still works!

IT'S TIME FOR OUR SUMMER _____.

(We can't bring ourselves to say it.)

Take up to 50% off at Family Britches.

MAKE TRACKS TO THE FAMILY BRITCHES WINTER SALE.

SAVE UP TO 50%.

Oversized postcards.

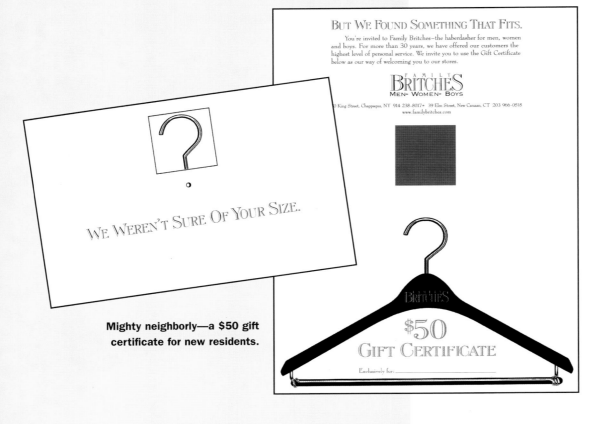

BUT WE FOUND SOMETHING THAT FITS.

You're invited to Family Britches—the haberdasher for men, women and boys. For more than 30 years, we have offered our customers the highest level of personal service. We invite you to use the Gift Certificate below as our way of welcoming you to our stores.

BRITCHES
MEN• WOMEN• BOYS

0 King Street, Chappaqua, NY 914 238-8017• 39 Elm Street, New Canaan, CT 203 966-0518
www.familybritches.com

WE WEREN'T SURE OF YOUR SIZE.

$50
GIFT CERTIFICATE

Exclusively for:

Mighty neighborly—a $50 gift certificate for new residents.

THINGS TO DO:

1. Get a $50 credit toward a new Southwick outfit

2. Men and women: Order 6 custom shirts, get 7th free

3. ♥ Valentine's Day gifts: Up to 50% off womenswear

4. Come in now through Feb. 28

5.

6.

7.

8.

9.

10.

BRITCHES
70 KING STREET
CHAPPAQUA, NY
914 238-8017   ❖   39 ELM STREET
NEW CANAAN, CT
203 966-0518

For Valentine's, a personal thoughtful touch.

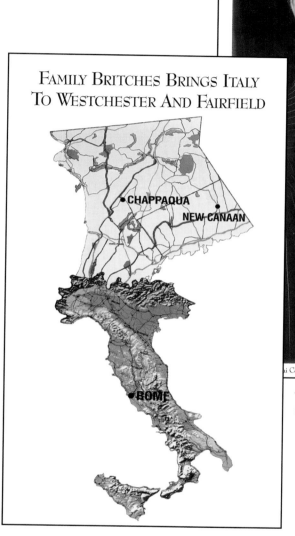

BUONGIORNO

Family Britches and the Italian Trade Commission invite you to join us for our Italian Fashion Festival. Come preview our spring collections and get a chance to win a trip for two to Italy.

▸ Paul & Shark Mens Collection: Saturday, March 29.

▸ MaxMara Womens Collection: Friday-Saturday, March 28-29.

▸ Corneliani Mens Collection: Saturday, April 5 in New Canaan and Saturday, April 19 in Chappaqua.

▸ Zegna Mens Collection: Saturday, April 12.

▸ Gran Sasso Mens and Womens Collections: Saturday, April 12.

▸ Zanella Mens and Womens Collections.

Come in and enjoy complimentary Italian specialties.

Italia
Life in I style

Italian Trade Commission
Government Agency

WIN A TRIP TO ITALY FOR TWO

Come to Family Britches and you could be on your way to Italy. Your trip includes two roundtrip tickets to Rome on Alitalia, three nights at a first-class hotel in Rome compliments of Italiatour, continental breakfast daily and more. Simply complete the entry form at Family Britches. No purchase necessary. Drawing will be held May 17.

FAMILY
BRITCHES
MEN • WOMEN • BOYS

70 King St., Chappaqua, NY 914-238-8017 • 39 Elm St., New Canaan, CT 203 966-0518

www.familybritches.com

FAMILY BRITCHES BRINGS ITALY
TO WESTCHESTER AND FAIRFIELD

This direct mail piece was sent to Family Britches' entire database.

---

relationship with the store.

Usually at the start of each season a letter goes to their made-to-measure customer and/or to their women customers. The letter is often a reminder to come in for his or her pre-season fitting while talking about some of the new selections available that season. The letter also provides the opportunity to announce upcoming trunk shows.

Mailers are also sent to their general customer base. Oversized postcards are used to announce semi-annual sales. A direct mailer was created for new residents in the area, which included a free $50 gift certificate (no strings attached!) by way of welcoming them.

This spring, an Italian Festival was the big thing. Working with the Italian Trade Commission and other retail businesses in town, Family Britches created a town festival. Each week, for six weeks in April and May, they held an event in-store in conjunction with a local wine shop, gourmet food shop, bakery, butcher, etc. There were wine tastings and Italian food specialties. To promote the event, a direct mail piece with the teaser "Come in for a chance to win a trip to Italy" was sent to Family Britches' list of 32,000. Ads were placed in local newspapers announcing the event and the contest. People came into the store with a coupon to enter the drawing to win the trip.

Another way Family Britches reaches out to customers is through its website, which has been up for about three years. Noting the website in its advertising gives people an opportunity to preview the store. Understandably, sales from it are minimal, but responses and inquiries are quite the opposite. Whenever a catalog is mailed to the 32,000 database, there is a significant increase in hits.

Family Britches, Chappaqua, NY
OWNERS: **Barry Mishkin, Richard Buggee**
ADVERTISING AGENCY: **Foreman & Resnick**
PARTNERS: **Rob Resnick, Tom Foreman**

Happily Ever After: The Bloomingdale's Home Planner

WHEN LOVE IS THE AIR, you can be sure retail won't be far behind. But in the mid-90s, love started taking a new turn. A culture was developing, whereby brides were abandoning their mother's tradition of registering at their department store. Instead, couples were becoming more selective, registering instead at a number of specialty stores with all kinds of popularly-priced goods.

This trend away from the traditional obviously hasn't boded well for department stores. Bloomingdale's, for one, definitely had a problem. Its Bridal Registry program had sunk to an all time low of 3% increases in year-over-year registrations.

That has had profound implications when you consider the kinds of high-ticket goods couples purchase. Bridal registries have increasingly become a two-fold proposition—getting the couple to register for the wedding, then holding on to them. Missing that can mean the loss of a fairly significant amount of revenue—not just opportunities for immediate sales with good margins, but more important to keep couples coming back and retain their business in the years ahead.

Bloomingdale's objective was forging this lifelong relationship. But the retailer clearly needed some marriage counseling to rebuild and reinvent its Bridal Registry Program.

The retailer turned to Emergence, a Richmond, VA-based strategic branding agency that the store was already working with relative to other direct-mail programs.

The first thing Emergence did was ask Bloomingdale's what sort of data they had on their typical customer. What they learned was that this customer was older, more highly educated, had traveled more and had a higher income than the typical department store registrant. There was also a higher incidence of second and third marriages.

The agency looked at the data and at the store itself in terms of what kind of promise Bloomingdale's could fulfill— what goods, what services, the things the couple can aspire to after their wedding, "Most stores spend all their time talking

about the wedding, not what Bloomingdale's does which is help with life after," said Pat Alderman, Emergence president.

That distinction is what led to the creation of a unique hard cover book, "Inspirations. The Bloomingdale's Home

Each book comes shrink wrapped to protect the dust jacket.

C O N T E N T S

Your home.

It's all about you:

where you live, where you entertain.

Our Home Planner will help you

create a home that's all your own.

Your sanctuary and your showplace.

Where you celebrate with friends.

Where you retreat for relaxing times

alone. We'll help to surround you with

an ambience that is uniquely yours.

These pages are filled with suggestions

for decorating and caring for your

home. From the basics of setting

the table to stocking your kitchen,

bedroom and bath...selecting your

furniture, mattress, bed linens and

lighting...planning a romantic getaway

and picking out luggage to take along...

indulging in cosmetics, fragrances

and a long, lingering bath...plus

planning for a year of sharing and

celebration. All this and more are

included in our Bloomingdale's Home

Planner, our gift to you. We hope

it will assist and inspire you while

designing an environment where both

of you will feel totally "at home".

1 Dining In
Page 6

2 Gourmet Kitchen
Page 52

3 Master Suite
Page 88

4 Personal Pleasures
Page 104

5 Interior Decor
Page 116

6 Home Finance
Page 126

7 Travel Plans
Page 132

INDEX

Recipes

A winter salad .... Page 25
The perfect martini .... Page 32
No-fail soufflé .... Page 44
Dinner in less than an hour .... Page 46
Fool-proof roast chicken .... Page 63
Roasted rack of lamb .... Page 65
Peachy orange shake .... Page 66
Royal caramel nut latté .... Page 72
Frittata .... Page 79
Devil's food cake .... Page 82
Cayenne-rubbed salmon .... Page 84
Cuban pork roast .... Page 84

Checklist

China checklist .... Page 8
Stemware & barware .... Page 31
Everyday flatware .... Page 40
Cookware & bakeware checklist .... Page 56
The basics on beds .... Page 91
Guest bedroom checklist .... Page 98

Tips & Techniques

Caring for china .... Page 8
Caring for crystal .... Page 28
Napkin folding .... Page 36
Caring for silverware .... Page 40
Soup basics .... Page 45
Cleaning your cookware .... Page 63
Removing spills and stains .... Page 100
Mastering a massage .... Page 112
Mortgage rates .... Page 127
Homeowners insurance .... Page 128
Useful 800 numbers .... Page 144
Shopping services .... Page 147

DINING IN
GOURMET KITCHEN
MASTER SUITE
PERSONAL PLEASURES
INTERIOR DECOR
HOME FINANCE
TRAVEL PLANS

Stair stepping divider pages make the Home Planner convenient to use.

Planner." Filled with nearly 150 pages of stunning photographs of items from specific manufacturers, inspiring editorial, checklists, techniques and tips on everything from how to roast a chicken and fold a napkin to mastering a massage, Inspirations. The Bloomingdale's Home Planner is a "must-have"—an invaluable resource for anyone, and an irresistible incentive to register.

Revised annually, the book is presented to every registrant—some 25,000 customers each year. The oversized (approximately 13¼" x 10¼") format was intentionally designed as a spiral. "We did it for two reasons—so it would lie flat if you were using it as a resource book, and so we could pick up pages for cost control," Alderman noted.

The Home Planner takes about three months to produce, with anywhere between a third and a half of the pages

being picked up. "Most of the time is spent in printing and bindery, because there is so much hand work with loose sheets that have to be spiral bound," Alderman said.

The book and registry have been promoted since the beginning. Over the years, ads have run locally in newspapers, in various publications nationally, including *Town & Country*, and in local and regional bridal magazines such as *Philadelphia Bride*. That effort evolved over time into ads in *Martha Stewart Weddings*, becoming a full fledged insert that picked up participating vendor's ads. (Vendors have the opportunity to go just in the book or have that full page picked up for *Martha Stewart Weddings*.)

In addition, there is a direct-mail component that follows the couple for 18 months after their registry "That's the period of time when couples themselves

will spend the most to complete their sets—the primary ways that you begin to build that sustained relationship," said Alderman. The direct-mail piece contains a certificate that gives the couple a certain percentage off to come into the store and complete their sets.

An additional incentive for the couple to return to the store is provided by a three-tier anniversary program for replenishment or completion of a registered collection. Each year for three years the couple receives a congratulatory direct-mail piece on their anniversary.

The program continues to pay off. Bridal registrations have increased at the rate of 16% to 25% each year resulting in significant growth in incremental sales.

BLOOMINGDALE'S

Sophisticated

Dining In

The book is filled with practical information.

ORREFORS Designed by Erika Lagerbielke and produced in Sweden, the Intermezzo stemware collection is designed with a rich blue, or a dramatic black, teardrop gracefully suspended in each stem. This distinctive shape and design has made Intermezzo an instant classic both domestically and internationally. It adds a well-defined pleasure to each variety of wine served from it. Shown: goblet, wine, flute, compote, wine carafe, tumblers and double old-fashioneds.

REED & BARTON Superb design does not go unnoticed. Reed & Barton stainless steel flatware gains approval for charm, flair and inherent beauty. Designed for entertaining in the 90s, these brilliant patterns are the perfect choice for the casual elegance of today's tablesettings. Shown left to right: "Golden Crescendo," "Country French" and "Longwood."

Interior Decor

household calculus

How much paint do I need? How much fabric should I order to cover my favorite chair? And what about carpeting? These are some of the questions we all need answered at one time or another. There are some simple guidelines.

To measure a room Start with a good measuring tape—a sturdy, retractable style at least 9-feet long is best—paper and a calculator. Now begin. Start with the walls, measuring floor to ceiling, excluding baseboards or trim. Then measure the width of each wall, including doors and windows. Multiply the width by the height for the total wall area. The next step is to measure the baseboards and trim—multiplying the length by the height of each. Ceilings call for measuring entire areas—the length and width of each. Then measure the width and length of each alcove. Finally, complete the multiplication and add them together for total ceiling space. In this instance, doors and windows are measured like walls—by multiplying the width by the height.

To order wallpaper Measure the room carefully, including alcoves and any irregular angles or columns. Measure the height from floor to ceiling. Then multiply the height by the width for each wall and add them together. Rule of thumb: a standard roll of American wallpaper covers about 30 square feet, about 25 square feet for imported varieties. Deduct one roll for every two doors or windows in the room. Then add two to three extra rolls in case of mistakes. Also buy extra for matching patterns.

One gallon of paint will cover about 400 square feet of base or flat coat; about half that, if the walls are new and thus more absorbent. Note: additional costs will require slightly less.

For carpeting Measure the room from the bottom of the baseboard to the deepest part of the door threshold, allowing for alcoves, doorways and other protrusions, plus the interiors of closets. Add three inches for trimming and extra if you are matching patterns. For stairs, measure each tread and riser, then add the height of a riser and width of one tread to the total length. Also, add a slight two inches to each tread to allow for padding, plus a half-inch for edges on open treads. On winding staircases, measure along the outer edge.

For shades Decide which kind will suit you best. For shades mounted inside the window frames—measure the width plus three inches, then top to bottom of the frame plus 12 inches. For shades mounted above the window—measure the width plus three inches, then the length from the

order to the bottom of the window plus 12 inches. For Roman shades—measure the width of the recess plus two inches, then the depth plus two inches. The lining requires the same amount.

For curtains and draperies To determine the length, measure from the top of the rod to the desired length plus floor to six inches for hems—plus floor to eight inches for headings and the diameter of the rod, plus one-half inch for casings. The width is double the length of the rod for fullness, triple for sheer fabrics, plus two to three inches for side hems and one inch for joining panels. Multiply the final length by the number of panels and divide by 36 for the number of yards needed.

For slipcovers Measure across the back and mark the center at the highest point, then measure from the top to the floor. Then measure from the inside of the back to the front of the seat plus five inches for tucking, then from the seat to the floor. Measure the arms from the outside to the floor, from the outside edge over the arm to the seat plus five inches and multiply each measurement by two. Then measure the front of the arms, times two. Add in the length, depth and width of loose cushions plus three to four feet for piping.

Shown above: Milling Road Collection metal table, Swain black and taupe chenille stripe sofa and Bloomingdale's Home Furnishings Design Studio bleachwood chair, Chinese vases and crackle bowl.

NOURISON The finest hand-tufted rugs on the face of the Earth make up the Nourison 2000 collection. These exquisite silk and wool carpets recreate the look of a 200-line hand-knotted rug at a fraction of the cost. Designed with intricate motifs and delicately tufted, these rugs are true works of art for the floor. With this fabulous line, Nourison has succeeded in creating the ultimate in luxurious, hand-tufted rugs.

Travel Plans

A Place In The Sun

The urge to get away has the lovely habit of taking control toward the middle of winter, wherever you live. Doesn't it? If a genie popped out of a bottle on one of those days and offered you a week's vacation anywhere you wanted to go, where would you choose? Dreams do come true. From St. Bart's to Singapore, your idea of visiting a place in the sun would become more than a favorite fantasy. Magically, it would become a real possibility.

We love vacations anytime of the year—winter, spring, summer or fall. To find the right spot, find inspiration in one of the new travel book stores or your favorite travel magazine, even by watching cable TV. And talk to others on the World Wide Web. According to one recent survey in the travel industry, 8 out of 10 Americans favorite US vacation spots are bright and sunny, as are one half of all foreign choices. And going to the beach follows eating delicious food as the most favored activity.

Now that you are geared up to get away, what would you pack and in what would you pack it?

Quality in luggage is a sound investment. Look for materials that can withstand the wear and tear of airline luggage handlers, the arduous trips through terminals and parking lots, even kids who use your suitcase as alternate seating or a trampoline. Ballistic nylon is a modern choice, because it is strong, lightweight and very durable. Nylon with leather trim is sturdy and stylish. Most luggage is constructed from hard plastics or in combination with strong fabrics of man-made fibers. Canvas provides a more casual look.

Luggage manufacturers have figured out how you can hold everything efficiently and safely, with a splash of style and color that is as modern as it is handsome.

TRAVEL AGENT TIPS

A good travel agent is like having your own personal assistant. Your agent is your private ambassador to carriers (airlines, boats, trains and buses) and properties (hotels, resorts, bed-and-breakfasts, reservation locations, etc.); and, yes, even tours/guides, transporters and entertainment options. Here are eight tips to help you get the best service.

1. Be honest about your full budget.

2. Advise the agent of your time frames. The more flexible your schedule, the greater your access to discount fares and other promotions. Travel agents can scan all airline and car rental companies at once in order to secure the lowest prices.

3. Check the newest immunization laws, customs regulations and duty-free allowances if you are leaving the country, even crossing the borders to our neighbors in Canada and Mexico.

4. Tell your agent about children, elderly or other companions. Pets, too. They can be of help to even the most demanding or finicky of travelers.

5. Alert the agent to your medical, diet and exercise needs, including non-smoking or smoking requests.

6. Advise your agent about your frequent flier/traveler programs for credit.

7. Ask for information about airport connections, bus and taxi services, fees, banks, foreign currencies, business contacts, etc. at your destination. You may need a special driver's permit if you'll be renting a car abroad.

8. Call from your trip for assistance with any problem.

9. Don't forget to ask your agent about baggage requirements. They still exist. For example, under-the-seat bags on airlines should measure 9"x14"x22" or 45" total.

LITTLE DIX BAY Just beyond a colorful barrier reef, lapped by gentle blue waters, lies the softly curving crescent beach of Rosewood's Little Dix Bay resort. Here, forested mountains are framed by sunlit skies. Little Dix Bay offers spectacular beaches, water sports, exquisite cuisine, tennis and more — all in a lush, secluded setting. This world-class Rosewood resort is located on Virgin Gorda in the British Virgin Islands. 1-800-928-3000.

LITTLE DIX BAY
A ROSEWOOD RESORT

"*Now join
your hands, and
with your hands
your hearts.*"
–William Shakespeare

The insert in *Martha Stewart Weddings* gives vendors another opportunity to promote their products.

From this day forward...

It's all about the two of you...
With so much to think about as you get ready for happily ever after, we're dedicated to helping you make sure no detail is overlooked. We offer personalized assistance and an easy, convenient way for you to register.

Register with us...
Let us tell your friends and family you're registered at Bloomingdale's. Once we've helped you select your gifts, we'll put your registry at the fingertips of all those who wish you well: your gift list will be on our website, http://www.bloomingdales.com, as well as in all our stores nationwide!

Advice from our experts...
Our experienced bridal consultants will guide you through our thousands of patterns of china, crystal, silver, linens and more, from the finest names and renowned designers. We'll even help you select wedding invitations and attendant's gifts. How about a pampering make-over with one of our beauty experts? Our experts will help you with all the little extras.

Our gifts to you...
Special gifts await you when you register with us. First, our Bloomingdale's Home Planner, 150 pages of inspiring ideas and photographs to show you just how to entertain. Second, our Bloomingdale's Wedding Planner, a resourceful guide for planning your special day. And there's more: you could be our Couple of the Month and win fabulous prizes, or the Honeymoon of your Dreams.

Call our toll free number or visit us on our web site...
We know you can't wait to get started, and we can't wait to help. Let us hear from you soon. 1-800-888-2WED or visit our web page at http://www.bloomingdales.com.

bloomingdale's
THE BRIDAL REGISTRY
CALL 1-800-888-2WED

SPECIAL ADVERTISING SECTION FROM THE BRIDAL REGISTRY AT BLOOMINGDALE'S

RALPH LAUREN Few things in life feel as luxurious as this. The "Diplomat" collection is designed in the tradition of the finest hotel apartment decor. Pure cotton imported sheets, shams, duvet covers and throw pillows, all with a rich floral design on a red background. With "Jean Michael" sheets with a reversible hem and white cuff, "Dignitary" navy 280-thread count Egyptian cotton sateen sheets, "Jardiniere" sateen duvet covers and velvet accessories and the "Aragon" fur pillow, Ralph Lauren shows how effortless it can be to pull together a simply elegant look.

RALPH LAUREN After a busy day of planning for your new home, shower and wrap yourself in one of these generously-sized 100% combed Egyptian cotton towels. Two-ply on one side for super absorbancy and one-ply on the other for softness, together provide your body with the therapy it deserves. Shown top to bottom: "Avenue" in white, sandstone, breakwater, balsam woods and cobblestone; "Avenue Quilt" in white, sandstone and breakwater. These are absolutely Ralph Lauren's most luxurious towels.

28   bloomingdales
www.bloomingdales.com

BLOOMINGDALE'S 1-800-888-2WED   29

Congratulations

The first in a series of direct-mail pieces designed to encourage return visits (and a customer for life).

...You did it! As you settle in to your new life together, you may notice that something's missing...One place setting shy of the perfect set? Short on sheets? Well, the best is yet to come. Stop by Bloomingdale's now to complete your gift registry list and get 10% off all the missing details.* Come in as many times as you like before your 6-month anniversary, and get 10% off each time! Pair your discount with our Dining Circle for extra value and no interest for 12 months. Visit our Bridal Registry to find out more.

Bring in this Bridal Card to Bloomingdale's and

take 10% off

any items remaining on your bridal gift registry list.
Enjoy unlimited use of this card for the next six months.
(See the back of this card for exclusions.)
Registry # _____ Offer valid until ___/___/___

bloomingdale's
The Registry at Bloomingdale's

Bloomingdale's, New York
AGENCY: **Emergence** (branding and strategic) Richmond, VA, (creative) Atlanta
PRESIDENT, **Pat Alderman**
VP/ACCOUNT GROUP DIRECTOR: **Milissa Cole**
ASSOCIATE CREATIVE DIRECTOR: **Amy Weaver**

The Power of Beautiful Branding

EAST MEMPHIS, Tennessee-based, Mednikow Jewelers' flagship store may bear a street address of 474 South Perkins Extended, but its address is well known throughout the city simply as Mednikow Plaza.

Mednikow is also well known as a venerable, family-owned business that has carried on a tradition of quality, service and integrity since the late 1800s, when Russian jeweler Jacob Mednikow emigrated to the United States. Today, the business is run by Jacob's grandson, Robert M. Mednikow—who holds the distinction of being his city's first registered AGS jeweler—along with Robert's wife and their two children.

The company opened a new store in Atlanta in 1995, marking its first expansion outside the Memphis market.

Although Mednikow represents a number of fine jewelry designers such as Mikimoto and big name watches from Rolex, Ebel and Patek Philippe, it differentiates itself from lots of other retail jewelers through its large house collection. More than half of the jewelry carried here is made in the firm's own workshops.

Mednikow says that he is indeed a different kind of jeweler. He's quick to admit that cookie cutter ideas don't interest him and that he takes a nonconformist, contrarian approach to his business, from his stores and the merchandise they carry straight through to the way in which he views and approaches his advertising.

"I want the customer to immediately know that she or he is in my store the minute they walk through the door. So when we were looking at building, we intentionally went to architects who had never done a jewelry store before. And we told them in no uncertain terms that we didn't want to look like any other jeweler."

Mednikow is also quick to point out his views when it comes to his retailing credo. "We believe that our customers are entitled to fine quality, immediate delivery and proper service. The only way to provide that is to make the jewelry ourselves," he says. "But there are still some fine jewelers from whom we buy. The man who makes our wedding rings makes rings for Tiffany & Co. and another craftsman does special order work for Cartier. But by establishing our own manufacturing arm, we have assured our customers a continuing emphasis on quality."

Aside from catering to regular customers with its requisite white-glove service and luxurious jewels and watches, Mednikow goes out of its way when it comes to providing something extra special for bridal shoppers. "We offer a Rolls Royce service for every bride whose fiancé buys an engagement ring and wedding ring from us. Our chauffeur-driven Rolls Royce picks her up and takes her to the church and sometimes from the church to the reception."

For this jeweler, who says he doesn't want to be "big, only excellent," targeted, believable advertising across newspapers, magazines and lush, full-color "image" catalogs, all created and produced in house, spreads the message. The idea here is all about consistently hitting existing and new luxury shoppers in the eye with lots of beautifully executed images "but with a warm, fuzzy feeling," explains Mednikow. (Ed. Note: Mednikow declined to release hard data on his com-

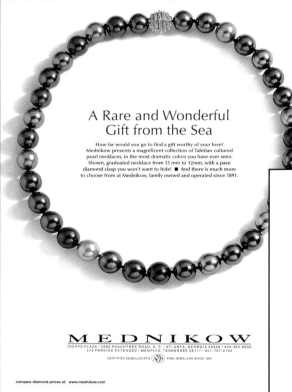

FOREVER YOURS

For your wedding day ... or to celebrate your anniversary of many years.
Mednikow chooses the most beautiful diamonds, and sets them
in precious platinum to create rings that are as brilliant as your love!
Top to bottom: $7,370, $19,750, $17,750, $42,250, and $20,750.
From Mednikow, the original Memphis family of fine jewelers.

MEDNIKOW

PHIPPS PLAZA / 3500 PEACHTREE ROAD, N. E. / ATLANTA, GEORGIA 30326 / 404-364-9900
474 PERKINS EXTENDED / MEMPHIS, TENNESSEE 38117 / 901-767-2100
CERTIFIED GEMOLOGISTS ⟨AGS⟩ FINE JEWELERS SINCE 1891

TRICK OR TREAT?

You're never too old for Halloween ... so give her a treat she'll enjoy all year.
Wonderful, whimsical spider pins feature magnificent Tahitian pearls and diamonds.
In sterling silver, eighteen karat gold, gold and platinum, or all platinum, from $400 to $1800.
A guaranteed cure for arachnophobia! At both Mednikow stores.

(And, speaking of webs, visit us online at www.mednikow.com)

MEDNIKOW

PHIPPS PLAZA / 3500 PEACHTREE ROAD, N. E. / ATLANTA, GEORGIA 30326 / 404-364-9900
474 PERKINS EXTENDED / MEMPHIS, TENNESSEE 38117 / 901-767-2100
CERTIFIED GEMOLOGISTS ⟨AGS⟩ FINE JEWELERS SINCE 1891

pany's annual volume or the percentage of that figure he currently spends on promoting his name and merchandise.)

"Every ad we do is sincere, non offensive, nonantagonistic and in good taste, plus we have every item in stock that we show in our ads, which only serves to heighten the fact that we've come to be recognized by our customers for our believability. The ads we present bolster confidence and security in the eyes of the viewer because that's exactly what they're designed to do," notes this jeweler.

While co-op partnerships with major vendors account for a portion of the company's on-going advertising program, Mednikow says that while he certainly takes full advantage of those dollars, co-op ads don't drive his advertising plans.

He brings the point home when he says he won't run an ad just because it is supported by co-op dollars. "Our goal and our signature over the years has always been the same; i.e., to portray beautiful jewelry in the finest way. Thus I won't run an ugly ad with bad photography, bad

copy and our logo not well represented, even if there's considerable co-op money involved. I'd simply cancel the ad and that would be that."

Mednikow is bullish on glossy, local magazines to tell his story, no matter if that story is about a Rolex watch or his own collection of beautifully colored Tahitian cultured pearl necklaces.

"We like doing business with these publications because they treat us with respect and let us know we're important to them. We know our contact person and regularly touch base with him. Overall, everything is done on a personalized basis. This is all akin to the way in which I run my own business and so dealing with the local books makes sense to me."

Addressing Mednikow's magazine campaign, well-photographed, full-page, full-color ads run with prime positions on a monthly basis in a full range of fashion and lifestyle publications such as *Memphis* and *Atlanta* magazines, *RSVP*, *Germantown*, *Jezebel* and *Playbill*.

When questioned as to why he does

not necessarily promote his name and image through slick, glossy national publications, Mednikow says that while the obvious high cost is a factor, there's a larger and more significant difference.

"We feel that to the huge, national books, we're an advertiser without a lot of clout. We're unimportant to them. So there's no guarantee of positioning for us. Additionally, we find that there's too much inconsistency in terms of a contact person we can work closely with from year to year."

Aside from magazines, the jeweler extends his story via eye-catching, full color and black and white newspaper ads in *The Commercial appeal* and *The Atlanta Journal Constitution*. "We like the frequency and deep penetration we receive from the $1/2$ page color ads we run every Sunday, as well as the visibility we receive from the 2x4 column black-and-white ads we place four days a week."

When it comes to his deluxe annual catalogs, Mednikow freely admits the books pay for themselves in terms of

SSSSSENSATIONAL!

MEDNIKOW PRESENTS BARRY KRONEN'S EXOTIC "PYTHON COLLECTION."
UNFORGETTABLE DESIGNS WITH BLACK, BROWN, AND CHAMPAGNE DIAMONDS,
SET IN EIGHTEEN KARAT WHITE GOLD. YOU'VE NEVER SEEN ANYTHING LIKE IT!
RING $3350. BRACELET, $6000. PENDANT WITH SILK CORD NECKLACE, $2500.
NEW TO MEMPHIS AND ONLY AT MEDNIKOW, FAMILY OWNED AND OPERATED SINCE 1891.

M E D N I K O W

PHIPPS PLAZA / 3500 PEACHTREE ROAD, N. E. / ATLANTA, GEORGIA 30326 / 404-364-9900
474 PERKINS EXTENDED / MEMPHIS, TENNESSEE 38117 / 901-767-2100
CERTIFIED GEMOLOGISTS (AGS) FINE JEWELERS SINCE 1891

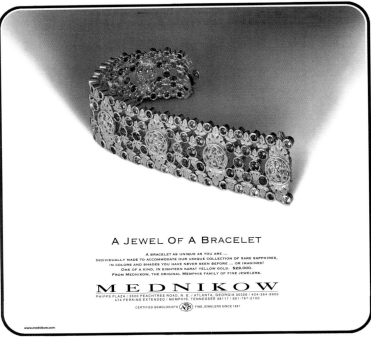

A JEWEL OF A BRACELET

A BRACELET AS UNIQUE AS YOU ARE ...
INDIVIDUALLY MADE TO ACCOMMODATE OUR UNIQUE COLLECTION OF RARE SAPPHIRES,
IN COLORS AND SHADES YOU HAVE NEVER SEEN BEFORE ... OR IMAGINED!
ONE OF A KIND, IN EIGHTEEN KARAT YELLOW GOLD. $29,000.
FROM MEDNIKOW, THE ORIGINAL MEMPHIS FAMILY OF FINE JEWELERS.

M E D N I K O W

PHIPPS PLAZA / 3500 PEACHTREE ROAD, N. E. / ATLANTA, GEORGIA 30326 / 404-364-9900
474 PERKINS EXTENDED / MEMPHIS, TENNESSEE 38117 / 901-767-2100
CERTIFIED GEMOLOGISTS (AGS) FINE JEWELERS SINCE 1891

FOR HIM ... FOREVER

NOT YOUR AVERAGE WEDDING RING ...
BUT THEN, HE'S NOT YOUR AVERAGE MAN!
FROM OUR COLLECTION OF UNUSUAL AND
WONDERFUL PLATINUM WEDDING RINGS,
IN "STEP" AND "BASKETWEAVE" DESIGNS,
WITH MILGRAINED EDGES. ■ $1265 EACH.

MEDNIKOW

CROSS YOUR HEART

YOU'LL FALL IN LOVE WITH DORIS PANOS'
"TATIANA" CROSS PENDANTS.
IN 18 KT GOLD WITH BRILLIANT DIAMONDS.
LARGE, $2800. SMALL, $2200.

MEDNIKOW

return on investment. Explaining that the catalog goes long and deep when it comes to branding his business in the eyes and minds of his clients, he does lift the veil to reveal that he spends around $150,000 for the 20,000 copies he annually sends out to customers and keeps in his stores for reference. "These catalogs contain at least 36 pages, if not more, and show at least 50% of our own jewelry. Again, we are not influenced by co-op money because we want to show what we want to show, not what other people want us to show."

The lush image pieces, which are generally mailed out around the first of November, feature personal notes from the Mednikow family, as well as stylized photography by NYC-based Ron Saltiel, clearly showing the jewels and watches against different colored backdrops. Haute couture-like glossy front covers, such as the white one from the 2002 edition featured a $77,500 yellow-and-white diamond bypass ring in platinum, shown casually resting alongside a blue and gold designer scarf. The scarf theme of this piece carried through to its back cover, but instead of another big diamond ring, the viewer saw a photo of a fantastic jewel encrusted gold Rolex watch—just the watch, the scarf and the Mednikow name. Not a Rolex logo in sight.

Moving ahead to the 2003 catalog, Mednikow points out that there is much more of an emphasis on image branding than ever before. "We're doing more embossing; we're showing more of our own items and we're showing fewer of them per page. We see this as a trend and we're taking full advantage of it to make a deeper hit with our customers at a very important time of year."

When queried on his views about the Internet, the jeweler freely admits that he sees the web as an important communicator and as a powerful brand builder for the present and into the future. "We've developed our own site, which has quite an editorial style look and read because we want to attract this shopping group, which is wide and varied.

It is our belief that we first have to grab these viewers with our message and then make them shop with us instead of going elsewhere to buy that national branded item. In so doing, we are also branding our own name and image today and for the years ahead."

Mednikow, Memphis, TN/Atlanta, GA
CEO: **Robert M. Mednikow**
PRESIDENT/COPYWRITER: **Jay Mednikow**
COPYWRITER: **Faith Stafford**
PHOTOGRAPHER: **Ron Saltiel,** New York, NY

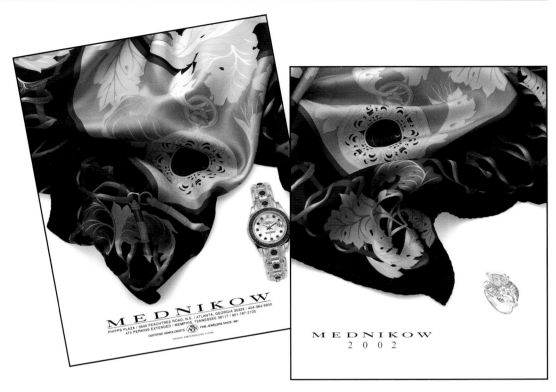

MEDNIKOW
PHIPPS PLAZA / 3500 PEACHTREE ROAD, N.E. / ATLANTA, GEORGIA 30326 / 404-364-9900
474 PERKINS EXTENDED / MEMPHIS, TENNESSEE 38117 / 901-767-2100
CERTIFIED GEMOLOGISTS — FINE JEWELERS SINCE 1891
WWW.MEDNIKOW.COM

MEDNIKOW
2002

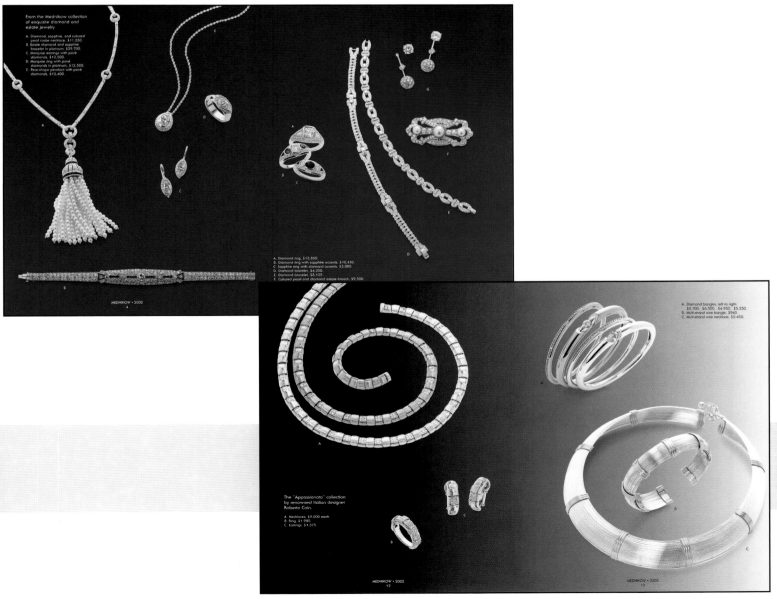

From the Mednikow collection
of exquisite diamond and
estate jewelry.

A. Diamond, sapphire, and cultured
   pearl tassle necklace, $11,250.
B. Estate diamond and sapphire
   bracelet in platinum, $29,700.
C. Marquise earrings with pavé
   diamonds, $12,500.
D. Marquise ring with pavé
   diamonds in platinum, $12,500.
E. Pear-shape pendant with pavé
   diamonds, $12,400.

A. Diamond ring, $13,850.
B. Diamond ring with sapphire accents, $10,430.
C. Sapphire ring with diamond accents, $5,000.
D. Diamond bracelet, $4,250.
E. Diamond bracelet, $8,125.
F. Cultured pearl and diamond estate brooch, $9,500.

MEDNIKOW • 2002
4

The "Appassionata" collection
by renowned Italian designer
Roberto Coin.

A. Necklaces, $9,000 each.
B. Ring, $1,980.
C. Earrings, $1,375.

A. Diamond bangles, left to right:
   $5,100, $6,500, $4,950, $5,350.
B. Multi-strand wire bangle, $940.
C. Multi-strand wire necklace, $2,450.

MEDNIKOW • 2002
12

MEDNIKOW • 2002
13

This magalog launched the current campaign "Life. And all its stores." It depicts the multi-faceted lives of King of Prussia's customers and how its stores are an intense part.

Targeting Multiple Markets

KING OF PRUSSIA, a mammoth mall 18 miles outside Philadelphia, is where shoppers in the tri-state area can find Neiman Marcus, Louis Vuitton, Versace, Hermes and Tiffany—all in one place. The mall is also home to Bloomingdale's, Nordstrom, Talbots and Crate and Barrel. It even has Penneys and Sears.

With eight department stores and 365 specialty shops, King of Prussia is clearly a lot of things to a lot of people. But although it is indisputably the upscale mall in the area and pulls from a vast market, the variety and selection of stores makes it not only for upscale shoppers but for middle and younger markets as well.

Widespread appeal to multiple markets is a situation that's increasingly common to many malls these days, as demographics lines are blurring. In the case of King of Prussia, marketing is right on top of those demographics and what the mall's customers are looking for. It not only knows from how far customers are traveling, but has extensive data from phone research and mall intercepts on the various segments that comprise King of Prussia's market. "An outside company conducts research for us on an annual basis," explained Elizabeth Paige, marketing manager.

That information has been indispensable for marketing and its long time agency, Lorel Marketing Group—particularly when it came time to develop a new multi-media campaign. "The strategic plan was to put together an advertising program to reach all the audiences in the market segments King of Prussia wants to target," said Lorna Rudnick, agency chairman.

The fact that the wide range of stores at King of Prussia appeals to many markets has been a challenge for creative as well as for media and marketing. Research is used extensively.

Creatively, in terms of positioning, it would be hard to ignore all those stores. (Not surprisingly, the campaign preceding the current one was "King of Prussia and Nowhere Else" indicating it was *the* place to shop.)

But in developing the current campaign launched in spring 2002, the decision was made to delve more into the customer's mind. The focus shifted to all the things

The magalog played off the hours of the day as they relate to the customers' day-to-day world.

their customers have to do in life, how the customer lives, and bringing shopping into that life. Hence, the campaign tagline, Life. And All Its Stores, depicting stores as an integral part of the to day-to-day things people do.

The primary vehicle in the multi-media campaign is direct mail, the most effective and efficient way to deal with segmentation. The program also includes television, outdoor and occasional radio and newspaper to support specific events, and a tourism component.

The direct mail elements are designed to speak to each of the mall's diverse audiences individually. The key vehicle for reaching the mall's upper income ($75,000+) shoppers is the twice yearly magalog, mailed to 100,000 homes.

The first piece, the spring 2002 magalog, used the device of the hours of the day and what had to be done in that day. For holiday 2002, the look of the book was changed. "We had gotten feedback that customers liked books a little smaller," said Rudnick. "We wanted to perfect bind it and make it look a little more like a book."

The feedback from that smaller 8½" x 8½" book determined repeating the size for spring 2003. The management team and Lorel wanted to bring the season to their customers in a unique and exciting fashion. Creatively, the goal was to create an intimate association between the customer's life, their dreams of spring, and

things fresh and new at the mall.

The key was in reflecting a reality, whether at work or at home, that the customer could truly identify with in his or her day-to-day life; to surrender to a favorite fantasy or escape to a place they can only find hidden somewhere in their own imagination. And that King of Prussia Mall, like no other shopping venue, offered them more of everything they want and need.

The true challenge came in actually executing that fantasy. Naturally, the first inclination is to load up the crew and fly away to an exotic location filled with palm trees and white sand beaches. A highly unlikely scenario given budgetary restraints.

That magical place the crew was looking for turned out to be in their own backyard—Longwood Gardens, the world's premier horticulture destination located in Kennett Square, PA. Longwood Gardens appeals to a very upscale clientele quite similar to that of King of Prussia mall. Longwood Gardens had never before allowed a commercial photo shoot, but the similarities in the target customer they share, as well as the win-win benefits of producing a tasteful, enticing catalog that spoke to the upscale customer prevailed.

The direct mail device for reaching the middle market is a "magalette"—an 8½" x 11" piece that opens up twice, doubling in size each time. Four stores are featured in each mailer. "The magalette format is

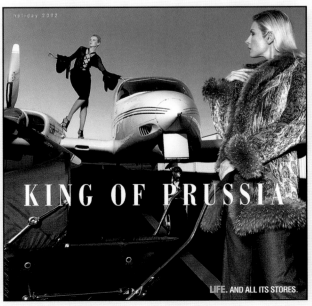

The format changed with Holiday 2002. The small 8½" x 8½" size felt more like a book.

The goal of the Spring 2003 magalog was to create an intimate association between the customer's life, their dreams of spring, and things fresh and new at the mall.

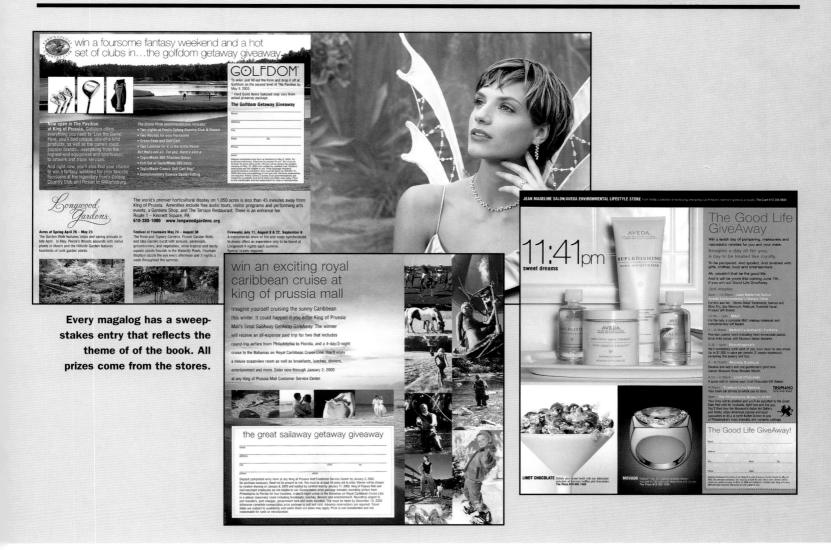

Every magalog has a sweepstakes entry that reflects the theme of of the book. All prizes come from the stores.

new," Paige explained. "Instead of the oversized postcards we used to do, they are actually broadsheets." This year seven magalettes, keyed to a specific selling season or event are being distributed to 45,000 middle market homes, some of which are different for each mailing. The mailings consist of a combination of King of Prussia's database and purchased lists which are then "merged and purged."

The mall has billboards up in three locations year round, which are changed four times a year. The strategy is to balance whatever is being done as a magalette at the time in order to cover all the bases. For example, during the back-to-school selling period, the billboards promote the mall's fashion stores while the magalette features stores for back-to-school shopping.

With so much of its marketing program geared toward targeting segments, it has nevertheless been important to hit the wider market as well. The thinking was that with all the direct mail being very segmented, that television was a way to cover the entire market network. There are 12 15-second spots which are rotated to run as two 15's back-to-back. The TV ads, like the direct mail and billboards, connect life to shopping and stores, again using the device of the time of day.

Each situation reflects real life in a humorous way. "King of Prussia wanted to make an emotional connection with the customer," said Paige. "The commercials are very warm and make you feel good!" Targeted to women 25 to 54, the spots run on approximately 10 stations in the Philadelphia market

Radio is another media that is utilized, albeit it less frequently. "It's the medium identified through market research as most effective to reach the teen market for spring and back-to-school," said Paige.

Print is used only for tourism or for a specific event when an ad may be placed in local papers. Tourism is promoted in drive markets to hotels, key tour operators, and travel planners. Brochures are distributed at local attractions, and other key distribu-tion centers. The brochure contains information about a savings booklet of exclusive coupons that is given at the mall. The savings booklet is not available from any other source, thereby providing tourists an additional incentive to visit.

The mall is also an active participant in the community service area. One particularly outstanding partnering was with the Main Line Art Center. In much the same manner as Chicago's cows of a few years past, the center "put on the dog." "They displayed 50 spectacularly decorated dogs in front of Lord & Taylor for three weeks prior to a gala auction and dinner event. Every dog was sold at prices ranging from $500 to $23,000, raising $325,000. "Main Line Art Center partnered with us for our marketing expertise, but we also helped them with our preferred customer mailing list—the same one we use for the magalog to get those prices," said Paige.

Once again, things just seemed to come together… just as most things King of Prussia does.

Cover from one of the magalettes.

Opened once.

Fully opened.

Back.

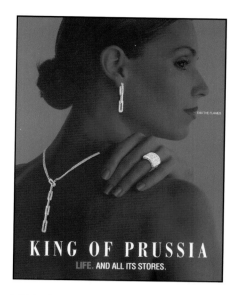
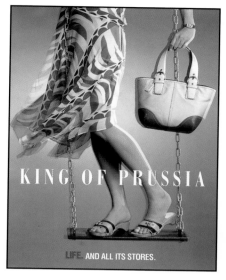

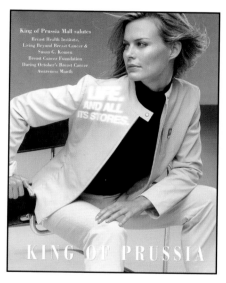

Magalettes are keyed to a specific selling season or event.

Billboards.

Mediterraneo Bamboo Club Morton's

exit 326

KING OF PRUSSIA
Golfdom
Talbots Mens
Bose

exit 326

"Late Again"

A man in a tuxedo, overcoat over his arm waits for his wife. As he checks his watch, she enters adjusting her jewelry. He is frozen by how beautiful she looks.

MALE ANNCR/VO: **7:18 p.m. Late again...**

SUPER: Swarovski

VO: **by Swarovski...**

She checks her dress in the mirror.

SUPER: Versace

VO: **by Versace... and by... Nordstrom.**

He holds up her shawl for her, then changes his mind and puts it down.

SUPER: Nordstrom

He checks his watch, then undoes his bowtie.

VO: **Life. And all its stores by King of Prussia**

"Chemistry"

A teenage girl and boy are sitting in a den, supposedly studying. Instead of reading, the boy is staring at the girl.

FEMALE ANNCR/VO: **4:28 p.m. Chemistry...**

SUPER: Wet Seal.

VO: **by Wet Seal...**

She feels his stare and looks up. He quickly looks back at his book. She checks him out a bit and smiles to herself, and returns to her book.

SUPER: Fossil.

VO: **by Fossil... and by... Borders.**

As he looks at her again, the girl, without looking up from her studying, reaches over and turns his book right side up. He looks at it and gives a sheepish grin.

SUPER: Borders.

VO: **Life. And all its stores by King of Prussia**

"Sleeping In"

Two people are asleep in a handsome sleigh bed as the bedroom begins to fill with morning light.

FEMALE ANNCR/VO: **6:46 a.m. Sleeping in...**

SUPER: Crate & Barrel

VO: **by Crate & Barrel...**

Camera moves over the fluffy down comforter.

SUPER: Domain.

VO: **by Domain... and by... Marmi.**

A large golden retriever comes bounding onto the bed. The couple is startled awake and try to fend him off with their pillows. The man picks up his wife's shoe and tosses it out the door. The dog goes after it. The man flops back in bed as his wife glares at him.

SUPER: Marmi.

VO: **Life. And all its stores by King of Prussia**

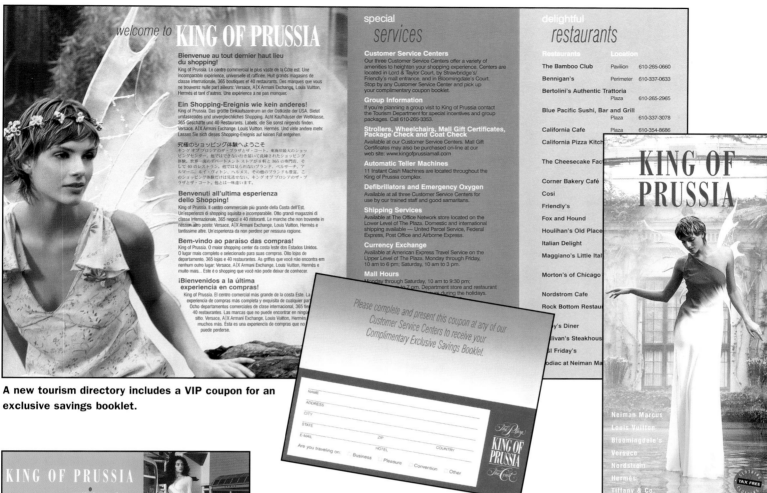

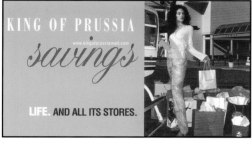

A new tourism directory includes a VIP coupon for an exclusive savings booklet.

Tourism flyer.

King of Prussia, King of Prussia, PA
MANAGEMENT COMPANY: **Kravco Company,** King of Prussia, PA
VICE PRESIDENT—MANAGEMENT: **Clinton M. Cochran**
King of Prussia Mall:
DISTRICT PROPERTY MANAGER: **Deane M. Shauger**
MARKETING MANAGER: **Elizabeth M. Paige**
AGENCY: **Lorel Marketing Group,** King of Prussia, PA
CHAIRMAN: **Lorna Rudnick**
CREATIVE DIRECTOR: **Carliss Million**

In these magazine ads the branding star, logo and branding statement come together as one to place the focus on the merchandise.

Star Treatment

MACY'S is unquestionably a department store institution. But like most department stores in recent years, its advertising has had a kind of institutional feeling to it. Now, in a move to keep the magic and wonder of Macy's shining bright, the retailer has embarked on a major new branding initiative, its first across-the-board branding in many years.

In doing so, Macy's joins a growing number of other majors in the category who are moving back to branding after veering toward promotion in recent years.

Why the swing back? "There's an adjustment taking place," says John Thomas, vice president/creative director. "Almost every major department store is looking at themselves from a marketing perspective to restore a better balance."

A lot of people would say this wake-up call is long overdue—a feeling Thomas echoes emphatically: "There's a numbing sameness in newspaper, and it's not the first time that we've all looked somewhat alike. You could put your hand over a logo and you wouldn't know whose ad it was. There's a point where it all just gets to be a blur." (Editor's Note: The department store category isn't the only one that's taken on the "me too" look. See RAW July, Copy Workshop.)

Undertaking a new branding initiative is a huge order. Macy's branding program is far-reaching, embracing everything from its logo, catalogs and TV spots, to image, trend, ROP and sales advertising. And that isn't the half of it.

"The reality of the situation is you have to come up with a system that allows you to brand yourself regardless of the nature of the message," says Thomas. "Everything from a designer statement to your clearance ad has to have some element of branding in it." That's quite a challenge when you think of the complexity and variety of print messages that a company like Macy's has to deal with on a daily basis.

When you factor in that the in-house agency at Herald Square does the ads for all of Macy's East—more than 100 stores from Florida to New England—you get some idea of the scope of the new work. Moreover, Thomas notes, "It's not just the number, it's the amount of versioning we do."

It's understandable then that in coming up with the new concept, Macy's wanted a simple device—something that would convey the special magic of the store, be immediately identifiable, and obviously, given the everyday demands of the advertising agenda, be flexible.

How do you capture the essence of a Macy's? The Herald Square store, which sets the tone for the entire chain, is an institution. From near or far, everyone wants to see "the world's largest store." "What Harrods is to

TOMMY HILFIGER. Star components... Ithaca striped polo. 59.50. Brigade chino pant. 49.50. Banded collar jean jacket. $59. Crochet camisole. $29. Wide leg pant. $54. Ribbed logo tee. $54. Cotton terry jacket. 49.50. Matching short. 39.50. Crewneck tee. $29. Cotton terry hooded sweatshirt. 69.50. Matching athletic pant. 49.50. Cap sleeve henley. $34. Stars and stripes skirt. $59.

MACY'S BY APPOINTMENT. LINDA LEE AND HER PERSONAL SHOPPERS CAN SHOW YOU ALL THE POSSIBILITIES. CALL 212-494-4181. OUTSIDE NEW YORK, 1-800-343-0121.

macys.com

Photography is shot in a way that expresses the upbeat, friendly and confident attitude of the store. Always clean and uncluttered, the page makes the merchandise the star.

BLACK AND WHITE TREND. Star performers... Dummy copy here about the different vendors. Fabric here. Misses 2-14. $245. On 2, Herald Square and select Macy's.

CHARTER CLUB. Swinging on a star. Fine gauge ribbed cotton twinset. Misses S-XL. Cardigan. $40 Crew. $35. Stretch cotton twill capri. Misses 4-16; petites 2-14. $40. MACY'S BY APPOINTMENT. LET LINDA LEE AND HER PERSONAL SHOPPERS SHOW YOU ALL THE POSSIBILITIES.

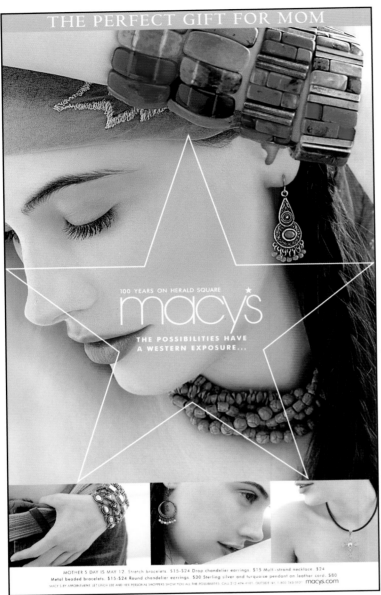

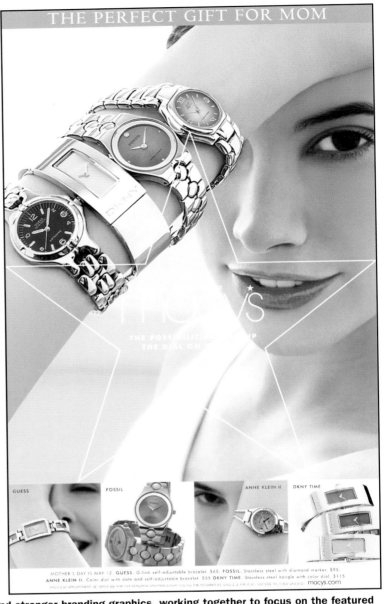

Newspaper ads have a clean, uncluttered look with streamlined propping and stronger branding graphics, working together to focus on the featured item or story and reinforce Macy's as a brand.

London, Macy's is to New York City. It's the preeminent department store retailer," says Thomas. "Primarily because of the high visibility of the annual events Macy's does—the parade, fireworks, the flower show—because of those kinds of things, people have an emotional connection to the store."

Clearly, Macy's has a special aura about it. One can see how in developing the branding, it wasn't much of a leap to using a star—this time as more than part of the logo itself, but expanded into a impactful graphic symbol that represents everything the store stands for—fashion, magic, wonder, theater, a total experience. "The star really jumped out," says Thomas. "Macy's already has equity in it, so at this point we

just reestablished the star as Macy's icon in a dramatic way. The big issue was how carefully do we have to think about the issue of consistency. Ultimately we came to the conclusion that there was room to maneuver primarily because the shape itself is graphically so identifiable. It's still a star!"

But changing a logo treatment, a management mindset and the infinite variety of creative treatments generated by new branding, was only the beginning of a complex creative process that according to Thomas was at least a year in the making. "One reason why was it had to be flexible. Every step was another step in merchandising and how we approach it, so we needed an arsenal of graphic components

that could be manipulated. Macy's is a high response machine because of its proximity to fashion."

In terms of copy, the branding statement selected to convey the optimism and define the brand in a single phrase is based on "the possibilities"—ever changing like the store, yet always the same like the brand.

While the response to the new initiative has been positive, Thomas acknowledges that it can be difficult in a business environment to "give up that much space to a graphic icon." The feeling now is that this is what's needed to get attention and establish the look. But he notes, "with time the star itself can become more subtle."

Right now, it looks like Macy's star is rising.

Newspaper ads feature the solid rendering of the star centered at the bottom of a single page on top of horizontal bars, the solid star holds together the look of the page. On double trucks, the star is placed on the right-hand page. Whether four-color or B/W, the star features Macy's logo combined with macys.com. ROP advertising covers a wide range—everything from full page trend and cosmetic/fragrance stories to 300L ads.

Catalog covers. The Spring book was one of the first direct mail pieces created with the new branding identity.

Valentine's Day catalog.

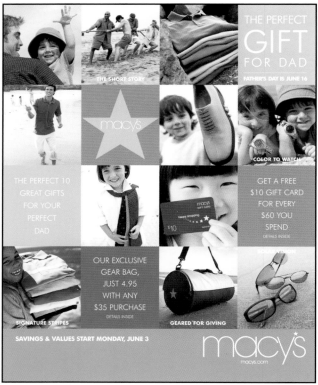

Father's Day catalog.

Macy's East, New York
AGENCY: **In-House**
EXECUTIVE VP/MARKETING: **Martine Reardon**
GROUP VP/CREATIVE DIRECTOR: **John Thomas**
COPY DIRECTOR: **Fylice Larsen**
DIRECTOR CREATIVE SERVICES/STOREWIDE: **Rick Pomer**
CREATIVE DIRECTOR/FASHION, HOME: **Heather Robinet**
DIRECTOR/BROADCAST: **Ed Sheehan**
OUTSIDE AGENCIES: **Amster Yard,** New York/
SFI Creative Group, New York

It's a Small World After All

"Our mission at Aveda is to care for the world we live in, from the products we make to the ways in which we give back to society. At Aveda, we strive to set an example for environmental leadership and responsibility, not just in the world of beauty, but around the world."

Horst Rechelbacher, Founder

AVEDA, the Sanskrit word for "all knowledge," is the concept that guides founder Horst Rechelbacher's approach to personal care products. The company is based on a holistic connection between beauty, wellness and environmental responsibility. Since Aveda's inception in 1978, the company has stayed true to Rechelbacher's vision by focusing the brand's efforts on creating plant-based products that stay true to its environmental mission. It's these raw materials that form the basis of Aveda's products,

since the goal is to use plant resources responsibly in an effort to safeguard the earth's dwindling supplies.

Even the company website, aveda.com, gives browsers info on Aveda's activism in the areas of global climate change, water and air pollution, habitat destruction, environmental toxins and waste generation, and offers tips on how individuals can make a difference.

Reinforcing the holistic message is Aveda's beautifully designed new color catalog.

Every other page in the 9⁷/₈" x 11¹/₄" catalog is trimmed horizontally to 5¹/₈". These short pages are the only place in the catalog that actual product shots appear. Here we show the first spread with the half page flipped to the right (it's actually "hidden" since it continues the image of the model), and then with the half page turned to the left (bringing products into view).

The center two sheets of the catalog are trimmed horizontally to form an eight-page mini catalog devoted to Aveda's range of hair care products. As with the other short pages, it at first appears "hidden" as it continues the larger photo.

The center spread with the mini catalog opened.

The center spread with the mini catalog flipped all the way to the left, revealing product shots.

untamed beauty.

Another example of the short page.

the substance of style.

Launched for fall/winter, the catalogs will be produced seasonally (with 35,300 catalogs printed and sent to approximately 150 U.S. retail stores, spas and Aveda concept salons). Even the catalog is environmentally correct since Aveda used soy ink on 30% post-consumer paper.

Visually exciting, the catalog reinforces the notion of a diverse world of beauty and its traditions. Hence the cover's tagline—One World, Many Voices. The models Aveda has chosen reflect this multicultural diversity. No cookie cutter faces here—all ethnicities are represented, from a dramatically made up African-American woman to an Asian beauty.

Even the copy places an emphasis on the firm's philosophy. Not only does it inform readers of the various products shown and the origins of their unique ingredients—it's a beautifully illustrated, mini-cultural history lesson.

In addition to the catalog, Aveda relies on magalogs (for sale at their stores, these feature the firm's entire product range), as well as frequent product sampling and giveaways at their retail stores, plus a "secret weapon"—a terrifically friendly and knowledgeable sales staff. Now, that's good karma!

Aveda, Minneapolis, MN
AGENCY: **Kevin White Photography,** Minneapolis, MN
PHOTOGRAPHER: **Kevin White** (trade hair beauty shots)
AGENCY: **JGK, Inc.,** New York, NY
PHOTOGRAPHER: **Ruven Afandor** (beauty styling, main pages)
AGENCY: **Faucher Artist Representatives NYC**
PHOTOGRAPHER: **Victor Schrager** (styled product shots)

Role Branding

*Communicating the image of the target consumer featuring her own lifestyle and persona. The strategy's focus is consumer centric with the **customer-as-a-brand**. Incorporating the way the customer brands herself — for example: aspirational "**id**" or perhaps the way the company brands itself through positional "**ID**", identification with the customer.*

"All the world's a stage and we are but players." Even when Shakespeare wrote this he knew we each have a role to play in our lives on this earth. While our reality may be different from the past, it still holds true.

The retailer's understanding of the customer requires an ongoing observation of and attention to what the customer's own image of self is—the "id." Borrowing from Freud and psychology to define the target consumer's "id" goes beyond demographics and focuses on the more multidimensional psychographics.

One of the best ways to create a dialogue with customers is to show them their own mirror image in the advertising, displays and promotion visuals. Some retailers have discovered the perfect "Role Branding" strategy, either by presenting their customers as they are or as they believe themselves to be.

They show an appreciation for a more realistic view of customers. Many customers do not like seeing the picture-perfect scenes and models in ads that do not resemble them or their lives. A refreshing break is when a retailer communicates how it truly understands the customer's values, attitudes, lifestyle, needs and wants. This is often the beginning of a close relationship that can be nurtured over time.

Developing this close relationship is similar to those in one's personal life. With honesty, respect and trust—providing more than what is expected—look at what these retailers see in their customers…

• **Real Lives** – *Crate & Barrel* chose "real people" to reach out to a new customer in the youth market, cast from the street.

"They're not posed; they're dressed in real clothes, depicting the way in which ordinary people live their lives at home." This authentic life feeling comes across in a whimsical, unusual way that entertains as it ties customer and product together: Consumer *id* meets retailer *ID*. See page 48.

• **Consumer Empowerment** – *Oakwood Mall* with General Growth Properties offers a little retail group therapy. The stylish illustrations and clever copy communicate fun, empowerment and personality—focusing on the malls' core customers' views and attitudes rather than the malls' offerings. This is consumer-focused marketing at its best. The images connect with women on emotional, personal "id" levels, making the relationship closer with the centers featured in the campaign— "brand personality ID." The malls empathize with people's needs for self-expression and self-fulfillment—"I shop, therefore I am." See page 50.

• **Who Am I?** – *Bootlegger* realized it had to reach its teen market with an emotional connection. Teens love to push the boundaries at the same time they have the serious teen issue of "identity" and how to "fit in." Finding their fit was a double play on repositioning the store in a newly competitive market, while speaking to irreverent teens who don't want the same old jeans ads. Bootlegger speaks the teens' edgy language. See page 54.

• **Make It Your Own** – *Saks Fifth Avenue* communicates directly to its target customer in a mutually beneficial way. From its

"Live a Little" campaign to the "Make it Your Own" campaign, it invites the customer to join in its "This brand, SAKS, is ME" connection. The strategy is to project an attitude and an excitement that matches the attitude and lifestyle of its customers, who want this retailer's experience over any individual apparel brands. Here the models are model-beautiful, but they present the idea that you too can "make this your own." See page 58.

• **A Part of You** – *H. Stern* knows that they have a market where a woman and her jewels still have an indelible relationship. For many of these customers, jewelry is aspirational and a part of the beautiful life. For others, it is a part of their sense of well-being. Elegant models provide the desired reflection of the modern sense of style and subtlety of understated opulence. Stern and its agency saw the "intellectual concept of jewelry as an extension of the wearer's personality and body." See page 62.

• **Family Photo Album** – *Pippers America* depicts "happy children doing happy things." Its photographer doesn't tell the kids what to do, he lets them just "be" and takes pictures of exactly what they would be doing normally. The naturalness and informal feeling communicates the comfort and quality Pippers wants its customers to feel in the clothes-shopping role of "Mom." See page 65.

Setting out to establish a difference can sometimes seem more difficult than it may need to be. Opening up to the honest, direct approach with customers is most refreshing and appreci-

ated. But first, *to thine own self be true*. A company must do some self-reflection and determine "who it wants to be." What are the retail brand's own beliefs, attitudes and values? How similar are these to its target consumers? What is the most effective way to build a close relationship between the retail brand and the target customer as brand?

The early days of retailing were a mix of instinct, passion and insight into the needs and wants of people. While that is still necessary, there is much more to building strong brands in this highly competitive world. Creating effective strategies to build and grow a brand employs a complex mix of disciplines and requires intellectual analysis of the brand, the company, its people, the product/service, and the most critical element, the consumer—all before a single ad or promotion is created.

Reality Check

We've all seen lots of beautiful furniture ads that tell the story via one or a grouping of colorful, well-photographed product shots. And they all do the job they've set out to do; i.e., sell that furniture to the viewer. But here's a campaign that really serves up the furniture message in a fresh, new way by weaving in just the right amount of lifestyle and whimsy to the mix.

When Tucker Tapia, the creative agency for Crate & Barrel, set out to create a new ad campaign for their client, their goal was to bring a fresh, different approach to each image. And they did just that by clearly playing up humanity, playfulness and a casual air across each of the four images they produced.

"We wanted to try something a bit out of the ordinary. We opted to shake things up just a bit in order to grab the viewer's attention and set the client apart from the competition," explains Jose Tapia, the agency's creative director/partner.

When it came to first conceptualizing the attitude for the full-color, four-page inserts, Tapia began with the idea of integrating an ethnically diverse array of "real people" models, cast right from the street, having fun with the furniture.

"We chose the people in the ads because to us, they portray the range of Crate & Barrel's customers; they're interesting, not trite and totally natural. They're not posed

in any way and they're dressed in real, everyday clothing," he says, adding that each big, bold image depicts the way in which ordinary people live their lives at home.

For Tapia, this kind of authentic life feeling comes across in a whimsical, unusual way with a mix of models (photographed softly or in an editorial-style, blurry way) shown dancing on a Peroba coffee table or playing "golf" on a Stillwater dining room table.

With an eye on producing a campaign that is anything but stuffy, Tapia's aim was to add younger viewers to the store's existing customer base. "We wanted to grab this important youth market and attract them to look at the ads. It was significant to have this audience immediately realize that the company has lots of terrific stuff just for them."

Overall, each image puts the company in a new light in terms of reflecting and accentuating the brand. The ads are highly personal, warm and inviting. They place the company on an intimate level, as Tapia

notes, by speaking one to one with the viewer. "We needed to reflect the fact that Crate & Barrel is not a huge, monolithic company. We did that by taking all of the attributes of each product and making everything across the campaign simple and fun for the viewer to see, read and learn about," he explains.

In approaching the distinctive, personalized story lines specifically created for each ad, the agency's copywriter and partner, Michele Tucker, says that in thrusting to a diverse crowd of readers, she first focused on lifestyle specific buzzwords, such as "Integrated," "Evolving," "Innovative" and "You Lead."

"We took each lead word, which gave life and meaning to the product it was describing and used it as a headline. Then we flowed each block of copy, which also contained words that told the viewer about that particular product, around that singular word."

The overall feeling here, explains Tucker, was to bring the viewer directly into each

ad—both visually and copy-wise—by way of strong images coupled with short, to-the-point words that give a personal account of the life of the person shown. "In addition, the words serve as a metaphor for each product," she notes.

While the Crate & Barrel logo appears in large, block-style white lettering at the bottom of the first and last ad, story lines run in either a black or white script style typeface from ad to ad. The reasoning for this treatment, explains Tapia, is to give the viewer added visual impact.

"While we naturally wanted to delineate the company's name and make that stand out on the page, we also wanted the photography and the copy to appear organic and fluid. So it was important that everything ebb and flow from ad to ad, while still maintaining continuity and tie together as an insert. Basically, what we wanted to achieve was to

take the viewer on a nice, little journey from beginning to end."

As for copy placement, Tapia allowed the type to flow from ad to ad, appearing sometimes at the top; sometimes at the bottom. "I looked at each image and decided to let that image dictate where the words should go. I wanted each word to appear as if it simply fell onto the page and came to rest in just the right spot. Nothing was forced and there wasn't any rigid format."

The campaign was shot by Chicago-based photographer Francois Robert and ran in lifestyle and fashion publications such as *Gourmet, GQ, HG, Vanity Fair, Vogue, Living Room, Elle Décor* and *Real Simple*.

Crate & Barrel, Northbrook, IL
AGENCY: **Tucker Tapia,** Chicago, IL
CREATIVE DIRECTOR/PARTNER: **Jose Tapia**
COPYWRITER/PARTNER: **Michele Tucker**
PHOTOGRAPHER: **Francois Robert,** Chicago, IL
MODEL CASTING: **Diane Vanaria Casting,** Chicago, IL

Evolving. In the beginning, there was a sofa. And you and your sofa were one. But what if you become two? Or three? What if three plays patty-cake on your pillows? Life's big choices include slipcovers. The couch is yours come what may. Spinnaker Sofa.

Innovative. Carving paths through mahogany and other traditions keeps dinner from becoming dull. We don't do dull. Stillwater Dining Table.

Group Therapy

MANY MARKETING directors are feeling pressured to do more for their centers but have less dollars to do it. Some people are using guerrilla-marketing tactics to deal with the new realities. Others are capitalizing on the power of partnerships and sponsorships—sometimes with vendors, but more commonly, with local community organizations or media, and with national charitable causes.

Still another group of shopping centers has found a viable solution in cost effective sharing—specifically, the group marketing campaign.

General Growth Properties, for example, has a program in which a certain segment of similar malls with limited marketing budgets, is able to share the same marketing campaign, making it more economical for everyone.

Each mall purchases the specific elements needed for its center. Oakwood Mall, in Eau Claire, WI, is one of eight small General Growth Property centers in the midwest which has participated in shared campaigns in recent years. With its 100 stores, Oakwood is what group marketing manager Johnna VanDeurzen, terms "a typical mid-market mall." "Oakwood has never had a huge marketing budget," she said. "But General Growth could always find a strategy that worked for several of its middle-market, mid-western centers. Group purchases make more sense. When you have someone else doing the same thing, you can steal and share, as long as you watch geographically that you're not crossing markets. There's really no downside."

Oakwood bought into the current small center group campaign "Let Yourself Go" across the board. The work of Omaha, NE-based agency, Sacco, the campaign takes an atypical approach to meet the branding and budgetary challenges GGP set forth to help each mall communicate a unique brand style.

"Let Yourself Go," is based on the idea that going to the mall can be therapy—presenting shopping as that healthy, therapeutic 'me' time everyone needs on occasion. The theme actually works on two levels—Let Yourself Go to the mall; Let Yourself Go—leave your stress, inhibitions and negativity behind.

"The idea of shopping being therapeutic is what appeals to me most about this campaign," said VanDeurzen. "It's humorous and comforting. We're all in the same boat—overworked women who don't have enough time. The mall is where we go for our little retail therapy."

The campaign incorporates illustrations that are stylish human representations. These images and their accompanying messages communicate fun, empowerment and personality—focusing on the malls' core customers' views and attitudes rather than the malls' offerings.

"It's good for mid-market people. They think it's a riot," said VanDeurzen. "We went from having a series of pretty fashion shots to something whimsical and fun that doesn't look like mall marketing. It's really a little bit out of the ordinary, especially for

Life's a Trip. DRESS Accordingly.

Thank You for Shopping with Us

Window static.

Inner Beauty is overrated.

*Oak*Wood Mall

Let Yourself Go

In-mall poster.

JANUARY SIDEWALK SALE

Don't Walk, Run!

January 17th – 20th, the biggest savings of the season are here! With discounts mall-wide from great stores like Younkers, Scheels All Sports, American Eagle Outfitters & Victoria's Secret, let yourself go!

The January Sidewalk Sale — top to bottom, inside & out — the coolest shopping event of the year, and it's only here at Oakwood Mall!

*Oak*Wood Mall

Let Yourself Go

HWY 53 AT GOLF RD. • MON-SAT 10 A.M. - 9 P.M.
SUN 11 A.M. - 6 P.M.
Oakwoodmall.com

Newspaper ad.

Oakwood Mall features five anchor stores - Marshall Field's, Scheels All Sports, Sears, JCPenney and Younkers. In addition, Oakwood is home to great stores like GAP/GAP Kids, Old Navy, American Eagle, Gymboree, Aeropostale, Bath & Body Works, and Victoria's Secret; a 12-screen Carmike Theater, children's play area and family restrooms.

THE ONE GIFT THAT'S PERFECT FOR EVERYONE

Gift Certificates are available at Customer Service in any denomination. They are redeemable at any Oakwood Mall retailer.

SHOPPING HOURS
Monday – Saturday 10am – 9pm
Sunday 11am – 6pm

Watch for extended hours during the holiday season.

...ent store and restaurant ...hours may vary.

OakWood Mall
Let Yourself Go

Phone (715) 839-7677

Located at US Hwy 53 at Golf Road
Eau Claire, Wisconsin 54701

www.oakwoodmall.com

OAKWOOD MALL DIRECTORY

Let Yourself Go!

Directory.

Hop To It!

The Easter Bunny arrives at Oakwood Mall on **Saturday, April 5th!** Bring the kids for fun and photos with Mr. Long Ears himself.

Through Easter in the Scheels wing.

OakWood Mall
Let Yourself Go

Located at US Hwy 53 at Golf Road
Eau Claire, Wisconsin 54701 • (715) 839-7677

www.oakwoodmall.com

Newspaper ad.

TV spot.

To appeal to the core woman shopper, the color palette is purposely feminine, using lighter pastels rather than bold colors to soften the impact of the visuals, which blend with the stronger verbiage.

this low-budget kind of center."

While the campaign appeals to a wide audience for perennial events such as Father's Day and back-to-school, it's designed to identify more with the malls' core women shoppers by employing psychographic, not demographic messages. Instead of focusing on aesthetics, or merchandise or store mixes that vary drastically from mall to mall, Let Yourself Go focuses on the human qualities of the shopper—— the vanities, frustrations, joys and challenges inherent in everyone's daily life— which are universally appealing.

Since the campaign is about attitude and emotion, it's universally applicable to each mall. Instead of using the standard 'beautiful model' shots associated with retail center advertising that would limit its appeal to certain age groups, the images connect with women on emotional and personal levels,

laying the groundwork for a more personal relationship with each of the centers.

The malls are represented as personalities that can empathize with people's need for self-expression and self-fulfillment. Headlines like "Inner Beauty is Overrated", "Heel Thyself" and "I Shop, Therefore I Am" reflect this individually expressive spirit.

"When we rolled out the campaign first quarter 2003, it was particularly well received," VanDuerzen said. "It will be our branding campaign for Oakwood Mall going forward for several years." Oakwood is utilizing all the elements in the campaign—newspaper, television and radio ads, outdoor, and in-mall collateral. The mall has one billboard and a significant amount of collateral—22" x 28" ceiling banners, table tents, window-static clings, and barricade signage among them.

While the in-mall collateral is ongoing

throughout the year, the ads are either event (for ex: "Sidewalk Sale") or season-driven. A typical schedule might include a ROP ad for holidays such as Mother's Day or Father's Day, several ads for back-to-school, and 15-20 placements for holiday in the main local paper as well as in publications for the visitors' and convention bureaus; TV spots on all the major cable and network stations in Eau Claire, and radio, for both back-to-school and holiday.

The broad creative platform affords virtually endless directions, enabling the campaign to evolve and grow over time. With a virtually unlimited amount of illustration applications, headlines and concepts, each of the malls has the opportunity to personalize an already personal campaign to better reflect its market dynamics, core shopper appeal and brand personality. In short, the campaign is working for everyone.

Isn't Life Delicious?

There's more to life than just great fashion. There's great food!

Stop by *The Ground Round*, or take a quick spin around The Carousel Café Food Court for tasty names like:

A&W, Big Ed's Chicago Style Hot Dogs, Great Steak & Potato Co., KarmelKorn, KFC, Magic Wok, Massads, Orange Julius, Osaka, Sbarro, Subway, and Taco Johns.

It's always a great choice.

River Hills Mall
Let Yourself Go

Exit at Hwys. 14 & 22 and County Rd. 3 S, Mankato, MN.
507-385-7450 • www.riverhillsmall.com
Mall Hours:
Monday-Saturday: 10 a.m. – 9 p.m. Sunday: 11 a.m. – 6 p.m.
A General Growth Property

Birchwood Mall
Let Yourself Go

Get Out There And Shop.

LAKEVIEW SQUARE MALL
Let Yourself Go

Get Out There And Shop.

"Let Yourself Go" lets people invest in their appearance and feel good about themselves— confident or free or playful or adventurous.

Find Your HAPPY Place
Capital Mall
HIGHWAY 50 WEST & TRUMAN BLVD., JEFFERSON CITY

Billboard.

I Shop, Therefore I am.

Colony Square mall
Let Yourself Go

Oakwood Mall, Eau Claire, WI
GROUP MARKETING MANAGER: **Johnna VanDeurzen**
MARKETING COORDINATOR: **Amy Resch**
AGENCY: **Sacco,** Omaha, NE
ACCOUNT EXECUTIVE: **Dawn Drazdys**
ASSOCIATE CREATIVE DIRECTOR: **Joel Barratt**
SENIOR COPYWRITER/STRATEGIST: **Thor Rosenquist**
ART DIRECTOR: **Scott Bargenquast**
ILLUSTRATOR: **Karen Wolcott**
MANAGEMENT COMPANY: **General Growth Properties,** Chicago

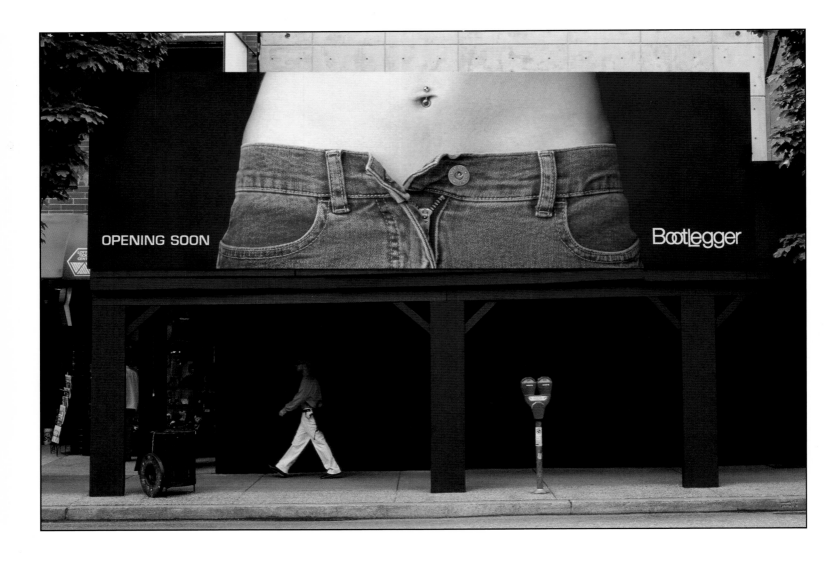

OPENING SOON

Bootlegger

Going for Edge

BOOTLEGGER, an apparel chain targeted to a young lifestyle, started in 1971 as a single store in Vancouver. In the seventies, it became *the* place to buy jeans in western Canada.

In the '80s, because of the arrival of Gap and other competition, Bootlegger retreated from its urban origins, opening many stores in the suburbs. By the late '90s, with more than a hundred stores, opportunities for expansion in suburban locations had maxed out. The company decided for future growth, it would have to get back to its urban roots. "We needed to stand out, and stand out for something

with our communication," said Kari Baker, marketing manager. That meant advertising with an edge to reflect the company's desire for an urban fashion image for a Vancouver store opening that was about to open and for Bootlegger stores in other locations.

In August 2002, a flagship store was scheduled to open on trendy Robson Street in Vancouver. To help create buzz for this important new store and position the brand as offering the hippest selection around, Bootlegger turned to Vancouver-based Rethink Advertising for three key projects. The first was to create some-

thing that would generate pre-opening excitement. The second and third projects were for ad campaigns that would be used for all Bootlegger stores.

One of the ad campaigns was a positioning campaign to launch the store. The other was a campaign to promote the latest in denim for back-to-school.

To get things off to a dramatic start for the pre-opening, Rethink developed an idea for a horizontal board that would be placed on top of the building six weeks prior to opening. The billboard showed a close-up of a woman with the button of her jeans open with the message,

"Opening Soon." When the store opened, a new board showed the woman with the zipper open and the message, "Now Open."

The campaign to position the brand and launch the new flagship store ("Find Your Fit") ran for three months from early August until early November in media such as skytrain station placards, bus sides, entertainment newspapers, radio and in store.

From the seemingly innocuous theme came three humorous executions that pushed the boundaries, while tapping into the serious teen issue of identity. "Mini storyboards showed various teens finding their "fit"—a boy who finds happiness with an older woman, the girl who would rather spend time with ice cream, a guy who would prefer to be with another guy. "The ads focused on the emotional side, what teenagers go though trying to find their fit, who they are," said Chris Staples, Rethink creative director. The theme has been so successful, it is being continued for upcoming work.

Jeans are an important part of Bootlegger's business. "That's where we started and what we've maintained throughout the years," said Baker. A big strength has been that it has more sizes and styles than the competition, but to attract its savvy market, variety wasn't enough. Bootlegger needed to get the message out that it was the place to buy fashion.

BOOTLEGGER

STRETCH JEANS — Bootlegger

LOW CUT JEANS — Bootlegger

DIRTY DENIM — Bootlegger

Radio :30, "The Perfect Fit"

A WOMAN SITS AT GOLDILOCKS AND THE THREE JEANS.

STORYTELLER: Once upon a time, Goldilocks was on her way to get some blonde highlights when she stopped by the brand new Bootlegger on Robson Street. She tried on three pairs of jeans.

SFX: zzzzzzip

GOLDILOCKS: These jeans are too skanky.

SFX: zzzzzzip

GOLDILOCKS: These jeans are much too tight.

SFX: zzzzzzip

GOLDILOCKS: These jeans are too skanky and much too tight... I'll take them.

STORYTELLER: And she lived happily ever after.

GROOVIN MUSIC UP

STORYTELLER: Bootlegger. Find your fit.

FLARED JEANS — Bootlegger

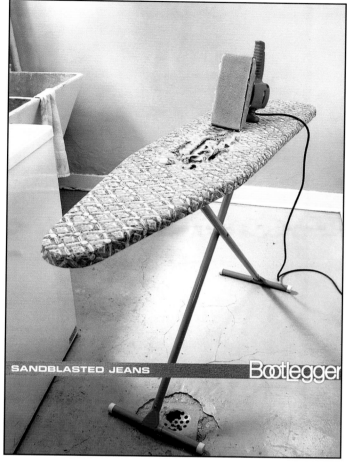

SANDBLASTED JEANS — Bootlegger

In working on the creative strategy for the campaign, the agency gave a lot of consideration to the shopping environment where the new store is located. "Robson Street in Vancouver is like Melrose Avenue in L.A.," said Staples. "There are a lot of hip sellers up and down Robson Street, including five or six places for young people to buy jeans. Bootlegger didn't have a lot of credibility as the place to buy fashion, so we decided to give them back the edge they'd had," said Staples.

The solution was the "Objects" campaign, developed to promote the latest in denim for back to school in a most unorthodox way. Instead of denim, each ad featured an object. "The last thing you want to do to establish your edginess or hipness is show another teenager wearing jeans," said Staples. "We wanted to zig, while everyone else zagged, edgy but not offensive. Things teenagers would find a little bit racy, but parents probably wouldn't get." The series appeared as window posters in all Bootlegger

Bootlegger, Richmond, BC, Canada
MARKETING MANAGER: **Kari Baker**
ADVERTISING AGENCY: **Rethink Advertising,** Vancouver, B.C., Canada
CREATIVE DIRECTORS: **Ian Grais, Chris Staples**
COPYWRITER: **Rob Tarry**
ART DIRECTOR: **Mark Hesse**
PRODUCTION: **Chelsea Miller**
STUDIO ARTIST: **Jonathon Cesar, Leanna Crawford** ("Ice Cream," "Cougar")
Genevieve Smith ("Football")

stores across Canada, and in newspapers and as bus shelters from mid-August to mid-October.

While there were a few e-mails about the advertising, there was surprisingly little controversy overall. On the contrary "It was well received by our stores," said Baker. "There was a lot of buzz!"

JUST DESSERTS

ALLOW US TO WHIP UP THE MOST DELECTABLE
CONFECTIONS, WORTHY OF A CONNOISSEUR.
WE LIVE TO SERVE.

CALL 1.800.429.0996 SAKS.COM

SAKS
FIFTH
AVENUE
MAKE IT YOUR OWN

Lightening Up

SAKS FIFTH AVENUE is one of those retail institutions of a certain age that inevitably commands respect. Refined, elegant, it's truly one of the Grande Dames of great stores. Yet Saks —like any long-established entity in the competitive retail world—can't afford to rest on its laurels.

"Any brand that has been around as long as ours has doesn't want to get lost in the past," said Kimberly Grabel, VP marketing. "You want to show you're about today."

Being about "today" to a large extent is being about individuality—a message that's inherent in what Saks did for spring with its current campaign "Make It Your Own." Its focus on individuality reflected a strategy Saks embarked on several years back with its "Live a Little" campaign.

One thing that made the recent effort different was the attitude it projected. Saks seemed to have more fun. "We

lightened up and loosened up a bit," said Grabel. "And that really has been the evolution of the strategy."

"It's also about keeping Saks modern, which is really its heritage" added Jan Richter, senior VP of creative. "We wanted to loosen up and still make it upscale, but aspirational, believable and real."

A tall order, perhaps. But, in actuality, Saks did a stellar job of communicating what the store represents. This was about Saks selling Saks (the implication being that Saks was where customers could find the special brands that reflect their individuality—that every customer has his or her Saks that they could make their own).

The campaign was carried out primarily as double-page spreads and multiple-page inserts in national magazines. There was some outdoor advertising and the big spring women's and men's books as well. The double-page spreads, in particular, illustrated the direction the strategy is taking. Rather than playing up its brands,

Saks branded the store instead.

Each execution featured a dramatic shot of a model and the Saks logo tagged with "Make It Your Own" on the right-hand page. The left-hand page consisted only of a brief block of brilliantly constructed copy, with the 800 number and website address at the bottom.

"These spreads are the purest essence of branding," said Richter. "What we've done that's different from our competitors is we're using smartly crafted copy. The other differentiating factor is we didn't mention brands. We thought that the experience, the verbiage and the attitude superceded the individual brand. It's more about the excitement and attitude."

The spreads ran in March and April in publications such as *InStyle, Vogue, Vanity Fair, The New Yorker* and *W Jewelry*.

The inserts consisted of multiple single-page pages with the same type of attitude-driven model shots as the spreads. The only element other than the copy block

While it appeared that Saks was targeting younger, it was more about the attitude. These are clothes that older women can wear as well.

on the first page of the insert was the Saks logo and a barely-there brand name tucked into the upper corner. Ranging in length from 12 to 16 pages, the inserts appeared in *Vogue, Lucky, GQ, Esquire* and *Details.*

The two spring core books provided an expansive showcase (the women's book was 140 pages; the men's—64) for the new attitude. The creative also surfaced outdoors in selected markets such as San Francisco, where Saks has been a consistent user of the kiosks on the streets. Las Vegas is another market where the retailer utilizes outdoor. The spring campaign could be seen on taxi tops and a series of billboards. "Las Vegas requires an outdoor presence," said Grabel. "We had a mobile billboard also running there for this campaign. Anywhere else I would never believe it!"

Taking it to the streets on a truck? Saks is definitely lightening up.

The copy was especially relevant—talking to people who appreciate an element of surprise.

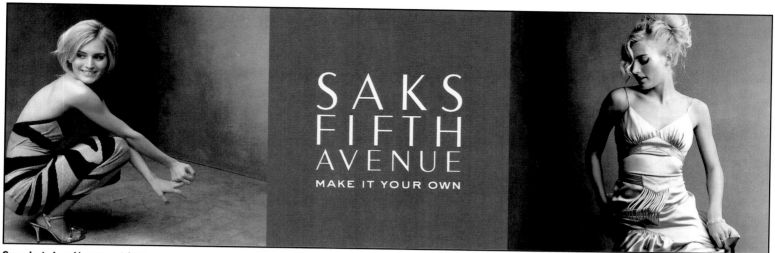

Sure bet: Las Vegas outdoor.

Catalog insert.

Catalog cover.

Saks Fifth Avenue, New York
SR. VP OF CREATIVE: **Jan Richter**
VP MARKETING: **Kimberly Grabel**
VP OF CREATIVE SERVICES: **Ann Skalski**
COPY DIRECTOR: **Laura Silverman**
PHOTOGRAPHER: **Diego Uchetel,** New York, Los Angeles

Kiosk – San Francisco.

Gorgeous, golden and glowing

HERE'S A JEWELRY campaign that, much like the luxury international retailer it hypes, blends just the right amount of beauty and sexiness with old-world charm and aucourant modernity. As the company's creative director, Roberto Stern points out, "Our mission statement is to always search the past for inspiration with a current interpretation, both for our gems and our advertising message. We want to portray who we are and what we do with strong merchandise and supporting visual statements that harken back to our beliefs, but also portray a high level of comfort and trust."

Keeping Stern's point in mind, it's not hard to understand why the essence of this jeweler's brand-positioning strategy is all about the concept of well-being. Since 2000, this haute luxe retailer has focused on a woman—as both muse and client—who is strong, independent, possesses a defined and modern sense of style and appreciates the subtlety of understated opulence.

Extending this attitude and cementing its image to the high-profile customer in a memorable way, H. Stern's 2003/04 ad campaign showcases four iconic, "optical illusion" type images—featuring important gems and watches in high-karat gold and diamonds—all specifically created to capture the intimate and indelible relationship between a woman and her jewels. Or, as Stern explains, "a personal, poetic way to position each image as a truest sym-

bol of the woman's personal style and keep our jewelry top of her mind in that way."

Furthering this story is the shimmery, gold H. Stern logo and "A Part Of You" tagline, which runs across the campaign. "The logo was created to stand on its own as another artistic element but also as another kind of gem. Naturally, we wanted to pop our name and tie it into the optical illusion of the ads, so we did the logo in gold as a three-dimensional element, which would be instantly perceived as precious and desirable even before any of the jewelry in the ads is noticed. The tagline draws the viewer right into the message of the campaign and links the imagery on a very personal level."

To clearly and instantly make the magic happen, Stern and Sophie Guyon, of the retailer's Paris-based agency, TBWA, came up with a campaign idea focusing on a magical, glowing aura to convey the special connection between a woman and her H. Stern jewels.

They then hired French photographer Christopher Micaud to shoot natural, sensual images that told the jeweler's story in tonal sepia (model/background) and color (gems). The campaign's glowing, 'golden' look was achieved through just the right combination of orange and blue lighting, which Stern says took many hours achieve.

Playing off the creative "magical touch" idea, every ad evokes the feeling that the jewelry stays with the wearer even when she's not wearing it. In one photo, we see an earring in the model's hand while the jewelry's shadow plays off her neck. In another shot, she removes a ring from her finger but a holographic halo of the ring remains in its place.

The creative process started with Stern and Guyon poring over illustrations depicting the intellectual concept of jewelry as an extension of the wearer's personality and body. Researching photographers, the pair located a book of Micaud's work and found that his pictures spotlighted beautifully lit clouds and different colors of backgrounds. Their interest piqued, they immediately called in originals of the shots; because says Stern, "We wanted to see what everything looked like before any com-

puter work or retouching was done, because we felt this was the best way to judge Christopher's talent as an art photographer, not a fashion photographer. We were looking for someone who could give us the feeling of still life on a person. I have nothing against computers, but they should only be used for a special effect or to enable versatility, never to correct mistakes. In our campaign, we were looking for an artistic photographer who'd only use the computer to give the images their magical touch."

The model, Leticia Birkheuer, was chosen, Stern adds, not only because of her beautiful face but perhaps more importantly because her serene features resembled those of a woman who had posed for old-world artists centuries ago.

The complete campaign runs simultaneously in the U.S., Brazil, Europe and Israel. In all countries with the exception of Brazil, strategic media planning was executed by the jeweler's creative agency TBWA/Paris.

The campaign launched with a *Women's Wear Daily* cover wrap (front/back) during New York's September 2003 Fashion Week, a placement specifically engineered to coincide with the 2004 spring/summer fashion debut of the jewelry. Queried on why the company chose this industry-targeted publication to break the ads, Stern says, "Everyone knows that *WWD* is the bible for cultural and lifestyle opinion leaders in New York City. However, we also know that it's the top fashion trade publication, whose readership goes way beyond just the

H. STERN

fashion universe. This type of placement allowed us to break barriers by surprising viewers and make them look twice at our ads because we showed up in an unexpected place."

Additional single and multiple page insertions appeared in publications such as *Vogue*, *W*, *W Jewelry*, *The New York Times* (main news section of the newspaper and the magazine), *Harper's Bazaar*, *Elle*, *Elle Déor*, *In Style*, *Departures* and *Gotham*. Supporting ads appeared on phone kiosks around Manhattan. International viewers caught ads in titles such as German and Brazilian *Vogue*, *Claudia* and *Veja*. For added visibility, ads showed up outdoors in Rio de Janeiro and Sao Paulo as well as in the windows and interiors of H. Stern's 160 worldwide stores.

H. STERN, New York City
CREATIVE DIRECTOR: **Roberto Stern**
CREATIVE AGENCY: **TBWA/Paris**
CD: **Sophie Guyon**
PHOTOGRAPHER: **Christopher Micaud,**
represented by Angela de Bona
STUDIO: **Pin Up,** Paris
MODEL: **Leticia Birkeruer, Mega Models**
MAKE-UP: **Thibaut Vabre (Angela de Bono)**
HAIR: **Bruno Weppe (Angela de Bono)**
FASHION STYLIST: **Adelaide**

Everything—from the unposed photos to the fabric spread splashed with happy kids—has a freshness about it.

Thinking Small

PIPPERS AMERICA is one of the more unusual retail businesses we've seen of late. Somewhat of a throwback to the handmade days of old, this children's wear company has nevertheless thrived for 16 years to the point where it's starting to split its seams.

The old-fashioned feeling starts with the clothes themselves. As Pippa Imrie, the designer who started the business when she was a mom with young children,

put it, "In this day and age when everything is so mass produced, it's nice to have something that 3,000 other people don't have. People are looking for something that almost looks like something your grandmother might have made."

Situated on Main Street in a small Long Island town, Pippers is a complete vertical operation. The retail store is in front, and much of the "manufacturing" is done on the premises. "People have always seen the

clothing being made," said Imrie. "The back is almost a loft with the shipping department, and the cutting and sewing department with seamstresses working at a big table. It's a bit small. Stuff is everywhere, but that makes it fun."

From all appearances, Pippers has been having fun every step of the way, from the free-wheeling manner in which the business started right up through its charming catalogs filled with "happy children doing happy things." Things are going so well, nothing seems to be too serious here, even the company's plans for what comes next.

The business had its beginnings when Imrie and her husband moved to the

Handknit V-Neck in
CHARCOAL

White Rib Shirt

Pippers Skirt in
CALAMITY JANE

Front Cover
Mock T-Neck in
BLACK lamby

Sailor Pants in
CHARLES

WELCOME TO PIPPERS FOR WINTER 2002!

Here we are! Sewing up a storm in Bellport, making each piece
of clothing especially for you and your child. As usual, we can-
not photograph all our styles and fabrics, so be sure to study the
swatch and style sheets carefully so you don't miss anything.
(for example, our stripey T-shirts which didn't make it to the
shoot). We've added a small holiday line which you can see on
the last page. If you're confused, we are happy to answer all
your questions and give advice.

from,
The People of Pippers

P.S. Thanks to our wonderful braves and squaws: Dominic,
Emma, Chappell, Wells, Flynn, Ava, Jonathan, Thomas, Juliana,
Cole, Lola, Olivia, Charlotte and Katherine

3

States from the U.K. 16 years ago with a baby and other small children. "My next door neighbor and I got to talking, and we decided we would start a little business," Imrie explained. "We went to the Salvation Army and bought old sheets. We bought a couple of sewing machines and I designed a small line. Then we went to a local bookstore and rented a window where we hung up our wares."

Two years later Pippers had a little store and its first catalog was somewhat of a family album. Imrie's husband, Richard, is a photographer. The family would go on vacation and take pictures of their kids running about. Later they would photograph their friends' children as well. Throughout the years they've never used professional models.

In fact, Pippers has never done a lot of things because that's what "should" be done. The pictures, for example, never have to be done in a certain way. "Richard doesn't tell the kids what to do, he lets them just be and takes pictures of exactly what they would be doing normally," remarked Imrie. "He's great at that." [Editor's Note: anyone photographing models of any age could borrow a leaf from Pippers.]

Everything about the catalogs, in fact, not just the naturalness of the photos, has an informal feeling. There are charming little homespun drawings on the price sheet and, of course, the clothes themselves. The copy, written by Imrie, is totally personal. In the winter 2002 catalog, which had an Indian theme, she thanked the "wonderful braves and squaws" whose photos appear on its pages. In fact, in every catalog, she makes it a point to thank each child by name.

The company does two catalogs a year, fall and spring. Over the years it has built a mailing list of about 25,000, which is never used in full. "Because we're so small, I hate the idea of doing random mailings," said Imrie. "We're very careful only to ship to buyers in the last two years and people who make catalog requests. We ship all over, even London."

In addition to the catalogs and the retail store, Pippers has a third sales "channel"—home parties. Started a few years ago in the southern part of the U.S., this small but fledgling operation, which are basically trunk shows, has three representatives who arrange for moms with young children to hold parties in their home. "This is nice, because there's not that much overhead," Imrie pointed out. "It's such an interesting way of selling. It makes us very accessible to a lot of people."

Held in spring and fall, there are approximately 12 of these home parties a season. It seems to be catapulting us to another level," she said. "I love selling by catalog too. Both are working well."

Grandmother would have been proud.

Imrie writes the copy herself. She always thanks the children by name.

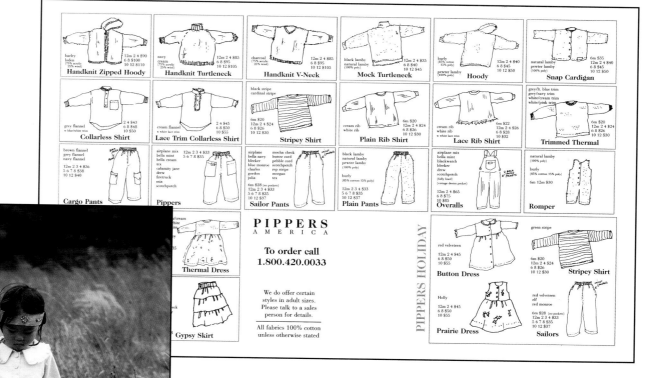

PIPPERS

$2.50

Fall/Winter 1998

PIPPERS
America, Inc.

Bulk Rate
U.S. Postage
Paid
Permit No. 259
Patchogue,
NY 11772

P.O. BOX 178 Bellport
NY 11713-0178

Or current resident

Order toll free: 1 800 420-0033   Fax: 516 286-0033

Connery

Pippers Skirts
Kids 2 4 6 $30
8 10 12 $32

Budding Roses

Toile

Stewart

Lace-Up Boots
Kids 10 11 12 13
1 2 3 $45
Adult 5-10½ (half sizes) $55
Brown or Black Leather

13

68

Pippers America, Bellport, NY
OWNER/DESIGNER: **Pippa Imrie**
PRESIDENT: **Wendy Benincase**
PHOTOGRAPHER: **Richard Imrie**
VICE PRESIDENT **Wendi Fucci**
TREASURER **Darren Beincase**

Caitlin. Lola. Jessica. Nina

Henry, Ali. Zoë. Lily. Lewis and Chloe and to

Thanks to all the children: Chico. Max. Tamsin.

PIPPERS AMERICA Inc.

WE'RE READY FOR A LONG, HOT SUMMER, AND HOPE YOU WILL BE TOO, AFTER LOOKING THROUGH THESE PAGES. REMEMBER, ALL THE STYLES ARE AVAILABLE IN A NUMBER OF DIFFERENT FABRICS, LISTED ON THE STYLE SHEET IN THE CENTRE SPREAD.

Have Fun—
Pippa

Richard for the handout pics.

White Lace
T shirt $20 Skirt
in Navy Gingham
with Daisy trim $35
Lace tank in Cream $18
Pippers pants in
Unbleached cotton $30
White canvas PIPPERS
bag $28

Fitness Branding

*How healthy is the brand? The "health" of a brand is its ability to use the media to communicate its fitness to offer choice and satisfaction through seamless service, merchandise assortments, personalized size and style information. The fitness workout includes building competitive **BrandPower** based on unique products, value prices and outstanding service.*

Improving the "health" of a brand begins with a treatment that improves its supply chain. This involves more than raising levels of productivity that reduce cost and increase profits. Retailers who communicate their brand fitness are indicating their ability to provide choice and satisfaction through merchandise assortments and personalized size and style information.

BrandPower can be achieved by retailers who are successful in making seamless service their regimen for fitness. Retailers can build merchant-muscle by using information technologies to gather and interpret customer data in real time and disseminate it through the store. This enables the store-as-a-brand to shorten the time it takes to personally service each customer.

An athlete works on the specific muscle groups needed to perform in each of the different sports. We're not referring to using steroids or creating ad hype—we are advocating BrandPower exercises by retailers to strengthen their appeals to their best customer segments. Fitness branding is communicated to customers that size matters—no "one-size, style, color or shape fits all."

Innovative retail marketers are turning to a number of different BrandPower tools to maintain the health of their brands and move their stores ahead of the pack. An essential part of a brand's fitness is its ability to interpret the media matrix that its customers have designed for themselves.

Traditional approaches to the analysis of the media mix and the messages that fit the mix may have to be scheduled for reinvention. A brand's media fitness depends upon its ability to understand its customers as media-makers themselves. The brand that is fit encourages its customers to get into the infor-

mation program and help send the message. They are indeed, by way of the technology, *media polyphasics* who can recommend the brand to their own audiences.

The brand's fitness program may include some or all of the following stretches and moves:

• **The Great Profile** – *Bellevue Square's* reinvention of its brand positioning is based on phone research it conducted for several years. It created a personality profile of the Bellevue shopper as "an independent thinker who stands out" (not "sticks out"— Talbot's slogan) for being and looking her best. They made it clear in their advertising that even an independent thinker values the opinion of an expert. See page 72.

• **The Pride in Well-Being** – *Pret A Manger* restaurants have a "loving attitude towards the foods they use" …offering a 90-second response to selections that contain ingredients with no preservatives from local suppliers. It has built up its power to serve "good food fast and fast food good." See page 78.

• **I Did It My Way** – *Dufferin Mall* appeals to the mind of its target audience. It builds brand fitness with an exercise in individual thinking about mall shopping. It positioning strategy focuses on "stand outs" in events and values. "Resist the ordinary" is Dufferin's message to urban young singles. See page 84.

• **Look at Me Now** – The *Mervyn's* store-as-a-brand has continued its message of "big brands, small prices." Recognizing that it

needed to upgrade the brand's fitness, it started to feature products in amusing situations that feature one-liners that begin with "in a perfect world…." For example, "In a perfect world, your body would defy gravity. Until then… COLE SWIMSUIT. (The very fit model is floating in space.) See page 90.

Fitness Branding has to rely on knowledge of the brand's diet and activities. Sometimes the brand's managers confuse marketing diets with selling activities. Marketing is *producing* what you can get people to buy. Selling is *having* what you can get people to buy.

A brand that is fit must have meaning, inspire trust and promise value. A brand's "body mass index" is most often based on the relationship of its quality to its price. A good example is the retail brand. Retailers have made their own store-brand products perform like producer brands. They have demanded that their suppliers of their store brands match the attributes and benefits of famous brands in every major category. The weight loss of the expense for research, development, marketing and advertising enables the retail brand to be priced lower, yet equal in quality to the name brand.

This message of *brand fitness* is being conveyed by brands that say…"we can do more for you—for less from you."

How to 'Be'

ONE OF THE FEW family-owned shopping centers in America today, Bellevue Square began as a family operation in a town a few miles outside Seattle, WA nearly 60 years ago. Today, Bellevue Square is a super-regional 1.3 million-square-foot shopping center in the heart of downtown Bellevue. It is surrounded by what have become the state's wealthiest neighborhoods—home to many of the techies who made millions of dollars in the dot.com heyday.

Over the years, not only has the "neighborhood" undergone changes, but like any retail operation of a certain age, so has Bellevue Square. One development, which has had a significant bearing on how the center markets itself, was the final closing in the early 1990s of Frederick & Nelson. Instead of putting in another department store, management used the three-story space to house 50 specialty stores and boutiques, some of which are locally owned.

This pivotal decision brought about the Bellevue Square of today. With its balance of 200 of the finest national tenants and its eclectic mix of distinctive single-owned or family-owned stores, Bellevue Square is considered to be the premiere upscale shopping center in the Northwest.

"We've been very influenced by high tech and the wealth that came to those folks at a young age," said Jennifer Leavitt, vice president – marketing. "Many of these area residents can afford to shop anywhere, so it has been important to make Bellevue Square the preferred place to shop." Despite the community's growing affluence and penchant for style, however, Leavitt noted that it isn't "showy." In fact it's still "fairly casual." "We try to find that balance between being fashionable and being over the top, so that we're not in a disconnect with our customers, and what they do in their lives."

Until two years ago, Bellevue Square had a long-standing approach of being all things to all people, but Leavitt noted, "We've gone through an evolution, especially from when our tenant mix was broader, with less of a focus on luxury tenants. We still have a very broad market, but we have a better understanding that we need to focus on the female customer—to

Bellevue Square's reposition is in its second year. These magalogs represent what "Be" was when it was launched in Spring 2002.

make us important in her life."

In 2001, with the idea of being all things to all people no longer the target, management asked Seattle-based Kendall Ross Brand Development & Design to help reposition the center. The challenge for the agency was not to completely recreate the image of Bellevue Square, but to redefine what it offered best.

The new positioning focuses on Bellevue Square as the destination for the best in personal style. Research showed that women ages 24-54 were spending the majority of their dollars on fashion and home purchases, and that they come to Bellevue Square because it offers the best fashion, home and dining choices in the area. Hence, the new tagline, "Style, Scene and In-between." Style (fashion), scene (home), and in-between (everything else).

Thanks to the phone research Bellevue has been doing annually for a number of years, the agency had an accurate picture of the customer. The agency was able to create a personality profile of the Bellevue Square shopper: an independent thinker who stands out for being and looking her best, and yet values the opinion of an expert. Embracing life as it is today is a high priority.

This profile became the inspiration behind the simple statement that has defined the campaign—"Be." At the same time, it plays off the center's name, "Be" underscores the idea of accepting and appreciating things as they are and enjoying the moment.

The concept grew into a platform for the entire campaign, translating first into bus cards, magazines and newspaper ads, then into radio. A quarterly magalog is a key element in the campaign.

"We've realized we have to narrow our focus to engage our customer more," Leavitt explained, "Not just telling her who we are but talking to her more in 'girl-friendspeak,' so that when she goes shopping, she says 'I'm going to my friend, I'm going to Bellevue Square.'"

"The campaign has been a two-year evolution from the first to the second, provid-

The original broadsheet had impactful visuals but was cumbersome to handle.

The current ads explore different ways "to Be," often including a female figure in the equation.

The first ads were more product-focused.

ing female customers with more information about who they are," said Leavitt. The friendly tone of the magalogs is a good example of how the campaign has evolved. Rather than typical editorial copy interspersed with vendor-produced advertising, the magalogs now feature shopping-savvy articles. These articles, written by experts in their field, share information on current styles in the voice of a knowledgeable yet friendly and approachable girlfriend of the targeted customer. The fact that the experts are real people, whose credentials are listed with their article, reinforces the credibility of the magalog and the relevance of Bellevue Square to its customers' lives. The articles relate to the core areas women shop the center for—fashion, home and all the things in between that make up their full and varied lives.

The look of Bellevue Square's ads has been evolving too. The initial ad campaign, which ran throughout 2002, was more product-focused than the version

Bold.

Be.

Vivid.

Daring.

Spring is looking fresher than ever with an abundance of daring details. From spontaneous stripes, to a bold new way to wear your style on your sleeve, find your passion for fashion, at Bellevue Square.

Bellevue Square
The BEST of EVERYTHING

Monday – Saturday 9:30 am to 9:30 pm
Sunday 11:00 am to 7:00 pm

bellevuesquare.com

bellevue square
STYLE, SCENE AND IN-BETWEEN

STRIPED TOP: CACHÉ

Distinct.

Heartfelt.

Be.

Cherished.

Celebrate the season at Bellevue Square with an unrivalled selection of gifts to astonish and delight. With more than 200 fine stores to choose from, you're sure to make wishes come true. Discover a world of holiday wonder – come shopping at Bellevue Square.

Bellevue Square
The BEST of EVERYTHING

Extended holiday hours.
bellevuesquare.com

bellevue square
STYLE, SCENE AND IN-BETWEEN

CANDLESTICKS: THE BOMBAY COMPANY.
CANDLES: ILLUMINATIONS. VASE: CRATE AND BARREL.
BEADED COASTERS: POTTERY BARN.

Be. Inviting.   Bring home the colors of fall.

Bellevue Square
The BEST of EVERYTHING

bellevue square
STYLE, SCENE AND IN-BETWEEN

Be. Vivid.   Refresh your home.

Bellevue Square
The BEST of EVERYTHING

bellevue square
STYLE, SCENE AND IN-BETWEEN

Be. Giving.   The gifts to please are at Bellevue Square.

Bellevue Square
The BEST of EVERYTHING

bellevue square
STYLE, SCENE AND IN-BETWEEN

Billboards.

Radio

SPRING FASHION :60

THE ANNOUNCER IS JULIE STEIN

TERRI: I'm a real thoughtful shopper. I like seeing what is out there and then making choices based on what's the most wearable and versatile in my own closet.

ANNCR: Terry Morgan, trend reporter, and owner of TCM Models and Talents talks about spring fashion, and Bellevue Square.

TERRI: This year is full of beautiful, romantic, feminine colors.

ANNCR: Bellevue Square brings you the best in spring Fashion.

TERRI: A lot of our fashion that we've been wearing in the gym is taking itself to the street.

ANNCR: And what about shoes for spring?

TERRI: Oh, shoes are yummy! (laughs) One of the key shoes for spring is silver metallic. They're sexy. They're definitely higher heeled, but they're comfortable.

ANNCR: The Square has a rainbow of happy hues to color your world.

TERRI: Bellevue Square has a wonderful selection of stores to shop. Everything from great active wear to beautiful evening wear. You pretty much can find it all there.

ANNCR: Now's the time to see what's fresh in fashion at Bellevue Square. Read Terri's report in Bellevue Square's Spring Catalog, or online at BellevueSquare.com

FALL FASHION :60

THE ANNOUNCER IS JULIE STEIN

ANNCR: Terry Morgan, trend reporter, and owner of TCM Models and Talents talks about new Fall fashion, and Bellevue Square.

TERRI: Accessories for this fall are a bit more matchipoo than they've been in the past (laughs)...

ANNCR: What do you mean by that?

TERRI: This fall, the gloves and the handbag and the shoes and the belt will all still be in the same family.

ANNCR: So what'll I find at Bellevue Square that's new and fun for fall?

TERRI: A look that's kind of fun that's coming back from the '80s is that "borrowed from the boys" silhouette where it's big on top and skinny on the bottom.

ANNCR: MMMMM (as in YES!) And what colors will be shimmering?

TERRI: There's great, you know, jewel tones. And if you don't feel good about wearing a bright red satin blouse, or a ruby blouse, you can sure put those on your feet and kind of be Dorothy with the Ruby Slippers.

ANNCR: Speaking of shoes...

TERRI: Well I always start at the shoes.

ANNCR: I know.

TERRI: If I find a great pair of shoes, then I will generally build an outfit around the shoes...

ANNCR: Uh huh...

TERRI: ...then I will generally build an outfit around the shoes...

ANNCR: It's always easy to find what you need at Bellevue Square.

TERRI: Bellevue Square has a wonderful selection of stores to shop.

ANNCR: Read Terri's trend report in Bellevue Square's Fall Catalog, or online at Bellevue Square.com.

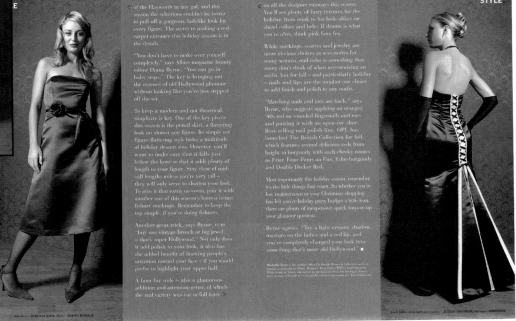

The original broadsheet has been reformatted into a user-friendly horizontal "book."

running now. In the newer version, graphic squares with a descriptive word enhance the main visual, and many executions include a female figure.

In 2003, the newspaper insert was reformatted as well. "We said, what if we turn this sideways and staple it?" said Leavitt. It was a major improvement over the initial large vertical broadsheet that had proved to be somewhat unwieldy. Distribution in the *Seattle Times* of the reformatted broadsheets has been increased to include more zip codes. (80,000 distribution for spring and fall, 100,000 for holiday.)

The timeframe and components of a typical media schedule are as follows: For fall, the magalog dropped in early August, followed by the broadsheet a week later. During that time bus boards started running. Several full-page ads ran in the *Seattle Times Pacific Magazine* (Sunday run). Radio spots aired concurrently with the fashion ads. "In the October time frame, we try to follow up with a special home-feature section the *Seattle Times* does and then theater programs, which tend to overlap during that time," noted Leavitt. Holiday is typically a five-week time frame, because unlike many other shopping centers, Bellevue Square doesn't set up until the day after Thanksgiving. "Our catalog and broadsheet drop early, but most of our print is geared in that five week period," Leavitt said.

In conclusion, Leavitt reiterated, "From a marketing perspective, everything is about trying to build preference. Part of the challenge for us is that our customer is wealthy enough to have choices. She can shop anywhere, New York, San Francisco…"

From our perspective, it looks like Bellevue Square and Kendall Ross know a thing or two about making the right choices as well.

Bellevue Square, Bellevue, WA
VICE PRESIDENT – MARKETING: **Jennifer Leavitt**
OWNER/MANAGEMENT COMPANY: **Kemper Development Company,** Bellevue
AGENCY: **Kendall Ross Brand Development & Design,** Seattle
PRINCIPALS: **David Kendall, Timothy Ross**

Fresh Thinking

ASK PEOPLE what they love most about New York City, and right up there with the great shopping, Broadway shows and museums is restaurants. New Yorkers have literally thousands of choices, so when a new eating place enters the market, the chances of making it a success are formidable. It simply doesn't get much more competitive.

When UK-based Pret A Manger, a 130+ take-out and sit-down chain featuring fresh, preservative-free food, decided to go global, it adopted a very aggressive marketing position. In entering international markets (the U.S., Hong Kong and soon, Japan), it has opted for using agencies located in each market, rather than one agency overall.

New York City, of course, is tricky for anyone. With consumers having so many places to eat to choose from, there's often a "been there, done that" attitude. But Pret A Manger has a fresh story to tell—a definite difference in terms of its food preparation, service and company philosophy. "The way they do business is different from here," said Hugh Hough, creative director of Green Team, the NYC agency charged with introducing the restaurant chain to New York City. "Pret uses ingredients from local suppliers, and there are no preservatives," Hough continued. "Their target is people who like good food fast, food that tastes good that's not junk."

Pret has a viable urban niche going for it. The company's loving attitude toward the ingredients it uses, combined with the fact that it's setup gets

people in and out in 90 seconds once they've made their selection, are attributes with strong appeal to time-deprived NYC foodies. Considering the quality of its ingredients, Pret offers good value. For customers, that trans-

Fashión Week buttons.

lates into an affordable luxury—something they can indulge in that won't break them.

The job became to get that message out and to build traffic at the 14 individual NYC locations. The idea was to get people in the shops just once, and the rest would be history. The campaign initially broke October 7 targeting 10 shops in midtown with a lot of ads on bus shelters and phone kiosks to drive traffic. "We made a quick buy of everything available to build awareness," said Hough. "We branded shuttle cars, bought City Lights (areas over parking lots), urban panels (signage at subway entrances), went into Bryant Park and gave out buttons during

Outdoor ads.

Coupons were handed out at openings at different shops.

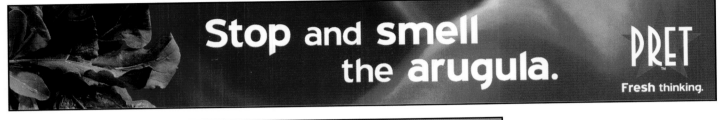

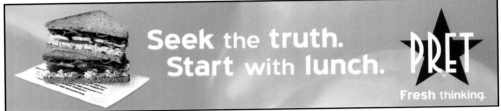

Subway ads.

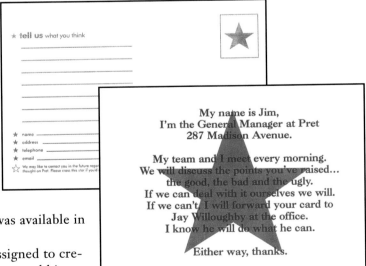

Pret means it when it says it cares about what customers think. Every store displays cards seeking feedback, like the one shown at left.

Fashion Week—whatever was available in October, we bought.

Two copywriters were assigned to create just the right voice—savvy and hip. "The ads have a little bit of an edge, not dumbing down," said Hough. "We wanted to be passionate about food and have fun, because food should be fun.

"We came up with the line 'Fresh thinking.' We needed to educate people to 'stop and smell the arugula.'" With that in mind, Green Team proceeded to photograph mouthwatering visuals that used an extreme close-up of a fresh item

of food as the background. The effect is delicious.

"A very important promotional component was educating people in what it is they're eating," Hough added. That voice and the concept of fresh thinking are reiterated again and again in what Pret calls "Passion Facts"—pithy statements that give the product its own per-

sonality. Educational as well as entertaining, Passion Facts turn up all over the place—in store on the walls, on tray liners, on Pret's website, packaging and more.

Pret is turning up all over the place too. The company's plan is to open a Pret a month in NYC.

Brochures designed to educate customers are displayed in-store.

Just a **taste** of what we sell...

Sandwiches
Super Club, Coronation Chicken, Avocado Parmesan & Arugula, Chicken Avocado, Egg Florentine, Bacon Lettuce & Tomato, Chicken Caesar, Turkey & Avocado, Thai Chicken, Tuna Salad on Rye, New York Brunch on Rye, Turkey Lunch

Baguettes
Brie Tomato & Basil, Tuna Salad, Salami & Mozzarella, Roast Beef

Wraps
Sesame Chicken, Hummus & Red Pepper, Tuna Nicoise, Green Thai Chicken

Salads
Range of Leaf and Pasta Salads

Bagels
Plain, Cinnamon Raisin & Sesame with Cream Cheese

Bakery
Muffins, Fresh Baked Croissants from France (Chocolate, Almond, Plain)

Cakes and Slices
Pret Brownie, Chocolate Chunk Cookie, Pecan Bar, Raspberry Coconut Bar, Carrot Loaf, Banana Loaf, Fresh Baked Cookies

Puddings
Chocolate Mousse, Cheesecake, Honey & Granola Yogurt Pot, Strawberry & Rhubarb Yogurt Pot, Blueberry Yogurt Pot

Coffees and Hot Drinks
Cappuccino, Latte, Mocha, Tea, Hot Chocolate

Cold Drinks
Orange Juice, Carrot Juice, Cranberry & Apple Cider, Lemonade, Raspberry Smoothie, Mango Smoothie, Strawberry Smoothie, Yogurt Smoothies, Iced Mocha, Iced Latte, Iced Cappuccino

Plus
Chips (Rosemary, Cracked Pepper, Sea Salt) and Fruit

To keep it innovative and exciting, our menu is constantly changing. We may already have replaced some of the above with equally delicious new items.

Call us about our delivery service and our catering menu.

© Pret A Manger (USA) Ltd 2002

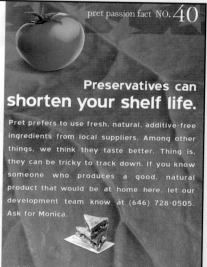

pret passion fact NO. 40

Preservatives can shorten your shelf life.

Pret prefers to use fresh, natural, additive-free ingredients from local suppliers. Among other things, we think they taste better. Thing is, they can be tricky to track down. If you know someone who produces a good, natural product that would be at home here, let our development team know at (646) 728-0505. Ask for Monica.

sandwiches ★ baguettes ★ wraps ★ breakfast ★ coffee ★ and more

* Passionate about food! *

At Pret A Manger, we're **obsessed** with food-quality. **fresh** food made with the sort of **ingredients** you'd choose to use at home. We're **not interested** in finding ways to **extend the shelf-life** of food. We don't mind that natural food goes bad quickly.

Fresh ingredients are **delivered** to **every** one of our **shops** each morning. Our sandwiches, baguettes and wraps are **made** throughout the day in **each shop**. The **team** serving on the registers will have **made** your **sandwich** this **morning**. At the end of the day, we give whatever we haven't sold to **City Harvest** to help feed people throughout **New York City** who would otherwise go hungry.

Numerous **Passion Facts**, many of which adorn our walls and packaging, **document** the **extraordinary** lengths we go to in **search of Pret-quality** ingredients. Our insistence that we keep Pret natural

pret passion fact NO. 38

Basil is high maintenance.

It's delicate. It bruises easily. It would be so much easier just to use pesto sauce, but alas, we can't. We just love the taste of fresh basil too much. So we order it in handpicked bunches, have it delivered to each of our shops daily, and place it on our sandwiches one leaf at a time.

means (among other things) that our ham is pale (not bright pink) and we delayed launching our pastrami and roast beef sandwiches until we could find meats guaranteed free from phosphates, hormones and antibiotics.

We are always trying to **improve** our menu...not just by introducing **new** recipes, but by **continually** reviewing all our 'classics' to make them even **better**. Probably only one sandwich idea in twenty makes it through our testing process.

It really **matters** to us what our **customers** think about our shops, our food and our hardworking wonderful people. If you have **something** to tell us, please call **646 728 0505** or email us via our website **www.pret.com** We would love to hear from **you**!

Jay Willoughby
(President)

pret passion fact NO. 5

Can a croissant get jet lag?

If they can, ours do. That's because they begin their lives in Bethune, France, a small village in Normandy. They're made there, then flown here, where we bake them in each of our shops. Try one with a cup of our Pret coffee in the morning, and be thankful you didn't have to travel as far to work as they did.

Start your day with a fresh baked croissant and coffee!

The idea of "Fresh thinking" applies to the way the chain does business as well as to its emphasis on preservative-free fresh food. Giving back is a priority. Every sandwich they don't sell is given to City Harvest, a NYC nonprofit that feeds the needy. Thanksgiving and Christmas promotions enabled customers to participate further in helping to feed others.

Thanks. Giving. Thanks. Giving. Thanks. Giving. Thanks. Giving. ★ Thanksgiving Day Lunch Sandwich ★ $5.75 Thanks. Giving. Thanks. Giving. Thanks. Giving. Thanks. Giving.
Turkey. Stuffing. Spinach. Cranberry Sauce. Mayo. Seasoning

pret passion fact NO. 38

Basil is high maintenance.

It's delicate. It bruises easily. It would be so much easier just to use pesto sauce, but alas, we can't. We just love the taste of fresh basil too much. So we order it in handpicked bunches, have it delivered to each of our shops daily, and place it on our sandwiches one leaf at a time.

sandwiches ★ baguettes ★ wraps ★ breakfast ★ coffee ★ and more   **PRET** **Fresh** thinking.

pret passion fact NO. 40

Preservatives can shorten your shelf life.

Pret prefers to use fresh, natural, additive-free ingredients from local suppliers. Among other things, we think they taste better. Thing is, they can be tricky to track down. If you know someone who produces a good, natural product that would be at home here, let our development team know at (646) 728-0505. Ask for Monica.

sandwiches ★ baguettes ★ wraps ★ breakfast ★ coffee ★ and more   **PRET** **Fresh** thinking.

Outdoor ads.

Loyalty Card counter card.

pret passion fact NO. 5

Can a croissant get jet lag?

If they can, ours do. That's because they begin their lives in Bethune, France, a small village in Normandy. They're made there, then flown here, where we bake them in each of our shops. Try one with a cup of our Pret coffee in the morning, and be thankful you didn't have to travel as far to get to work as they did.

sandwiches ★ baguettes ★ wraps ★ breakfast ★ coffee ★ and more   **PRET** **Fresh** thinking.

Pret A Manger, Ltd., London
ADVERTISING AGENCY (U.S.): **Green Team,** New York
CREATIVE DIRECTOR/PRESIDENT: **Hugh Hough**
CREATIVE DIRECTOR **Jimmie Stone**
ART DIRECTOR: **Brian Hurewitz**
SR. COPYWRITER: **Hank Stewart**
COPYWRITER: **Kate McConnell**
PHOTOGRAPHER: **David DiMicco,** New York

The original campaign targeting Urban Young Singles—a potentially lucrative market.

Standing Out Again

DUFFERIN MALL, near downtown Toronto, is an urban regional shopping center that has seen its core customer base change dramatically in recent years. Opened in 1957, Dufferin Mall was for many years one of the city's primary shopping destinations, serving a rapidly growing population. Two things occurred to change that.

First, newer and larger suburban malls were springing up in areas around the city, resulting in an erosion of Dufferin's primary customer base. Second, there was a change in the community immediately surrounding the center, which had been primarily a working class neighborhood made up of mainly European immigrants.

In the last few years, the area has seen a rapidly growing segment of "Urban Young Singles," young, well-

educated, upscale professionals who are attracted by the community's close proximity to downtown Toronto. Today this demographic constitutes approximately 50% of Dufferin's primary market.

The demographic shift led to extensive market research to evaluate the center's position and to determine what direction its marketing strategy should take. The findings revealed that while on the one hand, Dufferin was successfully reaching "Urban Ethnics," that was definitely not the case with the important new group who the research showed spent more per visit at Dufferin, even though they shopped there in considerably fewer numbers. In fact, the latter group accounted for only 23% of the mall's customers surveyed, despite representing half of the trade area population.

Clearly, Urban Young Singles represented significant untapped potential. But what was needed was a way of motivating them to come to Dufferin. The research had suggested that this group didn't perceive Dufferin as having what were the popular stores at the time.

Dufferin recently updated an innovative advertising campaign that had been designed to target these Young Urban Singles. The marketing initiative first got rolling in the late 1990s when a campaign was developed to make the mall stand out from its suburban competitors and position it as an "alternative" shopping center with a variety of stores. To substantiate this perspective and evoke an emotional response, the theme, "Stand Out, Resist the Ordinary" was utilized as the positioning statement and the

By expressing its individuality, Dufferin could be seen as having a quality that would appeal to Urban Young Singles.

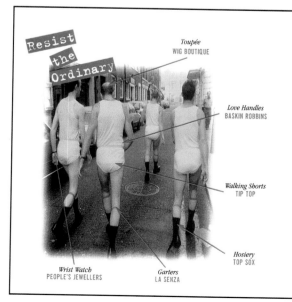

Evolution of a great campaign—Dufferin shows its colors.

overriding theme for the campaign.

The creative, which was done in black and white, was a stand out in and of itself. "It had a very urban edgy look," said Mary Thorne, marketing manager. The campaign ran for three years and was considered extremely effective.

So why change it? Some retailers run the same advertising campaign year after year. "If it ain't broke, don't fix it." They're content to continually reinforce their identity. But it's not as simple as that. One doesn't need to completely abandon the equity that has been established with a long-running campaign. Dufferin found a way to get the best of both worlds.

"We really had to come back to the table to ask what's the next generation," said Thorne. "You have to freshen it. The current campaign went to a full-color format for accessorizing. We also changed the logo creative slightly to mirror the more up-to-date color treatment."

But the original black and white

effect lives on in the form of utilizing black-and-white stock photography of individuals who typify the target group. Standing out from the norm, the images are enhanced with full-color accessories—ordinary items available from Dufferin's stores, presented in extraordinary ways.

This tongue-in-cheek feeling reinforces the fact that while the featured merchandise might be available at another mall, when purchased at Dufferin, it takes on a unique personality, one that appeals to the Urban Young Singles' penchant for individuality.

Media rates in the Toronto market are high, and Dufferin had a modest marketing budget. Prior to the campaign's launch, FSA ('forward sortation area') lifestyle data codes based on postal codes was analyzed to pinpoint streets and neighborhoods in the trade area where the target group resided. Direct mail postcards were chosen as the primary communication vehicle. A total of 12 different postcards (two dif-

ferent postcards during each of the six-week seasonal flights) were distributed directly to 30,000 households occupied by Urban Young Singles.

The jumbo-size postcards were designed to deliver a two-fold message—on the front was an image of a unique individual along with the center's positioning statement. The back was a silhouette of the individual, leaving only the accessories amidst a pattern of the store names where the featured merchandise could be found.

To help stretch dollars, the creative from the front of the postcards was also utilized in an outdoor advertising program. Outdoor is an important vehicle, because Urban Young Singles are frequent users of public transit. Divided into six four-week flights, the transit shelter campaign delivered highly visible exposure throughout the targeted neighborhoods. Similarly, platform posters were strategically positioned on the platforms of targeted subway stations

NOW OPEN
Telus, Moneysworth & Best, Shopsy's and Winners

Four different retailers were promoted on each postcard.

NOW OPEN
Roasty Jack's and RU2

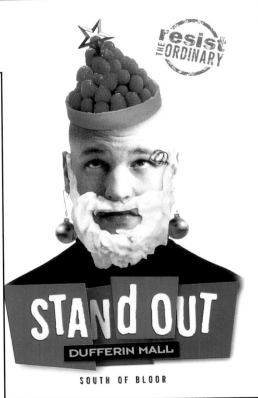

In-mall signage extended the campaign's visibility and promoted Dufferin's Stand-Out Events at all major entranceways.

during each of seven six-week flights.

The campaign's versatile format was utilized in the mall for event signage and to promote the center's merchandising program. Taking a twist on the positioning, the distinctive images promoted "Stand Out Events" and "Stand Out Values," the monthly in-mall merchandising program.

Since the new campaign, mall sales have experienced steady gains. The results of a research study conducted last spring confirmed that market share for Urban Young Singles had increased from 23% to 30%. This sizable gain translates into 58,450 more shopper visits per month from this vital group.

What a stand out!

MARKETING MANAGER: **Mary Thorne**
CENTER MANAGER: **Dave Wallace**
DIRECTOR, NATIONAL MARKETING: **Pamela Setzke**
VP, PORTFOLIO MANAGEMENT - EAST: **Don Burton**
ADVERTISING AGENCY: **True North Advertising,** Toronto
CREATIVE DIRECTOR: **Sal Ianturno**

In a Perfect World...

SINCE MERVYN'S opened its first store in 1949, it has continued to stake its claim as a neighborhood, family-focused department store. The company's guiding philosophy from the beginning (there are now more than 260 Mervyn's stores in 14 states) has been "Big brands, small prices"—a message that it continues to drive home. "We're always trying to find a fresh way to communicate it," said Lee Walker, senior VP marketing.

It's heartening to see a retailer stick with the same branding position for more than half a century. Mervyn's, of course, isn't the only one. But how many are as consistently able to avoid being stale? After all these years, despite what's obviously a challenge, Mervyn's keeps coming up with surprises.

How do they do it, we wanted to know. Unlike most retailers who rely either on one advertising agency, their in-house creative operation or a combination of both, Mervyn's reaps the best of many worlds. Walker explained that like Target, its parent company, Mervyn's utilizes the talents of many different agencies to get its message across. Different agencies have different strengths, and by not having the same agency do all the projects, the creative never feels tired. "Having many agency partners is part of how we do business." she noted.

Research also is part of the way Mervyn's does business. In fact, it was the result of research and feedback from cus-tomers (Mervyn's refers to customers as guests) that was at the heart of another example of Mervyn's exceptional campaigns "In a Perfect World..."

Research had determined that the chain's customers are 85% women, 25-54, mostly working moms with kids at home. Approximately 30% are Hispanic. "She's time-pressed and needs to make her budget stretch," said Walker. "We really try to present our brand in a way that's meaningful to her needs, and get the message across that we have a better product at a price."

In developing the "In a Perfect World..." campaign Walker and her team (one member came up with the line) worked in conjunction with Studio 1960,

In a perfect world, you'd have the energy of a 5 year old. Until then...MR COFFEE coffeemaker. $29.99

mervyn's
BIG BRANDS, SMALL PRICES.™

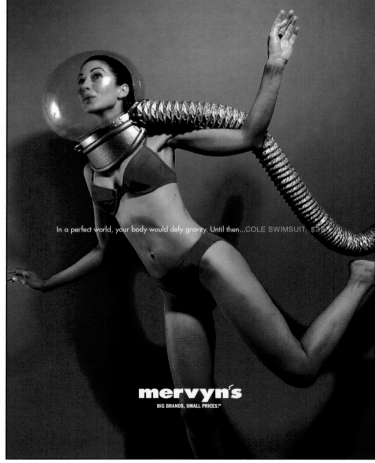

In a perfect world, your body would defy gravity. Until then...COLE SWIMSUIT. $3

mervyn's
BIG BRANDS, SMALL PRICES.™

a L.A. agency known for its creative images. Each of the 20 ads features a product (big brands at small prices) and then, in amusing situations, makes the product relate to the Mervyn's customers' world in a manner that evokes interest in the product. An ad for a coffee-maker, for example, spotlights the product with a muted figure in the background. The headline reads "In a perfect world, you'd have the energy of a 5 year old. Until then, Mr. Coffee Coffeemaker, $29.95." An ad for a swimsuit— "In a perfect world, your body would defy gravity. Until then…Cole swimsuits, $38."

All the ads are tagged with Mervyn's. Big brands, small prices.

Williams went on to point out that many of the ads ran in leading national magazines in an advertising environment in which a lot of the ads have lifestyle photography in them. Mervyn's ads look different. The person is always secondary to the product as hero, and every execution has its own monochromatic color scheme. "Part of our effort was to make sure we break through. That's why we did studio photography," she explained. "It's a way to show not tell," Williams noted. "It's a new twist to kind of show the product in a memorable way, not just talk about it."

The campaign also included three TV spots, illustrating various "In a perfect world" situations such as a woman in a donut shop with the voiceover beginning "In a perfect world, you could get all your favorites, and not feel guilty. You can, at Mervyn's (cut to various products, etc.

Big brands, small prices strikes again!

video	audio
OPEN ON EXTERIOR OF DONUT SHOP CUT TO WOMAN	**MUSIC:** ENERGETIC, FUN
CUT TO DONUTS	(MUSIC HITS)
CUT TO BAKER SERVING DONUTS	(MUSIC HITS)
CUT BACK TO WOMAN'S EXPRESSION.	**ANNCR:** IN A PERFECT WORLD…
	YOU COULD GET ALL YOUR FAVORITES, AND NOT FEEL GUILTY…
CUT TO STYLISH GRAPHICS AND PRODUCTS	YOU CAN, AT MERVYN'S…
SHOW PRODUCT AND NAME AS MENTIONED	
SUPER: NEW BALANCE	NEW BALANCE
SUPER: CUISINART	CUISINART
SUPER: UNION BAY	UNION BAY
SUPER: JOCKEY	JOCKEY
SUPER: MODERN LIVING BY MARTEX	FIND ALL YOUR FAVORITES…
SUPER: TOASTMASTER	
SUPER: NINE & COMPANY	NINE AND COMPANY
SUPER: DOCKERS	DOCKERS
SUPER: ADIDAS	ADIDAS
SUPER: ARROW	ARROW
MERVYN'S LOGO BIG BRANDS, SMALL PRICES.	MERVYN'S. BIG BRANDS. SMALL PRICES.

In a perfect world, there wouldn't be any homework. Until then…NIKE 'Entree' backpack. $20.99

In a perfect world, there would be 25 hours in a day. Until then…TIMEX watch. $29.99

video   **audio**

OPEN WITH HUSBAND ENTERING THE LAUNDRY ROOM AT HIS HOUSE.

HE LOOKS IN WASHING MACHINE...

ONLY TO FIND THAT HIS WHITES ARE NOW PINK. PINK T-SHIRT...

PINK ATHLETIC SOCKS...
PINK TOWEL...
PINK BOXERS...

FINALLY HE PULLS OUT THE CULPRIT...A RED BABY SOCK.

SHOW PRODUCT AND NAME AS MENTIONED

SUPER: GLORIA VANDERBILT

SUPER: VAN HEUSEN

SUPER: OSTER

SUPER: BEAUTYREST

SUPER: LEI

SUPER: SAMSONITE

SUPER: HANES

SUPER: MUNSINGWEAR

SUPER: TIMEX

SUPER: NIKE (WORKOUT)

SUPER: BIG BRANDS, SMALL PRICES

CUT TO MERVYN'S LOGO

MUSIC: INSTRUMENTAL – HIP, FUN

MUSIC

MUSIC

ANNCR: IN A PERFECT WORLD...EVERY SURPRISE, WOULD BE A GOOD ONE.

LIKE THE SURPRISING FINDS,

...AT MERVYN'S.

GLORIA VANDERBILT

VAN HEUSEN

OSTER

FIND ALL YOUR FAVORITES.

SAMSONITE

HANES

MUNSINGWEAR

TIMEX

NIKE

MERVYN'S. BIG BRANDS, SMALL PRICES.

video   **audio**

OPEN OF MAN STANDING IN AN UNDERSHIRT AND BOXERS

CUT TO MAN

CUT TO IRONING BOARD AND IRON

CUT BACK TO MAN

CUT TO IRON.

CUT TO MAN STARING AT IRONING BOARD

SHOW PRODUCT AND NAME AS MENTIONED

SUPER: SIDEOUT

SUPER: REEBOK

SUPER: GEORGE FOREMAN

SUPER: LEVI'S

SUPER: CARTER'S

SUPER: JANSPORT

SUPER: KITCHENAID

SUPER: LEE

SUPER: HAGGAR

SUPER: HANES (KID'S)

MERVYN'S LOGO
SUPER: BIG BRANDS. SMALL PRICES.

CUT BACK TO MAN

MUSIC: INSTRUMENTAL – HIP, FUN

MUSIC

MUSIC

ANNCR: IN A PERFECT WORLD...

EVERYTHING WOULD BE...EASY.

UNTIL THEN...

FINDING ALL YOUR FAVORITE BRANDS AT MERVYN'S IS...

SIDEOUT

REEBOK

GEORGE FOREMAN

LEVI'S

CARTER'S

FIND ALL YOUR FAVORITES

KITCHENAID

LEE

HAGGAR

HANES

MERVYN'S. BIG BRANDS. SMALL PRICES.

Mervyn's, San Francisco
SENIOR VP MARKETING: **Lee Walker**

AGENCY (print): **Studio 1960,** Los Angeles
CREATIVE DIRECTOR: **Andrew Mandolene**
ART DIRECTOR: **David Delgado**

PHOTOGRAPHER: **Rob Mandolene**
STYLIST: **Christina Soletti**
HAIR & MAKE-UP: **Patty Wheelock**

AGENCY (TV): **Ron Foth Advertising,** Columbus, OH

Co-Branding

Retailers are inventing a new era of brand associations and tie-ins between brands and celebrities, musicians, sports stars and teams, charities, artists, and other like-minded brands. Special events retail marketing is now an in-house necessity for the inventive retailer.

We've all heard the phrase, "You are judged by the company you keep." While that may not always be fair, it is one of the first levels of assessing the interests, values and similar beliefs of a friend, colleague or potential mate. This personal relationship concept has long been adopted into the promotional activities of countless companies, sports teams, non-profit organizations, media sponsorships and advertisers, not to mention endorsers of politicians.

Strategic Co-Branding is a synergistic tool that can generate more than the sum of each brand's parts. The two basic types of Co-Branding are:
• When two independent brands jointly endorse each other—e.g., American Express ads feature hotels, restaurants or retailers that accept the card. Credit cards are obvious examples for the mutual benefits of Co-branding.
• When one brand endorses the contents in part or whole of another brand—e.g., Intel Pentium chips inside an HP or Dell computer; Nutrasweet inside Nestea; DuPont Lycra in Donna Karan designs.

A retailer or host brand can benefit greatly from collaborating with a well-known producer, designer, credit card or magazine on a special event for a charity.

Retailers are in perpetual motion to build and keep drawing traffic into their physical stores and on to their virtual locations—websites and catalogs. Tie-ins and web-links help keep the brand in the customer's 24/7 world.

The goal is to make strategic associations with like-minded brands that will easily and quickly communicate a brand's image and keep it "top-of-mind" when a customer is considering a pur-

chase or a choice between brands.

This may not be a totally "new" strategy but it is one of the most effective and mutually beneficial. Inventive retailers and progressive brands of all types continue to seek out and build Co-Branding associations that keep their businesses vital to their target markets. There are no hard, fast rules to follow or traditions to adhere to with the new world of Power Retailers. They are creating more unique and unusual Co-Branding possibilities that are delighting customers.

• **Art Appreciation** – *H & M* brings a fresh perspective to the fashion scene not only in its fashions' cheap chic, but also in its advertising and promotions. The Co-Branding promotion teaming with Art Start and The Barnstormers artist collective targeted young, fashion-savvy customers by supporting talented young artists and musicians. An exciting, inspired tie-in that was a "perfect fit"—"Inventive and cutting edge, the artists' vivid works meshed perfectly with H & M's hip, creative approach...." See page 96.

• **A Star is Born** – *Holt Renfrew* partnered with *Vanity Fair* and American Express to launch FLICK, a national event celebrating the world of fashion and film, in conjunction with the Toronto International Film Festival. **"The goal was to deliver one-of-a-kind experiences to wow the customers."** Events can be small or large. Holt Renfrew matched this campaign to the magnitude of the film festival with a wide array of co-branded events—screenings of films, designer trunk shows and fashion shows, personal appearances, art and photography exhi-

bitions, silent auctions and even an exhibit of memorable Hollywood costumes. See page 98.

- **High-powered Fashion** – *Lord & Taylor* isn't selling automobiles, but matching or Co-Branding its own style image. To kick off a Father's Day promotion, L & T featured a few classic and new Corvettes in its Fifth Avenue windows tying into the 50th Anniversary of the 'Vette. "The Signature of American Style,"—Lord & Taylor—meets "an American Icon," the Corvette. "I don't think cars are removed from fashion; they represent fashion, function and lifestyle and a way to define your image." The brands deliver on helping the customer's **id** meets his **ID** in this multi-event, captivating promotion. See page 100.

- **Community Affair** – *La Maison Ogilvy* positions itself within the Montreal community as part of an "up market" image held by its own customers. Tie-ins were established with the best designer hotels, charity events catering to a specific customer profile, art exhibitions, cocktail parties and silent auctions that are part of its customers' social life and self image. "This has become an important factor in generating business and represents savvy thinking and an evolution in the brand's marketing strategy." See page 102.

- **Malls try Harder** – *The Gardens of the Palm Beaches* luxurious super-regional center has a strong calendar of events that promote its retailers, the ultimate in Co-branding. "The strategy is to position The Gardens as special in every way, from advertising and community programs to events and its own signature brand

identity." The mall Co-Brands a variety of events with local groups and media to serve their community. This is a *power retail center* that works hard to provide relevant tie-ins that are appreciated by its customers, its own retailers and its business neighbors. See page 105.

One of the most helpful tools of the creative person is what we call an "idea file." Since we are all after the illusive consumer's time, attention and dollars, retailers must keep trying to deliver the ultimate event, the solution to a customer's problem, the joys of shopping, entertainment and perhaps a bit of therapy. Anytime brands can join together to break through the competition's efforts with a better idea, the customer wins—and your creative "idea file" gets a new entry to stimulate your thinking.

Art Appreciation

WHEN SWEDISH retailing giant H&M launched its spring/summer 2003 advertising campaign, the purpose was twofold. The idea was to target the young fashion-savvy customer with a splashy series of ads sure to capture their attention while simultaneously supporting the creative efforts of talented youth from The Barnstormers artist collective.

Never heard of The Barnstormers? They are a collective of artists founded in 1999 by artist David Ellis after a pilgrimage to Cameron, a small farming town in North Carolina. The group paints explosive murals on barns, shacks, chicken coops and even 18-wheeler trucks! They're widely recognized for new media forms that combine time-lapse photography, large-scale installations, collaborative painting performances and sound. The Barnstormers exhibit internationally and are even the

subject of an upcoming documentary.

So where did H&M come into play? Since the retailer's latest ad campaign featured seven artists and musicians from the collective, an exhibition was timed in conjunction with the campaign launch.

Created by The Red Room, H&M's (Sweden-based) in-house team, the print campaign broke February 6 in *Teen*, *Vogue*, *Seventeen*, *Cosmo Girl*, *Interview*, *Paper* and *Time Out New York*. In-store signage, posters and billboards placed in the hip New York City neighborhood of Union Square were also utilized, as were splashy Barnstormers shopping bags.

Featuring the artists and musicians from The Barnstormers dressed in the retailer's spring collection, the candid images by photographer Sasha Eisenman conveyed a spirited, individualistic approach to life and fashion. The artists were captured in the

process of creating a series of paintings on walls, canvases, a car, and even a boat!

This artists' collective "was a perfect fit for the print campaign," noted Karen Belva, H&M's spokesperson, thereby inspiring the retailer to sponsor the exhibition from February 7 through 23 in a gallery located above its SoHo store.

Inventive and cutting edge, the artist's vivid work meshed perfectly with H&M's hip, creative approach and "we kind of knew that this was the angle to go for and a perfect fit for our company," stated Belva.

The exhibit incorporated The Barnstormers collaborative painting, juxtaposed artwork created by young people from the New York City–based, nonprofit organization, Art Start. The media got a sneak preview at a cocktail party complete with a silent auction benefiting Art Start. An interactive "Collaboration Room" featured a

T-shirt $5.50

Shirt $25

team from Art Start who created a series of large-scale "live painting" murals, which evolved continuously throughout the exhibition. In our book a compelling reason for repeat visits to the gallery, and downstairs to H&M for a little shopping fix.

"We wanted to bring to life the inspiration and spirit of the ad campaign with this unique art exhibit. Teaming with Art Start, who serve city community organizations, shelters and 'last chance' schools, gave us the opportunity to share the experience with the kids from their programs," said Belva.

To further maximize the benefit to Art Start, H&M donated 1,000 T-shirts, created by Art Start artists and The Barnstormers. The specially designed, limited edition tees were sold at H&M's SoHo store, the gallery and through Art Start's existing tee shirt business, with proceeds directly benefiting the organization.

Jeans $39

H&M (Hennes & Mauritz) New York, NY
AGENCY: **In—house, "The Red Room"**
PHOTOGRAPHER: **Sasha Eisenman**

A Star is Born

For Fall 2003, Holt Renfrew, one of Canada's leading retailers, partnered with *Vanity Fair* and American Express to launch Flick, a month-long series of national events celebrating the world of fashion and film. Events were scheduled at each Holt Renfrew across Canada.

"As the 'official retail sponsor' of the Toronto International Film Festival, we wanted to maximize the opportunities inherent to this role and the strong synergies between film and fashion," said Andrew Jennings, president and managing director of Holts. He further stated that the goal was to deliver one-of-a-kind experiences to wow the customers. And wow them Holts' did, by offering a dazzling array of more than 30 events at the Toronto flagship alone, plus dozens more at each outpost across the country. The scope of these events were pretty spectacular and included photographic installations, fashion shows, a screening of an original short "art" film, designer trunk

shows and personal appearances, art and photography exhibitions, silent auctions, and an exhibit of top Hollywood costume pieces.

One of the most sought after invites was the Toronto flagship store's exclusive gala, with special guest Graydon Carter, *Vanity Fair's* editor-in-chief. This was some bash! Among the 1,600 guests who walked the red carpet (yup, just like a real movie premiere), were luminaries such as Seal, Benecio Del Toro, Naomi Watts, William H. Macy, and many more. Media coverage

was extensive and included powerhouse TV show *Entertainment Tonight*. The spectacular party was also simulcast on a Jumbotron set up outside so passersby could get in on the action vicariously. Guests at the gala could enter a draw for a chance to win two tickets to the 2004 Golden Globe Awards in L.A. plus passes to Vanity Fair's coveted, star-studded, pre-Golden Globe bash. In a clever move, Holts even got the Bloor Street store location cordoned off to traffic for the event! Now that's covering all the bases.

INSIDE HOLT RENFREW
AUGUST 2003

Flick

This fall, from September 2 to October 4, 2003, Holt Renfrew and *Vanity Fair* in association with American Express present Flick, a star-studded celebration of the fashion, style and glamour that is and always will be Hollywood.

An unprecedented event, Flick puts glamour in the spotlight and shouts, "Hurray for Hollywood." It showcases the glitz and the allure of all things Tinseltown including the stars, the designers, the clothes and even the paparazzi.

The wide range of events will include everything from previews of the latest

fashions and accessories, as well as an exclusive private shopping night, makeovers, gifts-with-purchase, exciting contests and so much more.

We're pulling out all the stops for this exclusive, once-in-a-lifetime extravaganza. So don't miss out on any of the excitement - join us for a month of irresistible in-store activities at all Holt Renfrew locations across Canada.*

Flick - it's not a dress rehearsal. Starting September 2, 2003, we are ready for our close-up.

*Except Winnipeg. These events are just a sampling of what's happening in store. Please note that the events vary and may be subject to change. Contact your store for more details of events listed above. To view other events and news, visit our website at www.holtrenfrew.com

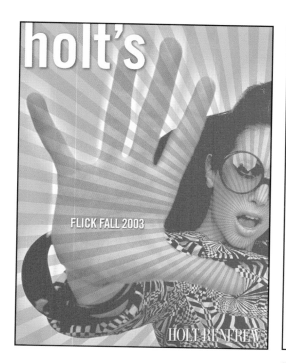

holt's

FLICK FALL 2003

HOLT RENFREW

star style

Hollywood: from film to fashion

BY AYSE LONG

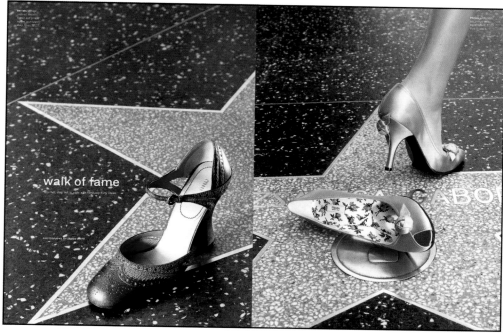

walk of fame

This fall, step out in style with famously flirty shoes

PHOTOGRAPHY BY JAMES WORTH

FLICK

FLICK

FLICK

This clever little flip book was handed out as part of the media press package. Sometimes, pictures really are worth a thousand words!

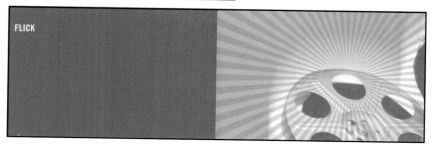

Two American Icons Team Up for a Classic Salute to Dad

DON'T THINK Lord & Taylor is getting into the automobile business. The quintessential style store simply jump-started its Father's Day business by parking a few classic Corvettes, along with the sports car's newest model, in its Fifth Avenue windows. But, there's more. The chain totally added onto the hoopla when it unwrapped its Corvette Concept Shops, featuring a collection of 50th Anniversary commemorative merchandise inside all of its 84 stores.

Lord & Taylor recently came up with a novel way to say Happy Father's Day right along with promoting its special occasion business by way of what it terms, "The Ultimate Fashion Accessory" when LaVelle Olexa, senior VP of fashion presentation, reached out to Chevrolet to work on a tie-in between the store, which proclaims itself "the signature of American style" and the Corvette, which is viewed as an American icon.

Prior to the holiday, several classic Corvettes, circa 1955, 1966 and 1978, were driven right into the store's Fifth Avenue windows. The actual installation,

which, according to Olexa, was a wild combination of a party on the street and putting a ship in a bottle, began on the evening of Tuesday, May 21 with the cars arriving at around 8 p.m. It took an outside crew until the early hours of the next morning to remove the glass plates, hoist the sportscars on platforms, and squeeze the vehicles right into the windows, sans any fender benders, of course. The framed windows showcased only the cars and showed no merchandise. However, the nine additional windows, which wrap around the store and entranceway, featured special Father's Day gifts and merchandise in conjunction with the Corvette theme. All windows were on view to the public until Tuesday, June 18.

Along with the vintage 'vettes, the chain unveiled the automaker's new 50th Anniversary edition for 2003, one week before a similar model served as the pace car at the Indianapolis 500 race. Blow-ups of photos of Corvettes belonging to various private owners, along with human interest stories supplied the backdrop for the windows. The smallest Fifth Avenue window showed a die-cast Corvette model car atop a slanted checkerboard flag patterned runway. Here, shoppers were invited inside the store to visit the first-floor Corvette outpost shop and register to win prizes. Additionally, on June 13, New York customers had the opportunity to have their pictures taken in a Corvette,

along with a professional race car driver, as well as receive a special commemorative edition of *Car and Driver* magazine

As Olexa says, "Corvette represents a sleek modern approach to styling, and that's the direction we are taking with our store, which is modern and up to the minute, but not avant garde or cutting edge. We know that there is a renewed interest in sports cars today and therefore this kind of classic salute is appropriate for Father's Day as well as Lord & Taylor. I don't think cars are removed from fashion; they represent fashion, function and lifestyle and a way to define your image."

The concept shops, which were in all L&T stores through Father's Day, showcased Corvette-inspired merchandise, a special edition gift card promotion featur-

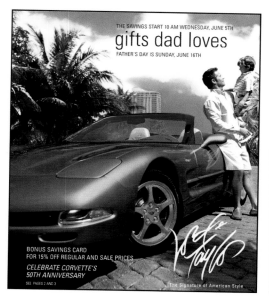

ing a 1953 Corvette and prizes such as a two-day, all-expenses paid trip for two to the Justin Bell GT Driving School in Palm Beach Gardens, FL.

All shops featured a consistent look (merchandise, marketing and prizes) in order to tie together the feeling of the fun Father's Day Event across all markets. Colorful Corvette style checkerboard flag patterned floors, Alpha caps and overlays, 25 in. x 60 in. graphics, and 5.5 in. x 7 in. toppers with the theme of "It's a Gift for Dad" all appeared in the shops, while accompanying signage (22 in. x 28 in. posters) ran storewide. The only difference in the storewide promotion was the exclusive New York windows.

Lord & Taylor supported the entire promotion (windows/interiors) in all of its markets via full-color, full-page ads in newspapers such as *The New York Times* and a full-color, 51-plus page "Gifts Dad Loves" catalog, which was mailed to cus-

tomers and placed in the stores. The catalog, which hit at around the same time the windows went up, also contains a toll-free number to order the 2003 Corvette.

This reporter visited the New York store during the Father's Day promotion and was captivated by how perfectly the excitement in the windows/interiors, coupled with the marketing and the merchandise all fit together. Obviously, Lord & Taylor's Father's Day Promotion is a prime example of just how well planning ahead can work.

Lord & Taylor, New York, NY
SENIOR VP/FASHION MERCHANDISING: **LaVelle Olexa**
VP/VISUAL MERCHANDISING: **Michael Salinas**
CREATIVE DIRECTOR, VISUAL MERCHANDISING/WINDOWS: **Manoel Renha**

Tradition with a Twist

IT'S TWELVE O'CLOCK noon and business is bustling, when suddenly the unmistakable sounds of a bagpipe are heard. Yes, this is just another typical day at La Maison Ogilvy, one of Montreal's leading department stores, and at 136 years old, a true grande dame!

As the bagpiper—in full kilted regalia—wends his way through the store, shoppers and passersby stop and acknowledge the brand's Scottish roots. While it's this heritage that has made Ogilvy a leader in retailing among a discerning clientele, (think of London's Harvey Nichols and New York's Bergdorf Goodman as its retailing equivalents), according to Errol Pereira, Ogilvy's vice president of marketing and visual presentation, the brand's image goes beyond that of a traditional merchant.

On a recent trip to Montreal, *RAW* sat down for a conversation with Pereira and got the inside scoop on what sets Ogilvy apart from the crowd, and how the brand has managed to hold on to the traditional customer and still satisfy the needs of the younger, fashion-forward shopper.

Interestingly enough, it's a very specific ambiance that is key to the brand's success. Imagine an atmosphere that's European in flavor, and as if the customer were in someone's residence rather than a typical department store. Pereira went on to say that "people consider us to be upmarket. We have built up a very successful customer base with both men and women." Therefore, in positioning Ogilvy as an upscale brand, direct mail works better than newspaper or magazine ads.

Six catalogs are produced each year in house, with names culled from the retailer's own mailing lists. "We mail out 350,000 copies, with half in French and half in English, he added. We direct mail 60,000 copies, and the rest are distributed in both French and English newspapers."

A glance through the latest fall catalog reinforces the store's image as more than just a place to shop. On the inside cover is a personal letter from Pereira. Instead of promoting the merchandise it gives the reader a rundown of some of the best designer hotels in town, complete with addresses. Taking this a step further, the various hotels are then used as chic backdrops for the fashion shots. Copy is kept to a minimum and positioned on a neutral band of color. The designer's name, price points, and (most useful to our way of thinking), the phone number and extension of the particular boutique are listed. In every catalog, these chatty letters reinforce the brand's personal marketing approach. However, it takes more than a cosy atmosphere and beautiful catalogs to lure new shoppers and excite the core customers. With this in mind, Pereira informed *RAW* that upcoming plans call for changes on the ground and main floors, with an expansion of the Vuitton boutique as well as the cosmetics area. In essence, marketing to the fashion forward consumer entails focusing more on luxury brands.

Ogilvy also takes an active role in Montreal's social life by participating in many charity events that cater to a specific customer profile. In addition, art exhibitions, cocktail parties, and even silent auctions are held. And guess what? The store has the perfect setting. Located on the fifth floor, Tudor Hall, is a baronial

OGILVY

Dear Friend of Ogilvy,

As you open this autumn catalogue and discover a world of exciting new fashion, you'll also open the doors to some of the city's most fashionable hotels.

It seemed only natural that we photograph the latest designs and styles available in the many boutiques at Ogilvy, inside some of Montreal's greatest designer, boutique hotels. Although we adore all the beautiful fashions and all the great hotels this city has to offer, unfortunately we could not include them all.

We hope you enjoy this taste of what Montreal and Ogilvy have to offer.

Hôtel Le St-James
Stepping into the lobby of Hôtel Le St-James is like slipping into an haute-couture evening gown...luxurious, elegant and oh-so-sophisticated. This hotel is a veritable palace offering European charm and grandeur that never go out of style. Each of its 23 rooms and 38 suites is a unique décor experience, as tailor-made rooms provide the utmost in comfort and luxury.

Hôtel Nelligan
This intimate boutique hotel is a unique blend of contemporary décor set in traditional Old Montreal architecture. Just like Ogilvy, it's truly "a world within a world". Imagine fireplaces, stone and brick walls, a spectacular fountain, a garden atrium and the Verses restaurant with contemporary cuisine and a classic wine cellar, not to mention many other convenient and stylish accessories.

Le Saint-Sulpice • Hôtel-Montréal
Located in the shadow of the Notre Dame Basilica, Le Saint-Sulpice is "la pièce de résistance" when it comes to luxury hotels. Gold Award Winner 2003 for accommodation from 50 to 149 rooms, this all-suites hotel is enhanced by countless elegant details reminiscent of the great euro-establishments.

Sofitel Montréal
Imagine transforming a suit from the 70's into an amazing and glamorous new look for today. Once a classic 1970's office building, this magnificent hotel ideally located on elegant Sherbrooke Street is now a stunning example of contemporary style and design. This artistic structure is best described as "a crystal by day and a lantern by night" thanks to a façade that plays with the transparency and reflection of light making it shine both day and night.

Loews Hôtel Vogue
A unique blend of classic old-world charm and new-world style... this hotel really lives up to its name. The Hôtel Vogue is always in vogue. With plush furnishings, a luxurious atmosphere and an envied downtown location within the Golden Square Mile, this hotel means business and pleasure.

Errol Pereira
Vice-President Marketing

SAINTE-CATHERINE AND DE LA MONTAGNE, MONTREAL   514-842-7711   WWW.OGILVYCANADA.COM

HÔTEL LE ST-JAMES
355, rue Saint-Jacques
Montréal (Québec) H2Y 1N9
Telephone: (514) 841-3111
Toll Free: 1-866-841-3111
Fax: (514) 841-1232
www.hotellestjames.com

HÔTEL NELLIGAN
106, rue Saint-Paul ouest
Montréal (Québec) H2Y 1Z3
Telephone: (514) 788-2040
Toll Free: 1-877-788-2040
Fax: (514) 788-2041
info@hotelnelligan.com
www.hotelnelligan.com

LE SAINT-SULPICE • HÔTEL-MONTRÉAL
414, rue Saint-Sulpice
Montréal (Québec) H2Y 2V5
Telephone: (514) 288-1000
Toll Free: 1-877-SULPICE
Fax: (514) 288-0077
www.lesaintsulpice.com
www.concorde-hotels.com

SOFITEL MONTRÉAL
1155, rue Sherbrooke ouest
Montréal (Québec) H2A 2N3
Telephone: (514) 285-9000
Toll Free: 1-877-285-9001
Fax: (514) 289-1155
www.sofitel.com
www.accorhotels.com

LOEWS HÔTEL VOGUE
1425, rue de la Montagne
Montréal (Québec) H3G 1Z3
Telephone: (514) 285-5555
Toll Free: 1-800-465-6654
Fax: (514) 849-9819
www.loewshotels.com

RODIER BOUTIQUE ON 2 842-7711 EXT 269
LOCATION HÔTEL LE ST-JAMES

CARACTERE AUBERGINE SHORT WOOL COAT 6 TO 14 $995 • AUBERGINE VELVET PANT 6 TO 14 $475 • PINK STRIPED CRINKLED BLOUSE 6 TO 14 $545
BOUTIQUE CAPSULE ON 3 842-7711 EXT 274 SHOES BY OGILVY SHOE SALON
LOCATION: HÔTEL LE ST-JAMES

AQUASCUTUM LONDON BOUTIQUE GROUND FLOOR 842-7711 EXT. 210
LOCATION: HÔTEL LE ST-JAMES

space that reinforces the feeling that one is attending a swanky party at a private residence rather than a department store. On average, 500 people are invited to these coveted special events.

Last but not least, tourism plays a part in the brand's marketing strategy. What works now? Placing videos in all the leading hotels in Montreal and the provinces, "in which the merchandise featured is fine tuned to play up to the various taste levels." Considering the various types of hotels and the customers they attract, (from trendy boutique to old-garde establishment), this has become an important factor in generating business and represents savvy thinking and an evolution in the brand's marketing strategy.

Now about those bagpipes…

La Maison Ogilvy Inc., Montreal, Quebec
VP MARKETING AND VISUAL PRESENTATION: **Errol James Pereira**

Outclassing the Competition

THE GARDENS of the Palm Beaches, a luxurious super-regional center in retail-rich Palm Beach County, Florida, consistently stands apart from the competition. The key is a combination of preparation, imagination and organization.

Marketing makes sure that everyone is on the same page, literally, The Gardens distributes an Events & Promotional Merchant Calendar to all retailers in January of each year. The calendar includes dates for mall events, advertising/media flights, holidays, mall closings and public school closings, enabling retailers the opportunity to plan their in-store events, promotions and advertising efforts with mall-wide events and advertising schedules in mind.

The strategy is to position The Gardens as special in every way from advertising and community programs to events and its own signature brand identity. The newest campaign, "See. Be Seen. Be Seen Shopping," emphasizes fashion and retail selection. "This campaign definitely focuses on our retailers," said Jeannie Roberts, marketing director. "It allows us the opportunity to tailor the fashion image and featured retailers based on the publication's audience and shopping season. The retailer listing bar also serves as a great way to introduce new retailers. It's very flexible!" Full-page 4C ads run monthly in regional lifestyle publications—*Palm Beach Illustrated, Ocean Drive* and *VIVE.*

All the advertising is the work of its agency, Panzano & Partners. In addition to magazine advertising, the media plan includes radio and newspaper (primarily for special events), direct mail, outdoor and television. Two :30 image TV spots "Mom" and "Home" run throughout the year. While the action takes place on the upper two thirds of the screen, the bottom is devoted to retailers. "We seasonally change the store names as new stores open," Roberts noted. The spots air on a rotation schedule (each spot has been done in five versions featuring different selections of Gardens retailers) on the local NBC, ABC, CBS and FOX affiliates during key shopping periods and in conjunction with major mall events.

Out-of-home advertising has proven very successful as well. The Gardens billboard has a prominent interstate location, where it's estimated that more than 120,000 adults view it daily. In addition, two backlit Duratrans are located in the baggage claim area of Palm Beach International Airport. "As a super-regional shopping center in Palm Beach County, where airport traffic was +14% in April 2003, it is imperative to

The merchant calendar is a great way to distribute information and facilitate advance planning. The creative reflects a combination of The Gardens' "signature series" campaign and the customized fashion campaign.

Television: "Home"

VIDEO: The footage runs on the top two thirds of the screen, with the bottom edge being a drop shadow over a white field. On the field run the names of key retailers. The retailer names come in succession. The first name comes up and fades down, leaving one or two letters which float to a new place where other letters fade up revealing the next retailer.

The location is a large home with porch and garden.

SFX: Original music.

VIDEO: Opens on close-up of young, professional couple outside of the home.

VO (FEMALE): Our dream home. It's been our labor of love. (As couple walks into house.)

VO: And since we discovered The Gardens, it's become more love than labor. (As woman makes bed.)

VO: Just last week, I found the perfect frames for our wedding photos there. (Man walks down hallway with box in his arms.)

VO: And it's also where I'll get the dress for our first anniversary. (Couple in kitchen.)

VO: When you have so much to look forward to, sometimes you forget to stop and enjoy it. (Medium shot of couple on Adirondack chairs at sunset. Cut to close-up.)

VO: Somehow, I don't think that will be a problem. (Wide shot of couple. Fade to white.)

VO AND ARTCARD: The Gardens of the Palm Beaches. See. Be Seen. Be Seen Shopping.

introduce the shopping center's message to business and leisure travelers alike," Roberts pointed out.

The Gardens has long been known for its unique events. Many are museum-quality exhibits. "These remarkable events have been the backbone of how we set ourselves apart," Roberts said. "We have been able to find these exhibits that have never been in a shopping center environment before." To wit: The Gardens has hosted a Princess Grace exhibit and a chil-

dren's interactive geography exhibit, "Earth to You" in conjunction with the Smithsonian.

This spring, The Gardens of The Palm Beaches was the first shopping center to host the largest collection of Princess Diana gowns exhibiting in the United States. The exhibit was made available through Pink Ribbons Crusade, an organization whose mission is to continue the work of the Princess of Wales in fighting breast cancer. Visitors could view the stun-

ning exhibit in the mall common area at no charge; however, in an effort to benefit local breast cancer awareness, while increasing mall traffic and sales, one weekend of the exhibit was devoted to a fundraising sales promotion. A portion of sales at The Gardens was donated to a local breast cancer awareness organization. As a result, $7,500 was donated to the organization.

The event was promoted through radio spots, in-mall posters, newspaper ads and

Full-page, 4/C ads run in regional lifestyle publications.

Duratrans.

Posters help promote the fashion shows.

Radio: Fashion Show

SFX: Original music

FEMALE VO: To some of us, clothes aren't merely clothes. They're fashion.

Fashion is that extra spring in your step that comes with a new pair of shoes, that subtle feeling of confidence that a new dress can give you.

The Gardens of the Palm Beaches understands that feeling. We understand fashion. So we invite you to join us at our stylish showcase, our Spring Fashion Shows. These energetic runway shows will feature spring's best styles from Gardens' stores, including Bloomingdale's, Ann Taylor and Sisley.

Discover the newest trends from Banana Republic, Adrienne Vittadini, Coach and many more.

It all takes place in Grand Court this Saturday at 1 and 4 p.m., and again on Sunday at 3 p.m.

And while you're there, be sure to visit The Princess Diana Dress Collection, featuring six beautiful gowns owned by the late Princess.

The Gardens of the Palm Beaches.
See. Be Seen. Be Seen Shopping.
I-95 to PGA Boulevard East in Palm Beach Gardens.

handouts in-mall. More than 15,000 people visited the Princess Diana dress collection during the 16-day exhibit.

The mall hosts a variety of other types of events (in addition to the usual Santa, the Easter Bunny, etc.). One such event, "Taste of the Town," benefited customers and a local food drive alike. Partnering with a local NBC affiliate, The Gardens invited 15 restaurants to come in and provide tastings for customers who could either give a $5 donation or canned food for the gastronomic experience.

The Gardens of the Palm Beaches is also known for its professional fashion shows. For spring, the latest looks from more than 40 Gardens retailers were presented during three shows. They were supported by radio spots, in-mall posters and newspaper ads. More than 2,000 people turned out.

There are also back-to-school fashion shows, which are related to one of the more unusual programs it offers. That program, Fashion Camp, is an enormously popular summer-long program, now in its eighth year. It consists of seven Saturday workshops for boys and girls, ages 6 to 18, broken down by age group. The "campers" learn about fashion, nutrition, and proper etiquette, and they have an informal fashion show in which everyone is invited to participate.

Those who had good attendance throughout the program are invited to participate in the Gardens back-to-school fashion show. "Fashion Camp is so popular we sell out every year," said Roberts. "The enrollment for the program has to be capped at 200. Everyone loves to be in the fashion show. It's another thing that sets us apart."

Each show is professionally choreographed and includes an energizing combination of music, lights and fashion. Newspaper ads and posters feature a teen model, as well as carefully selected Gardens retailers that appeal to the BTS shopping audience. Radio spots are also utilized to support the event.

Never one to let an opportunity pass by, The Gardens direct mails a new resident piece to more than 2,000 newcomers in its effective trade area each month. "There is an influx of new residential developments in our market; therefore, introducing the shopping center and including trackable bounce-back offers for select stores and restaurants is a strategic effort to capture this audience," Roberts said.

And to make sure that all consumers get the message that The Gardens of the Palm Beaches is a center unlike any other, there is the distinctive signature series—a recognizable identity that was introduced at The Gardens in 2002. It consists of a simple elegant design on items such as shopping bags, gift bags, savings books, gift certificate envelopes and mall directories.

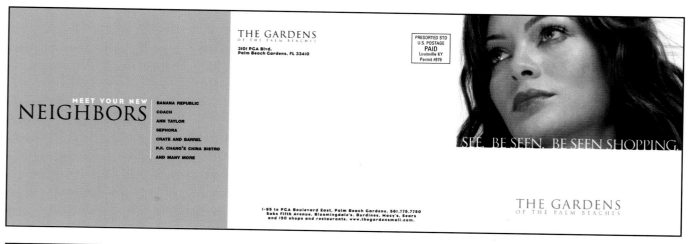

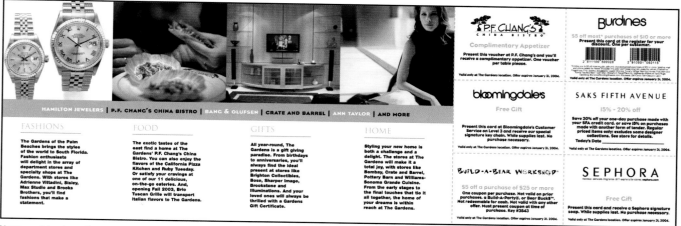

New resident mailer.

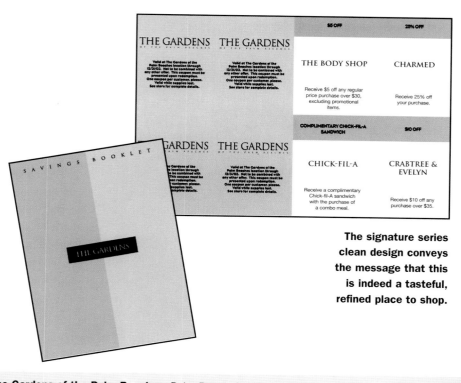

The signature series
clean design conveys
the message that this
is indeed a tasteful,
refined place to shop.

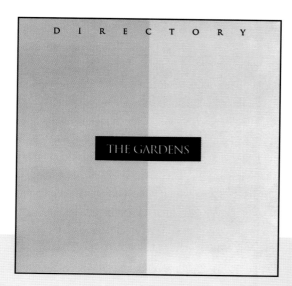

The Gardens of the Palm Beaches, Palm Beach Gardens, FL
MARKETING DIRECTOR: **Jeannie L. Roberts**
ADVERTISING AGENCY: **Panzano & Partners,** Moorestown, NJ
MANAGEMENT COMPANY: **The Forbes Company,** Southfield, NJ

Channel Branding

Integrating all channels of communications to develop a holistic approach to communicating with customers. From opt-in fashion newsletters to personal shopper PDA services, the range of new tools for building emotional connections with the brand is exploding.

Too many marketers ignore the importance of distribution. **Channel Branding** is a multichannel strategy for retailers to communicate how convenient and desirable their systems and services are to their customers. In order to control a brand's appeal, you must control its distribution—and now this means more than from producer to seller. It involves seamless service, online shopping experiences and the timesaving that an efficient and informative merchandise department location plan has to offer. **Channel Branding** is now a complex of matched media-mix that provides opportunities for building strong relations with customers.

The advent of e-business and e-tailing has provided unique opportunities for "non-physical" distribution. 24/7 shopping and services are more and more available. Nine-to-five opening hours are not enough any more. Waiting two weeks for an order is a no-no sale.

Channel Branding is a strategy that works to create a persona for the brand. It is a process for making the brand a friend who is always there for a customer. It creates a "romantic" or "emotional" relationship that says "I'm here for you when you want me—I'm ready when you are."

The retailer uses its own mix of marketing communications to keep **evolving** its positioning. An example is a retailer who has had to reposition a well-known brand image from a classic supplier to fashion change-makers. The store's present customers, who have become accustomed to its way of serving their needs, now see new technologies for channels and media capable of changing their entire shopping experience. The retail brand must evolve with a new style without losing its identity. This

may require some reinventions of store design, merchandise assortment, category range, co-branding and brand extensions.

- **Bebe** is an international specialty store chain that has brought its own brand of online shopping to its target market. It has re-profiled its customer from the typical junior and missy demographics to a contemporary bridge apparel shopper. Its customer is not profiled as junior or missy, but rather as a woman who has a distinct awareness of her own sensuality. And it has created a website, **bebe.com**, with a special selection of apparel and accessories that confirms this self-image. See page 112.

- **Famous Footwear,** known for its value specialty stores, has added trend-right and fashion-orward styling to its price appeal. It has a multi-media strategy that includes ads on TV and radio, in newspapers and vendor co-op tabloids for its "surround channel branding." For example, its research found that the demands on women's time inspired the creation of "moms on a mission," a 17-market radio ad campaign, and TV ads in six of its major markets for back-to-school shoe shopping. See page 116.

- **Caché** sends out a warning to its customers that its fashions "are not for the faint of heart." Its creative strategy positions Caché with "a *culture branding* approach to mine the beliefs and value systems of its clientele." Its multichannel marketing communications encourages the customer to surf **caché.com**, sends constant direct-mail promotions, and projects its image on giant billboards in New York City's Times Square, promising: *"admiration from women and desire from men."* See page 119.

• **Ikea** operates in more than 30 countries worldwide. Its creative strategy incorporates playful humor that is designed "to educate consumers about Ikea, and to change their relationship with home furnishings." It departs from the traditional communication channels, "exploring new media or ways to use traditional media in new ways." Its creative approach is to poke holes in the consumer's reasons for holding on to old decorating ideas, and let them see how they could replace them with (Ikea) pieces more in line with their passions or interests, and definitely in line with their budget. See page 124.

• **Lloyd Center** has used channel branding to reposition itself a "fun place." Its strategy was to create a new holistic brand positioning for the entire mall. The objective was to focus on the *mall experience* rather than the product and price. The message is that Lloyd Center offers emotional experiences that surpass the low-price kicks offered by a discount retailer. The TV spots captured "the real experience that happens to real people like you at Lloyd Center every day." These spots, plus a new print campaign, developed a customer fan club that related to the funny one-liners and comedy dialogues in every ad. A connection was made. See page 128.

A retail brand, as never before, needs to *break through* the current state of 24/7 marketing, the ad clutter and the consequent consumer big-brand back lash. In the process for building its brand power, the retailer should constantly be asking: What is a brand? What does my brand mean to my customer? Do I really have a brand, or merely a non distinct one-of-a-category, -product, -store or -service?

A product, store or service becomes a brand only when it offers attributes, benefits and commitments that differentiate its brand meanings to consumers. Communicating through non-traditional and traditional channels, in new and different ways, is expected by today's consumers. The retailer's BrandPower strategies should be designed to increase the customer's understanding of the brand and how they value its attributes and benefits. Creating power for a brand requires the retailer's knowledge of its functional and emotional appeals, its lifestage and lifestyle associations and above all, its differentiation. The retailer should know why having a favorite brand is important to the customer. In building reasons to favor their brand, retailers can use our brand appeals model, *"FAVORITE."* It is based on the following reasons for favoring a brand:

Finding out where to find the brand or store.
Assigning responsibility for its performance.
Values based on quality, related to cost to the buyer
Opportunities for self-indulgence.
Risk reduced through trust.
Image of the brand adding to self-image.
Testing my own ideas.
Experiencing it in a new way.

Any, or any combination of the above, can create unique value propositions that make the consumer choose the brand and encourage the customer to stay with it.

BEBE

Online. On the money.

WHETHER OR NOT TO WEB—that is the question for many retailers as they continue to debate the merits of setting up an online store. When a major player like Fingerhut closes down, it can have an unsettling affect on the "should we's?" or "shouldn't we's?" On the other hand, there are companies that are finding that as with any new business model, it's what you do with what you've got that ultimately makes the difference.

Home page.

That has certainly been true for bebe.com, the latest venture for a company that has been pushing the envelope for more than 25 years.

When bebe first came on the scene in 1976, three categories dominated the women's wear market—junior, bridge and missy. Having pinpointed a demographic that was neither junior or missy, bebe aimed to break the mold by offering stylish women a distinctive line of contemporary bridge apparel with an unmistakable hint of sensuality. The original concept stuck and bebe has been on a successful trajectory ever since.

The company has grown to the point where it currently operates 160 specialty stores in the United States and Canada, and licensed bebe stores in Greece, Israel, the Middle East and Singapore, as well as the online store, bebe.com.

According to Julie Kessler, online marketing manager, bebe first opened what was pretty much a bare-boned online store three and-a-half years ago. "About eight months after the launch, we started staffing up, hiring a full-time designer, operations manager and marketing manager (me!). Realizing the potential of online sales, the company invested in new technologies and relaunched the site with a new back end in the fall of 2000 and then refined and optimized it again in November 2001." The staff continued to grow to its current 17 people, encompassing every area from design, marketing and merchandising to production, operations, customer service, engineering and fulfillment.

Having a stable site coupled with a full selection of merchandise offerings, bebe felt that the time was right to initiate marketing dedicated to promoting the site and increasing traffic numbers.

How the company went about achieving these goals demonstrates the importance of making the right choices. With a limited online marketing budget to work with, they decided the most effective way to obtain more online shoppers would be to produce a printed piece and utilize store traffic primarily for distribution to drive sales to the web—rather than leaning heavily on direct mail.

Every season, bebe has been running an image campaign with its own theme and imagery to promote the brand and drive store traffic. It has been customary to produce a brochure highlighting the campaign that is mailed to bebe's top 20,000 customers and distributed to the retail stores. The brochure is followed immediately by a postcard, which is used by the stores and corporate for customer communication. (The postcards, which were available for the duration of the campaign from mid-October through the end of December 2001, are so popular customers often collect them.)

For holiday 2001, the brochure took on a new role as the focal point for promoting bebe.com. "This is the first official piece of collateral that we have produced specifically for bebe.com," says Kessler. "The purpose of the brochure was to introduce new and current customers to bebe's online channel." Distributed in mid-October when the new ad campaign launched, the brochure was distributed as bag stuffers in the U.S. retail stores, in completed online orders and through direct mail.

The look and attitude of both the brochure and the postcard served as the inspiration for an additional collateral piece—in a fold-out format—that rein-

Brochure.

Holiday launch e-mail.

forced the season's imagery and brand consistency (branding is clearly a high priority at bebe, which invests between 3.5% and 5% of its annual sales in its high-impact image ad campaign). "The purpose of this companion piece was to introduce and educate new and current customers to bebe's online channel, reassure them that bebe.com is an easy and safe shopping experience, promote online gift shopping

and offer visitors the free shipping incentive," Kessler explains. The piece included the free shipping promotion, which started on November 15. It was distributed in store from November 15 through December 20.

A total of 100,000 of these pieces were produced and distributed to all bebe stores in the U.S. In addition to being placed on counters, they were used as bag stuffers. The piece was also included in every shipped bebe.com order.

During 2001, bebe had produced a set of four magnets with the bebe logo and the imagery from each season's campaign. For holiday, the bebe logo was replaced with the bebe.com logo. The magnets were given away with every purchase made on bebe.com. "This has proved to be a strong incentive for online shoppers to follow through with a purchase on the site,"

says Kessler. "We have found that it has even become a collectible for bebe fans!"

One of bebe's main objectives is to continue to build up its opt-in database. A key part of its strategy has been to capitalize on its strong retail presence to expand the consumer database. "After simply adding an e-mail field to the in-store mailing list cards, we have increased our database an extra 12,000 names in a short period of time," says Kessler. "We also added an e-mail sign up field to the site's home page and have seen a substantial increase from this feature as well."

Additionally, bebe has found sweepstakes to be a strong draw for obtaining additional e-mail addresses. "Last year we ran an online sweepstakes offering a bebe shopping spree as the prize. We received over 32,000 entries and from that number a total of 22,000 new e-mail addresses, says Kessler. Several e-mails a month highlighting promotions and/or merchandise are sent to these opt in e-mail addresses, which she adds "result in a burst of traffic to the site."

GWPs have also proved to be a strong and cost effective strategy to spur purchases online. Every month a different GWP (recent examples include a logo key chain,

Postcard.

Get in the mood
for holiday glamour...

at **bebe.com**

Fold-out piece.

...e an entrance this
...holiday season in something
...and irresistible from

bebe.com

...online boutique features fabulous possibilities

...aking the season by storm: **showstopping**

separates, party-perfect outfits, stunning

accessories, and the sexiest heels.

Treat yourself then select a little something for all of

those bombshells on your gift list. bebe.com offers

you limitless ways to give the gift of glamour.

Free shipping
never goes out of style.

Get it with every order of $125 or more

from bebe.com. Your shipping charge will

automatically be deducted at check out.

Offer good only at bebe.com. Offer effective at 12:01 a.m. (PST) Nov. 15, 2001. Ends at
11:59 p.m. (PST) Dec. 20, 2001. Three-day standard delivery charges will be automatically
waived for qualifying online orders over $125. $125 merchandise total does not include sales
tax, discounts or shipping and handling. This offer is good for standard shipping within the
United States to the first 'ship to' address in your order. If you choose overnight shipping,
additional charges may apply. Standard delivery service is Federal Express 3-business-day
shipping, so orders should arrive in 3-5 business days. Offer subject to official terms and
conditions. Visit bebe.com to review official terms and conditions.

Make an entrance this

holiday season in something

sexy and irresistible from

bebe.com

Our online boutique features fabulous possibilities

for taking the season by storm: **showstopping**

separates, party-perfect outfits, stunning

accessories, and the sexiest heels.

Treat yourself then select a little something for all of

those bombshells on your gift list. bebe.com offers

you limitless ways to give the gift of glamour.

Ring in the holiday season
by shopping bebe.com. It's fun, fashionable
and brings you these fabulous features:

- Place your order(s) by Dec. 20 and you're guaranteed to receive them right on time for the holidays.

- Leave the wrapping to us. Each gift arrives elegantly wrapped in bebe logo tissue and gift box.*

- Enjoy a secure shopping experience with quality service from a fashion brand you can trust.

- Got an online return or exchange? Mail it back to us or return it to your closest bebe store.

- Call our Merchandise Request Center at 1-877-bebe-NOW for assistance with locating those bebe fashions you can't find online or in your local bebe store.

- Choose how you'd like your orders delivered. We offer standard delivery (3-5 business days) and overnight shipping, both via Federal Express.**

- Shop our collection of up-to-the-minute fashion by category, find out the latest bebe holiday looks, and take advantage of special holiday offers.

- Can't decide how to surprise those style mavens on your shopping list? Give them the gift of shopping with a bebe gift certificate.

* footwear and larger items can't be gift boxed
** please note that we do not ship outside the 50 United States

FAQs
Fashionably Asked Questions

Q: What's bebe.com's return policy?

A: Online holiday gift purchases may be returned to your nearest bebe store or via mail by Jan. 7, 2002 for merchandise or store credit.

Q: How can I contact bebe.com?

A: bebe.com Customer Service can be reached Monday through Friday, 8 a.m. to 6 p.m. PST. Call 1-877-bebe-777 (1-877-232-3777) or e-mail us at askus@bebe.com.

Q: How do I know if the items I've selected fit?

A: We invite you to use our Size Chart, located in the Customer Service section of bebe.com. Simply follow the detailed measurement instructions to find the fit that's right for you. If you need further assistance, please feel free to call bebe.com Customer Service at the above number.

Q: I'm not comfortable entering my credit card information on the Internet. How secure is your site?

A: We aim to provide you with a safe and convenient online shopping experience. When placing an order online, your information is transmitted using Secure Sockets Layer (SSL) technology, the approved industry standard. For more details, please visit the Customer Service section of bebe.com.

Q: How can I learn the latest news from the world of bebe?

A: Sign up for bebe e-mails when visiting bebe.com.

cosmetic bag, logo camisole, etc.) is offered. "We have been careful to gradually increase the purchase amount to a level that is not only profitable for us, but also is comfortable for our customer," Kessler notes.

For holiday, bebe had events in Los Angeles and San Francisco to promote holiday fashions and to support a cause benefiting breast cancer research. Cards promoting the website were stuffed in goodie bags for the party goers, with the intention of driving this traffic to the site.

The site was also promoted with a listing in *Elle* magazine's e-commerce guide in the December issue.

The company now includes a reference to bebe.com on the inside left side of the print ads along with the toll free number.

The combination of savvy marketing, both online and off, combined with an investment in staff and refinement in technology, has definitely paid off, says Kessler. "During the past holiday season, bebe.com saw an increase in sales of 170% over last year."

But bebe is not resting on its laurels. Says Kessler: "In the upcoming year we will focus more on driving sales between the channels."

Events cards.

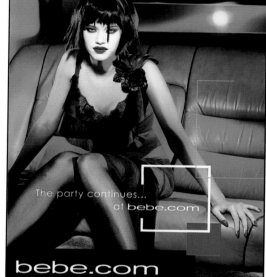

Bebe Stores, Inc., Brisbane, CA
ONLINE MARKETING MANAGER (bebe.com brochure, magnets, bebe.com screen shots): **Julie Kessler**
COPYWRITER MANAGER (bebe.com brochure, magnets, bebe.com screen shots): **Paul Cannon**
WEB DESIGN (bebe.com brochure, magnets, bebe.com screen shots): **Neda Saffarnia**
GRAPHIC DESIGN (bebe.com brochure, magnets, bebe.com screen shots): **Jonathon Kong**
PR/MARKETING DIRECTOR (bebe brochure, postcard, ad campaign): **Sally Kruteck**
ADVERTISING MANAGER (bebe brochure, postcard, ad campaign): **Sandra Alvarenga**
AGENCY (bebe brochure, postcard, ad campaign): **Lambesis Agency**

Locker Stocker

FOR FAMOUS FOOTWEAR, the country's largest chain selling value-priced, brand name footwear for the family, back-to-school is far and away the most important time of year. "It's our holiday," said Scott Cooper, senior vice president of marketing. "The six-week back-to-school season is when we drive in excess of 20,000,000 people to our stores." (The company operates more than 920 stores in every state, plus Guam and Puerto Rico).

Famous Footwear, which has always been known as a value specialty store, is in the process of moving toward the position of offering consumers an assortment of fashion, trend-right styles each season in addition to great prices.

The company has done considerable research in developing this positioning. Certain of the findings, particularly the demands on women's time, are evident in the campaign Famous Footwear

mounted for back-to-school. It called all "moms on a mission" with a 17-market broadcast advertising campaign around its Locker Stocker back-to-school shoe promotions.

The multimedia Locker Stocker campaign also included a national print advertising campaign and five weeks of in-store promotions with themed displays and special savings. Eight-page

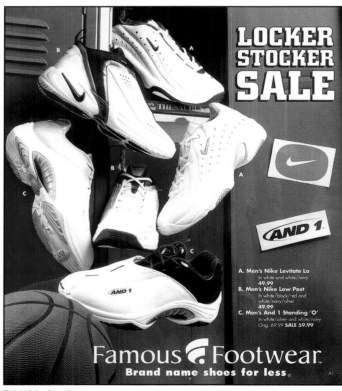

Tabloid circulars.

RADIO SCRIPTS

Famous Footwear Back to School Locker Stocker—STEPHANIE'S MISSION

MISSION MOM MUSIC UP AND UNDER

STEPHANIE (WITH INTENSITY): I went over the plan one last time: get in, load up, get out. Flawless. As I gripped the steering wheel, I pictured my destination. (RHAPSODIZING A BIT) Name brands as far as the eye could see. Shoes for the whole family. And the prices. Oh, the prices. (SUDDENLY EXCITED) There it is! The friendly logo beckons me like a moth to a flame. Famous Footwear's Locker Stocker price sale. Buy one pair get the second pair of equal or lesser value at half price. Just what I need to stock up for back to school. (TEETH CLENCHED IN DETERMINATION) Let the mission commence at Famous Footwear.

MUSICAL FLOURISH

STEPHANIE (DRAMATICALLY): The sign at the door screamed out to me "Locker Stocker 1/2 price sale." (COLDLY CONFIDENT) "I'm on my way" I said. (LIKE SHE'S DESCRIBING AN OUT-OF-BODY EXPERIENCE) The next half hour was a blur: box after box just flew into my cart. Skechers. New Balance. Nike. And 1. Adidas. (DIGRESSING SLIGHTLY) Even some cute little Aerosoles for me. (BUILDS TO A CONFIDENT, "HIGH-FIVE-MYSELF" CONCLUSION) It was like taking candy from a baby. Mission accomplished. Locker. Stocked. I. Am. So. Good.

MUSIC: CONCLUSIONARY FLOURISH

ANNCR: Famous Footwear's Price Locker Stocker Sale. Famous Footwear. For Moms on a mission.

Famous Footwear National—MYSTERY OF THE MISSING LOCKER

(ALL SFX IN THE MANNER OF AN OLD TIME RADIO MYSTERY LIKE "THE HARDY BOYS") DRAMATIC THEME MUSIC.

JUSTIN: Egads Michael. Your locker... it's... it's... MISSING.

MICHAEL: First our mom is missing. Now my locker.

MICHAEL: I've an eerie hunch they are somehow connected.

JUSTIN: Look, on the floor... a torn flier.

MICHAEL: Our first clue! It says...

JUSTIN (READING): Fam Foo Loc Sto Have Price Sale

MICHAEL: Who is this Fam Foo?

JUSTIN: Wait! Here's the rest of the flier. Put them together

BOYS TOGETHER: Aha!

DRAMATIC MUSICAL EMPHASIS

MICHAEL: Famous Footwear's Locker Stocker Half Price Sale

JUSTIN: Buy one pair get the second pair of equal or lesser value at half price.

MICHAEL: Nike, Skechers, New Balance, And 1, Adidas.

JUSTIN: Mom's at Famous Footwear!

MICHAEL: Let's go!

MOM Not so fast boys.

BOYS TOGETHER: Mom?

MOM: Okay, I admit it. I did it. I took your locker to Famous Footwear, stocked it at the Locker Stocker Half Price sale... and here it is.

SFX: LOCKER SLAMMING INTO PLACE

BOYS TOGETHER: Holy Locker Stocker Half Price Sale!

ANNCR: This week only at Fam Foo... um... Famous Footwear's Price Locker Stocker Sale. For moms on a mission.

tabloid ads ran in national newspapers in the same markets as TV and radio as well as additional markets. The first was a vendor-funded co-op tabloid, followed by a half-off promotion, then a 20% to 40% off promotion that included a savings coupon on the front.

"Locker Stocker was an umbrella theme that gave us continuity," said Cooper. "Our intent was at any point, people knew there was a Locker Stocker sale this year." Besides the TV and radio spots, that point could have been any of the five ROP ads, three eight-page tabloid circulars, or in-store signage and display.

The television commercial begins with a pair of puzzled young boys staring at an empty space in a bank of junior high lockers, only to have the mystery solved when Mom wheels up a locker fully stocked with shoes.

"We wanted to produce something

Having a mom take her son's locker from the school, wheel it into a Famous Footwear store and then bring it back filled with shoes, much to the chagrin of her son, makes the ad unexpected and entertaining.

unique and creative for back-to-school that told the full story of mom's mission at this time of year," said Cooper. The idea came out of talking to moms who shop during that time who are feeling increasingly time-pressured from long lists of back-to-school errands. The research showed that these moms want one stop that crosses the gamut—young kids, older kids, junior girls or guys who just want basketball shoes. "We played to those insights," Cooper noted.

Mom comes into play in the radio commercials as well. There are two versions of the Locker Stocker radio ad, one offering a variation on the missing locker theme and the other narrated by a tough, shopping-savvy mom relying on Famous Footwear to help her succeed at the seemingly monumental task of back-to-school shoe shopping.

The Locker Stocker television ads appeared throughout the month of August, in six markets—Atlanta, Chicago, Dallas, Phoenix, St. Louis and Madison, WI. Radio spots ran in 11 markets—Cleveland, Columbus, Ohio, Denver, Houston, Kansas City, Minneapolis, Oklahoma City, Philadelphia, Pittsburgh, Rochester, NY and Wichita, KS. The creative for the television ads was developed by The Hiebing Group, Madison, WI.

Meanwhile, anyone who walked into a Famous Footwear store knew immediately that the Locker Stocker sale was underway. Every single end cap had a locker on it with shoes hanging on pegs. "It was fun," said Cooper. "Some of the stores' personnel would write graffiti on them!"

Famous Footwear (a division of Brown Shoe Company, Inc.), .St. Louis, MO
SENIOR VP OF MARKETING **Scott Cooper**
CREATIVE MANAGER **Steven Welch**
VP CREATIVE SERVICES: **Dick Brunning**
MANAGER OF VISUAL MARKETING: **Nettie Heimeri**
ART DIRECTORS: **Dick Kallftrom, Brenda Bickel-Bonds**
VP MARKETING **Jay Gillespie**
DIRECTOR OF PLANNING: **Scott Sensky**
ADVERTISING AGENCY: **The Hiebing Group**, Madison, WI.
CREATIVE DIRECTOR: **Barry Callen**

MANAGEMENT NOT RESPONSIBLE FOR LOST OR STOLEN HEARTS

CALL 1.800.788.CACHE **SURF** www.cache.com

CACHÉ

YOU'VE BEEN WARNED

Warning: Caché clothes are not for the faint of heart. The retailer is aggressively advertising to those who want to get noticed.

Out There

CACHÉ IS GOING all out to change its image. Having long ago established itself as a source for upscale after-five apparel, the retail specialty chain has embarked on aggressively repositioning its brand. The objective: to communicate the fact that Caché is a lot more than special occasion wear.

While Caché has built on the occasion niche for some 20+ years—to the point where it has grown to nearly 200 stores nationwide—in recent years it has expanded its product toward more fashion-forward apparel and accessories.

"Sportswear has always been important to us, but we've refined it to have broader appeal," said Lisa Decker, vice president marketing. As a result, management decided last year that it was time to market Caché as an all-occasion retailer, underscoring the fact that not only does it specialize in the occasion wear that it's known for but also in day wear and sportswear. "We've begun to talk about the depth of our merchandise," says Decker. "This is the first time we have aggressively pursued building and expanding the brand to develop the recognition that Caché should be getting and having at this point."

New York–based advertising agency Cossette Post was selected for the nation-al rebranding effort. "We wanted to reposition the brand to get current and prospective customers to shop the store, but we also had to give them a brand position to get new customers," said Frank Sampogna, chairman and COO of Cossette Post. The agency used what it terms its "Culture Branding" approach to mine the beliefs and value systems of Caché's current and future clientele prior to developing the campaign.

Focus group research uncovered that the Caché woman sets her own stage and makes her own rules. The campaign reflects these findings and makes a strong emotional connection with the customer.

The tagline, "You've been warned," reminds female customers that wearing Caché clothes can evoke an emotional response from others—admiration from women and desire from men.

"We're using Culture Branding to

CALL 1.800.788.CACHE   SURF www.cache.com

! MAY CAUSE
SHORTNESS OF BREATH

CACHÉ
YOU'VE BEEN WARNED

**The idea behind the these headlines
is this woman is proud to be very
body conscious, sophisticated and
exuberant about herself.**

help Caché take advantage of its sales
momentum in a soft retail market," said
Sampogna. "A lot of retailers are pulling
back now," Decker added. "But we're
somewhat of a contrarian retailer. We are
in a place where our merchandise is
right, our store locations are right, and
we're going at it with both barrels! We
tripled our media placement budget this
year over last year."

Decker describes the new multimillion-
dollar advertising campaign, which
launched in April, as "all encompassing."
Not only did the company change its
national advertising, but all other venues
in which the consumer would come into
contact with Caché (what Decker refers to
as "consumer touch points") were
wrapped in this new branding effort.
Those "touch points" include a pull-out-
all-the-stops domination of New York
City's Grand Central Terminal and other
dramatic out-of-home venues, full-color
ads in high-profile magazines, direct mail,
and a new website.

Unquestionably, the most dramatic
aspect of the campaign was the domination
of Grand Central Terminal. Caché virtually "owned" the busy station—every piece
of ad space available in Grand Central
from April 15 through May 15. There
were 72 pieces of creative ranging in size

from 26" x 50" to a walloping 5' x 90'—
dominating everything from floor graphics, vertical panels and glass displays to
vertical kiosks and corridor wallscapes.

Why such concentration in New York
City when Caché is a national brand?
Consider: Fashion editors, the media and
people from all over stream through the
terminal each day. The objective was to
generate buzz. The station isn't called
Grand Central for nothing!

Other out-of-home media included a
wraparound billboard in Times Square
that was 120 feet across and bus boards
traveling throughout the city. Currently
there are also billboards in Miami and
Dallas and ads on mall kiosks nationwide.

The high-visibility campaign extended
to magazines as well. Caché is advertising
in six publications this year versus one last
year. The schedule calls for four to five
ads over the course of
the year in *Vogue*,
Harper's Bazaar, *Jane*,
Marie Claire, *Contents*
and *Flaunt*.

The ads feature head-
lines pronouncing the
powerful effects that
Caché clothes inspire. One
version says: "Management
not responsible for lost or

stolen hearts." Another warns:
"May cause shortness of breath."
The new campaign's striking
backgrounds and the model's
sexy pose embody the sophisticated Caché woman.

Caché is also conducting a
targeted direct mail program
that talks to special customers. "Direct
mail is one of the best ways to drive traffic
into our stores. We have a very large and
qualified database that we continue to
grow at store level," said Decker. "We can
target our direct mail to suit the consumer's needs—and how she shops."

The majority of the direct mail pieces,
which are mailed approximately every six
weeks, are promotional with specific
inducements such as a percentage off or a
savings coupon. Each reiterates the new
branding message in a provocative way. A
mailer for a private dress sale, for example,
carried the warning, "Caution: may cause
spring fever!"

Any way you look at it, Caché is definitely out there.

! SAVINGS ADVISORY:
GOOD THINGS COME
TO THOSE WHO SHOP

CACHÉ
YOU'VE BEEN WARNED

**Direct mail is
primarily
promotional.**

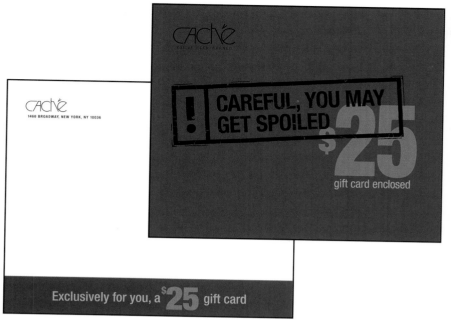

CAREFUL, YOU MAY GET SPOILED

$25 gift card enclosed

Exclusively for you, a $25 gift card

GIFT $25 CARD

04302

Caché

Redeem this card through 04/30/02 at any Caché

After all, this gift is only for our **very best customers**. Use it towards any purchase at any Caché from now through **April 30th**. And it's just in time for our **Spring arrivals**. Everything from the **coolest capris** to the **sexiest dresses** in **bright Spring colors**. Make an entrance in **striking solids** or show off your wild side in **animal prints**. Or mix it up. Because whether you're at work or at play, in these fashions you'll really heat things up.

Caché
YOU'VE BEEN WARNED

CAUTION: MAY CAUSE SPRING FEVER

The website—another consumer "touch point."

CAUTION: FANTASIES MAY OCCUR

Big impression—the Times Square billboard.

CACHÉ

Direct mail reinforces the new branding message.

At Caché, we're welcoming the **warmer weather** with savings. Present this coupon from now through **May 27th** and **save $30** on any Caché dress. This exclusive offer happens only once a year, just in time for our Spring dress collection. **Sparkle, shine** and **shimmer** in this season's trendiest prints and bold styles that holler, **"It's Spring!"** So whether you're at work or at play, in a **Caché** dress all eyes will be on you.

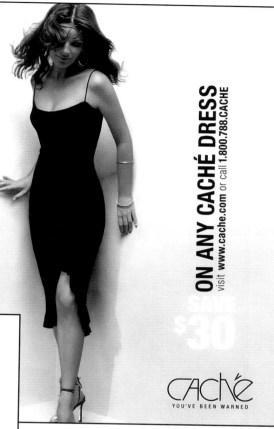

ON ANY CACHÉ DRESS
Visit www.cache.com or call 1.800.788.CACHE

SAVE $30

Caché
YOU'VE BEEN WARNED

Direct mail is consistent—and continuous—with new pieces going out approximately every six weeks.

! **CAUTION: MAY CAUSE SPRING FEVER**

PRIVATE DRESS SALE

Caché
YOU'VE BEEN WARNED

1460 BROADWAY, NEW YORK, NY 10036

$30 **SAVE** **Save $30** on any dress now through **Monday, May 27th, 2002.** For more information, visit **www.cache.com** or call **1.800.788.CACHE (2224) Monday–Friday, 10am–6pm EST** and reference promotional offer code D05272.

Cache Inc., New York
PRESIDENT/CHIEF OPERATING OFFICER:
Thomas E. Reinckens
VP MARKETING: **Lisa Decker,**
AGENCY: **Cossette Post,** New York
CHAIRMAN/COO: **Frank Sampogna**
CREATIVE DIRECTOR: **Richard Ostroff**
CLIENT RELATIONSHIP MANAGER: **Dorothy Cohen**
VP/MEDIA DIRECTOR: **Margot Grady**
PHOTOGRAPHER: **Mark Liddell**

Who are You Calling Crazy?

WHEN AN AD CAMPAIGN is lampooned in the satirical newspaper *The Onion* within months of its launch, clearly you've attracted attention. That is the case for Ikea's "Unböring" campaign, created by Miami-based agency Crispin Porter+Bogusky and launched last fall. "We were pretty pleased by that," says Rick Humphrey, management supervisor of the campaign at CP+B. "Whenever you penetrate pop culture, you know you've gotten far more out of your ad dollars."

According to Christian Mathieu, Ikea's external marketing manager for North America, while each Ikea country organization independently handles its own marketing—the company operates in more than 30 different countries—all are guided by a similar playfully humorous approach. "Ikea's advertising goal is to educate the consumer about Ikea, and to change people's relationships with home furnishings,

using playful humor, unconventional thinking and a 'human' approach," he says. "In our efforts to push through the clutter, we are always looking to break advertising conventions…we are always exploring new media or ways to use existing media in a new way." CP+B's campaign meets that goal, boldly making fun of consumers with irony and wit.

Humphrey explains that the inspiration behind the campaign essentially came from the consumer research the firm did in preparing to pitch Ikea. "We set out to discover how consumers feel about home furnishings, and realized that North American consumers change their spouses more often than they change their furniture." They found that in general, North American consumers are essentially boring when it comes to their home furnishings. They tend to buy safe and lasting pieces, and keep them, even if they no longer fit their

lifestyle. "When we realized that, we saw the campaign as an opportunity not only to educate the consumer about Ikea, but revolutionize the home furnishings business as well," says Humphrey. He pointed out that in certain markets, Ikea already has a dedicated customer—"Ikea fanatics," he calls them—who look at home furnishings with a soft goods mentality. "They see their home as an extension of themselves, and buy home furnishings that express their personality and style," he says. One goal of the campaign was to reach and convert more people to this mindset, and "liberate them" from the idea that redecorating was risky rather than a means of self-expression. Says Humphrey, "Our approach was to poke holes in people's reasons for holding on to old items, and let them see they could replace them with pieces more in line with their passions or interests."

Besides being generally a bigger cam-

The $99 KLITTEN chair, helping uproot the notion that wobbly, uncomfortable furniture is your lot in life. Visit unboring.com. **IKEA** unböring

The $29.95 SKYAR floor lamp, helping uproot the idea that a beautifully lit room costs an arm and a leg. Visit unboring.com. **IKEA** unböring

Lamp spot.

paign for Ikea, CP+B's concept brings a different media mix to Ikea's past efforts in North America, with a stronger focus on television spots and print ads, the introduction of other print collateral material, wild postings, as well as carrying on the striking outdoor advertising that verges on installation art that Ikea is recognized for. While the various ads all feature the "Unböring" theme, each focuses on a different aspect of the Ikea message.

The print campaign focuses on "old furniture gravity" and the idea of letting go of items that no longer make you happy or fulfill your needs either esthetically or practically. Ads show people pulling out old furniture literally rooted into their floors over a photo of a stylish replacement item from Ikea, as well as the price.

Moo cow milk pitcher spot.

This message is reinforced by the first set of TV spots, which poke fun at people's tendency to hold on to household items when their environment could be vastly improved by replacing it with something they like better. In fact they are "crazy" if they don't. The first spot in the campaign, directed by *Being John Malkovich* director Spike Jonze, follows a woman as she leaves an old desk lamp with the trash on the curb and replaces it with a new one. As sad music plays, a Swedish man appears and says, "Many of you feel bad for this lamp. That is because you are crazy. It has no feelings. And the new one is much better." As he finishes speaking, the Ikea logo and "Unböring" tagline appear. A second, similar spot aired a few weeks later, again accusing viewers of being "crazy" for feeling sad about a tacky milk pitcher that breaks.

A second pair of TV spots, directed by Wes Anderson, writer and director of *The Royal Tenenbaums*, sent an overall brand message: "You can find everything you need to feel at home." They open on what seems to be a glimpse at an intimate moment in a couple or a family's life, only to reveal that they are taking place in an Ikea showroom as they are shopping for furniture. In the first spot, a couple is arguing about their relationship, when an Ikea sales associate

Relationship argument.

Daughter is pregnant.

walks up and says, "So… What do you guys think?" and the camera pulls back to reveal they are in an Ikea showroom display. The couple looks around and say, "It feels good. We'll take it."

The second spot features a daughter revealing to her parents that she is pregnant. As her father rants about her creepy boyfriend, an Ikea associate again appears. "By giving a picture of shoppers in our stores having the most extreme and intimate conversations, which we take to exaggeration, we effectively communicate that the Ikea shopping experience and product designs are exactly what customers want and are comfortable with, making it feel

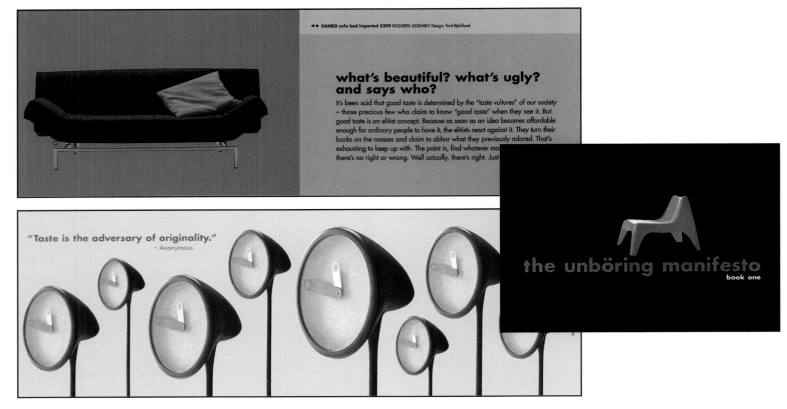

DANBO sofa bed imported $399 REQUIRES ASSEMBLY Design: Tord Björklund

what's beautiful? what's ugly? and says who?

It's been said that good taste is determined by the "taste vultures" of our society – those precious few who claim to know "good taste" when they see it. But good taste is an elitist concept. Because as soon as an idea becomes affordable enough for ordinary people to have it, the elitists react against it. They turn their backs on the masses and claim to abhor what they previously adored. That's exhausting to keep up with. The point is, find whatever ma____ there's no right or wrong. Well actually, there's right. Just ___

the unböring manifesto
book one

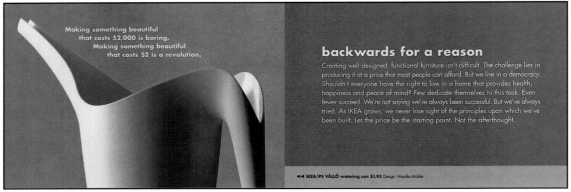

"Taste is the adversary of originality."
– Anonymous

Making something beautiful that costs $2,000 is boring. Making something beautiful that costs $2 is a revolution.

backwards for a reason

Creating well-designed, functional furniture isn't difficult. The challenge lies in producing it at a price that most people can afford. But we live in a democracy. Shouldn't everyone have the right to live in a home that provides health, happiness and peace of mind? Few dedicate themselves to this task. Even fewer succeed. We're not saying we've always been successful. But we've always tried. As IKEA grows, we never lose sight of the principles upon which we've been built. Let the price be the starting point. Not the afterthought.

IKEA/PS VÅLLÖ watering can $1.95 Design: Monika Mulder

an unböring sum of parts

When you add up all the things that make IKEA IKEA, you can tell we aren't like other companies. IKEA started in Sweden and its heart remains there to this day. And as everyone who's grown up in Sweden has learned – either from their mom or dad, or from society in general – everyone should be given a chance to enjoy life.

ILEN trolley table/TV bench $35ea. Max load 55lbs. REQUIRES ASSEMBLY Design: Annika Grottell ▶▶

just like home," said Gina Raiser, advertising manager for Ikea North America.

A new element of the "Unböring" campaign is the use of mini books. The first of the books, "The Unböring Manifesto," explains the Ikea philosophy as well as its origins and includes photos of a variety of Ikea products, from bigger pieces to small accessories. A second book, "Prepare For Unböring," is a handbook to help shoppers physically and psychologically prepare to go shopping and make decisions about what to buy. In addition, the mini books are an engaging way to tie the whole campaign together.

The "Manifesto" book, which appeared first, balanced the initial message of the campaign, that of replacing old, meaningless items with new ones, by focusing on Ikea's origins and dedication to great design at great prices. "Prepare" returns to the idea of changing the relationships people have with their furniture. It takes the idea to a witty extreme, posing questions

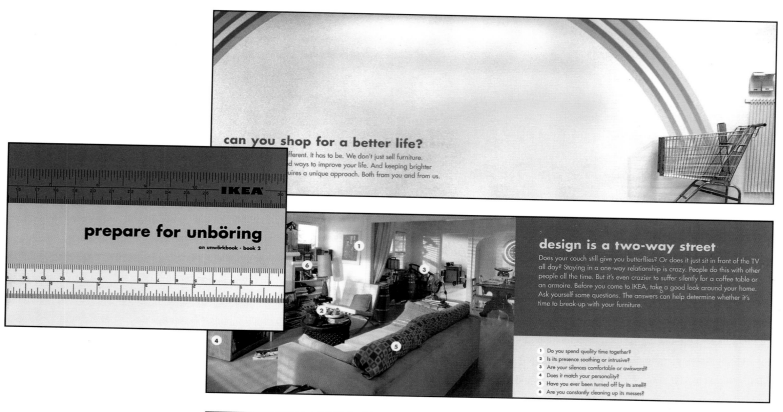

such as, "Does your couch still give you butterflies? Or does it just sit in front of the TV all day?" and suggests that it might be "time to break up with your furniture."

"It's hard to tell stories like these in a 30-second spot or a one-page ad," says Humphrey. "These books offer a very powerful way to deliver a deeper, richer message," he says. The books can be used in a variety of ways—from inserts in magazines to direct mail to handouts in the stores. "One of the key pillars of our marketing strategy is to educate consumers about Ikea and tell the story of how Ikea arrives at great, quality designed products at such low prices. The books are a great way to deliver this deep and rich content," Mathieu says.

But is it smart to call customers "crazy"? Both Mathieu and Humphrey say the response to the campaign has been great.

And Humphrey says he's even gotten phone calls from people who liked it. "That's really rare," he says, "Usually you only hear the negative stuff." Apparently it's like getting parodied in *The Onion*.

AGENCY: **Crispin Porter + Bogusky**
CREATIVE DIRECTOR: **Alex Bogusky**
ASSOCIATE CREATIVE DIRECTOR: **Paul Keister**
MANAGEMENT SUPERVISOR: **Rick Humphrey**
ACCOUNT SUPERVISOR: **Marianne Pizzi**
ACCOUNT EXECUTIVE: **Julie Spiegel**

Product Print Ads
ART DIRECTORS: **Paul Keister, Dave Swartz**
COPYWRITERS: **Bob Cianfrone, Roger Hoard**

Lamp and Moo Cow TV spots
ART DIRECTOR: **Mark Taylor**
COPYWRITER: **Ari Merkin**
AGENCY PRODUCER: **Rupert Samuel**
DIRECTOR: **Spike Jonze** (Lamp),
Clay Williams (Moo Cow)

PRODUCTION CO.: **MJZ Productions**
DIRECTOR OF PHOTOGRAPHY: **Rodrigo Prieto**
EDIT HOUSE: **Spot Welders**

Kitchen and Living Room TV spots
ART DIRECTOR: **Paul Stechschulte**
COPYWRITER: **Tom Adams**
AGENCY PRODUCER: **Rupert Samuel**
DIRECTOR: **Wes Anderson**
PRODUCTION CO.: **Moxie Pictures**
EDIT HOUSE: **Lost Planet**
EDITORS: **Adam Schwartz, Geoff Hounsell**

Manifesto Book
ART DIRECTOR: **Mike del Marmol**
COPYWRITER: **Steve O'Connnell**
AGENCY PRODUCER: **Julieanna Wilson**

More Than Stores

LIKE MANY OLDER MALLS, Lloyd Center, Oregon's largest, faced increasing competition from newer centers and large discount stores. No longer able to depend solely on the immediate trade area around it, Lloyd Center needed to go beyond being merely convenient in order to attract people who could just as easily choose another place to shop

In the mid '90s, to increase its appeal, Lloyd Center embarked on a campaign using a spokesperson—a local actor dubbed Lloyd (for Lloyd Center). "He was very funny," said Chris Moore, account supervisor at the mall's agency, McKee Wallwork Henderson Advertising. "The campaign did what it needed to do, creating the perception of Lloyd Center as a fun, exciting place."

But after running seven years, the campaign hit a snag. The local actor was becoming successful too and was no longer affordable. A financial decision was made to develop a new campaign.

"We wanted to extend that feeling of branding the mall as a whole, not the stores," said Moore. "The department stores do their own campaigns throughout the year. The problem is a lot of them have taken a very price-focused effort. What a shopping center as a whole fears is we're training consumers to only shop on price. What we wanted to do with mall branding was not to focus on one element or one store or shopping. Going forward we really wanted to focus on the experience, the summation of the experience of all those things that are going on—the benefits of shopping at Lloyd Center as opposed to a discount retailer"

The mall's management company, Glimcher Realty Trust, had Morris & Fellows conduct research for Lloyd Center. The in-depth study, called MAXtrak research, incorporated mall intercepts and substantial economic and geographic data. Among the findings was that the mall's target is a professional working mother in her 30s or 40s, who's a little more sophisticated than the typical shopper and often pressed for time.

This woman enjoys shopping, nevertheless, and does it frequently. She seeks the experience itself as much as the products she's out to buy and is excited and expectant each time she shops. The research also found that if you were to ask this woman how to improve Lloyd Center, she would want more of a feel that it's where things are happening. (She'd love it if her husband actually liked going there!) A frequent response was that Lloyd Center is what they used to go downtown for—shopping, eating, people watching, and always something going on.

This information—the experience of shopping in a shopping center—was to prove instrumental in developing the new campaign, "More Than Stores." "There was a lot of information," said Moore. "We

2 pairs of shoes. 3 new shirts. 27 rides on the escalator.

LLOYD CENTER   More than stores.

One friend + one day of shopping = getting over Todd.

LLOYD CENTER   More than stores.

All the guys know that the mall is the place to meet girls.

LLOYD CENTER   More than stores.

went through it and also used our experience and history with Lloyd Center. We took the hollow phrase 'shopping experience' and kept the target very much in mind. Experience isn't a word, it's what you live through."

It's almost impossible to look at any of the print executions or TV spots without having the "Aha!" reaction. Said Ann Grimmer, marketing director, "More than anything else these ads capture the true spirit of Lloyd Center. Our customers can relate to them because they portray real experiences that happen at Lloyd Center every day."

As part of the transitioning period from the spokesperson campaign, the center started running black and white print ads about a year and a half ago.. Prior to that, they had not done a lot of print. Television was, and still is, the primary medium. What made the addition of print work was an opportunity presented by the local Portland daily, *The Oregonian*. The paper had a large banner ad space on the weather page that it had not been able to sell on a regular basis. "Lloyd Center negotiated with the paper and was able to make a good deal," said Moore. "They're able to run ads, predominately in color, on a weekly basis.

Four new :30 TV spots, which are rotating equally, broke in April. The spots are running on one network (NBC) in Portland and on cable. The majority run from 6 p.m. to 11:30 to reach both working and non-working women. The plan is to run the ads for a couple of years to reach people during peak shopping seasons—spring, back-to-school and holiday. "We're not trying to level out the year," explained Moore. "This is a budget decision of course. We thought we could reach a broader audience, rather than buying networks.

"The cable is scheduled to run over eight networks to ensure reach. Because the creative is so strong, we're going with a reach buy rather than with the frequency a lot of campaigns would need," he added.

The food court. It's like a daycare for husbands.

Mother-daughter moments rarely take place on sandy beaches.

Dear Diary: went to the mall for clogs. Found something better.

Shop. Shop. Giggle. Giggle. Shop. Shop. Giggle. Giggle.

27 rides on the escalator.

"Escalator"

Music throughout.

Cut to kid on escalator. Open on a kid at Lloyd Center dragging mom into a toy store.

SUPER: 11 places to beg for toys.

Cut to kid on escalator. Cut to kid dwarfed by a gumball machine.

SUPER: 5 gumballs in two hours.

Cut to kid on escalator. Cut to kid at the pet store holding a hamster.

SUPER: 1 new friend.

Cut to the kid getting off the down escalator with mom and dragging her onto the up escalator.

SUPER: 27 rides on the escalator.

Close up on kid looking up and mom with a thankful smile.

SUPER: More than stores.

Cut to logo frame with Lloyd Center logo.

2 friends and no diet.

"Todd"

Music throughout.

Open on two women shopping. They approach a dressing room with their arms full of clothes.

SUPER: 3 new looks.

Cut to the women in a nail salon getting a pedicure.

SUPER: 30 minutes of pampering.

Cut to the women having a drink at

Stanford's Restaurant.

SUPER: 2 friends and no diet.

Cut to women leaving the mall carrying a bunch of bags in each hand.

SUPER: 1 day getting over Todd.

SUPER: More than stores.

Cut to logo frame with Lloyd Center logo.

1247 things to eat.

"Food"

Music throughout.

Cut to the guy eating _____.

Cut to the guy eating _____.

SUPER: 34 Places to eat.

Cut to the guy eating a plate of fries.

SUPER: 1247 things to eat.

Cut to the guy eating _____.

Cut to the guy eating _____.

Cut to the guy eating _____.

Cut to a close up of the husband eating

wings. He has a little b-b-q sauce on his face.

SUPER: And she thinks you just had wings.

She leans over and wipes it off with an accusing look.

SUPER: More than stores.

Cut to logo frame with Lloyd Center logo.

1327 places to meet girls.

"Places to sit"

Music throughout.

Open on an elderly man at the mall sitting on a mall bench.

SUPER: 1327 places to sit.

Cut to the man in a department store sitting on a barco-lounger. Cut to the man at the food court.

SUPER: 1327 places to relax.

Cut to the man sitting on a bench by the

ice rink. An elderly lady comes and sits next to him.

SUPER: 37 benches.

They both notice each other and smile.

SUPER: More than stores.

Cut to logo frame with Lloyd Center logo.

Lloyd Center also targets tourism because of its proximity to the Portland Convention center.

The directory reinforces the charm of the campaign.

Ads promoting special events capture the essence of the campaign without copying it.

Lloyd Center, Portland, OR
MARKETING DIRECTOR: **Ann Grimmer, CMD**
ASSISTANT DIRECTOR OF MARKETING: **Rosemary White**
MANAGEMENT COMPANY: **Glimcher Realty Trust,** Columbus, OH
ADVERTISING AGENCY: **McKee Wallwork Henderson Advertising,** Albuquerque, NM
ACCOUNT SUPERVISOR: **Chris Moore**

Clone Branding

Cloning the brand relies on "brand DNA" analysis to transfer those genes that will impart character, personality and performance to new brands from known brand successes.

We now have a retail format mix almost too flexible to identify and define. With so many different types of retailers presenting so many similar merchandise categories, it is difficult to tell the difference between a super market and its **clone**, the super market-drug store. So when it comes to brand power for a product or store, we are in a power struggle for competitive differentiation.

Brand image promotion for today's retailers has to be more than advertising to create awareness of a name, logo or slogan. They have to use integrated marketing and communications to position a **value perception**. Brand value is derived from "brand DNA." ***Brand value*** **in the mind of the consumer specifically relates *benefits* to *costs*. And for the consumer, costs are more than price—they are also time costs and emotional costs**.

A retailer can *clone* attributes and benefits values throughout its brands with the following associations and promises:

- **PERSONALITY PLUS** – *Pacific Sunwear's* advertising is a good example of cloning the customer's California personality into its product. Pacsun positions its brand with a differentiating U.S.P. (Unique Selling *Personality*). See page 134.

- **CUSTOMER-AS-BRAND** – *Pacific Sunwear* identifies its customers as its brand. *Pacsun's* DNA is based on its genetic and authentic authority on California lifestyles. It helps its customers become their own brand by using a teen panel to identify teen trends. See page 134.

- **SELF-IMAGE INNOVATOR** – *Joseph Abboud* has a brand image that suggests an innovative kind of thinking about men's appar-

el. Its thoughtful advertising consistently reflects its understanding and knowledge of the increasing market of *successful* men. Abboud features *real* successful men in its advertising, who provide self images for their customers. See page 137.

- **FRONT RUNNER** – *Timberland* clones a brand image that has been up front in promoting the outdoor life by transmitting its rugged genes to a new territory, the streets of the city. See page 140.

- **VALUE-SAVVY** – *Community Home Supply's* strategy is to clone its customers, valuing them as a prime source into a value as an upscale source. Its extensive merchandise assortments for kitchen and bath are designed to make its customers feel good about their "shopping savvy." See page 142.

- **INDULGE YOURSELF** – *Testoni's* brand image is associated with "an utmost attention to detail in design and quality." Its customers' busy lifestyles range from business meetings to evening parties. Testoni's models are cloned from its customers. It provides "a frame of reference for the product." See page 146.

A major key to Clone Branding is solutions. Retailers who offer solutions for customers are building value throughout their retail and producer brands. They also know how to integrate store services with each of their merchandise categories. They customize solutions and communicate this knowledge to target segments. They involve the customer as a partner in the creation of these solutions.

When customers are helped to find genuine solutions in a store, the satisfaction makes the brand image more than just awareness. A good example is Home Depot. Its stores clone its brand into do-it-yourself counselors on the floor. They also inform customers of trustworthy carpenters, electricians and plumbers who can set up and connect Home Depot's products in the customer's home.

Coming up with solution strategies that really help the customer fulfill wants and needs is too often easier to say in an ad than to follow through in customer relationship management. In a retail world confronted by increasing price competition and category commoditization, brand value is built throughout by what the store *does*, as well as what it *says* in its advertising.

Retailers are dealing with consumer knowledge that indicates that more and more consumers are not buying the product, but rather the image associated with it.

Retail brand value management requires that the retailer sees itself as a service business as well as a product provider. Brand value must not only be an association with solutions, it should also be a promise of satisfaction with usage. And a retailer should not make the mistake of thinking that the customer's brand concept of solutions and promises will hold up over the long term. Advertising the brand must be constantly reinforced by customized communications and services.

The question of how to clone value throughout their brands is one that retailers should be asking. What is emerging in brand management is the realization that **mass media advertising is often ineffective for retailers. The need for non-traditional matched media is growing.** For example, in-store

media special events and sponsorships are creating more credibility for the store-as-brand in the minds of customers.

Retailers are also creating brand-cloning strategies that rely on the association of their brand(s) with other images and other brands. Michael Jordan, himself a brand, was an inspiring association for Nike to clone. A brand's image can best be evaluated by an assessment of customer loyalty to it. While harder to obtain now, customer loyalty itself needs to be defined through its DNA, attributes and benefits. Is the brand a trusted friend? A personal counselor? An esteem-building supporter? And can it be counted on to be right-on-fashion?

Building BrandPower is more than a marketing objective. It has to be an ongoing commitment to managing the brand to fit the customer's management of self image.

That Southern California

I N MANY WAYS, Pacific Sunwear, a retailer of California lifestyle apparel, accessories and footwear for active teens and young adults, epitomizes the American dream. The American retailing dream, that is. This is a company that had an idea, started small, managed to change with the times, and ended up as a public company with hundreds of stores nationwide. The company's advertising also has an aspirational quality.

Pacific Sunwear (commonly known as Pacsun) began as a small surf shop in 1980 in Newport Beach, California. What made it different from the other shops

whose business stalled when the beaches emptied out during southern California's wet, cool winters, was Pacsun did what its customers did. It headed to the mall—becoming the first surf shop to move into California's popular mall locations.

A sea change occurred when Pacsun opened on the East Coast. The retailer's surf brands (mainly shorts and T-shirts) weren't warm enough for much of the East Coast. Pacsun had its vendors modify their surf and skate brands to include long pants and sleeves. Sales began to climb. In 1993 the company went public. More changes followed, most notably the

introduction of juniors and shoes.

Today there are more than 749 Pacsun stores in the United States and Puerto Rico. The reasons for the company's success? Many say it's the ability to listen to its customers and to change.

The most significant change in recent years has been a new emphasis on the junior side as it became increasingly apparent that the real opportunity in the teen apparel business was the junior segment. They opted not to focus on boys, a segment that was not nearly as dynamic. In fourth quarter 2001, corporate made the move to be in the junior

Del Mar   Hot-air balloon   Sky surfing   Touching clouds   Sweater weather   OMG!   Sunset   Freedom   Down-to-earth   Landing gear   A star in stripes

Girls: Billabong, Independent, Roxy, Tilt   Guys: Breakdown, Bullhead, Dickies, Hurley, O'Neill, Transpine   For store locations: 888-4pacsun, www.pacsun.com or aol keyword: pacsun. Ask about the PacSun Credit Card.

Thing

apparel business. The change in strategy was started at the store level. It was then reflected in the advertising for the first time in February 2002.

At the heart of their target is the 17-year-old. "As this age group starts to spread its wings a little bit, the values of freedom, liberation, and independence are very, very important," Blett pointed out. "California has always represented those values as much if not more than anything else."

Not surprisingly, Pacsun's advertising is geared toward communicating those values. Also not surprisingly, the advertising agency charged with conveying

that freewheeling spirit—Doner's Newport Beach office—is located right there at the heart of it in the epicenter of young, fun, surf and sun country.

In creating its print ads Doner started with Pacsun's core values. "It's a southern California company all the way," said Tim Blett, president. "The buyers, the designers, all the brands are quintessential California."

"That gets to what we're trying to sell strategically—to establish Pacsun as a brand, the authentic authority on California lifestyle," Mark Weinfeld, account executive added.

Focus group research is where Pacsun gets much of its information about trends and about what kids like about what they're doing. The agency has augmented the use of the company's teen panel to

give insight into the teen market as it moves forward.

The advertising campaign consists solely of print ads, which have worked so well they are essentially the only consumer advertising the company does. (Pacsun does have a website packed with contests, music prizes, a chance to win a shopping spree, special offers and an online newsletter.)

Many of the elements in the shots are very iconic to southern California. "They're not just traditional beach shots," said Weinfeld. "You're never going to see Hollywood Boulevard. You're going to see classic California icons like palm trees, piers, roller coasters—that legendary culture that these kids very much relate to and aspire to."

The double-page spreads with a split

Girls: Billabong, O'Neill, Roxy, Tilt   Guys: DC, Billabong, Bullhead, Transnine, Quiksilver, Split

For store locations: 888-4pacsun, www.pacsun.com or aol keyword: pacsun. Ask about the PacSun Credit Card.

Associating the boys and girls with what they're wearing is a smart way to advertise the brand names carried.

PACSUN

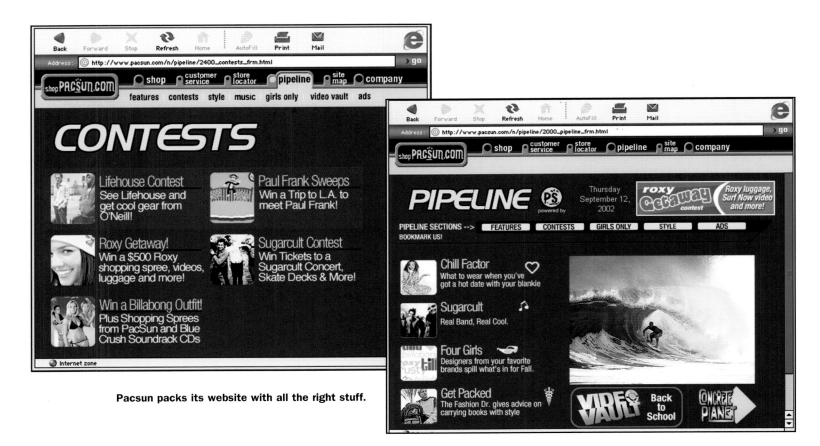

Pacsun packs its website with all the right stuff.

visual on each page have an editorial look. Generally, the time involved in producing an ad is about 2½ months though sometimes three ads may be shot at one time. "We do new ads four times a year," said Weinfeld, "so we're basically always working on them."

With the new emphasis on juniors, the media has changed too. The ads run every month in *Teen People, YM* and *Seventeen*. Sometimes they run as "double doubles" (two spreads back to back).

As important as the look of the ads is the tone. The copy points come from the research. "We're very careful not to come off as a corporate entity," said Blett. "It can be a challenge speaking to this audience in their language."

Seems pretty cool to us.

Pacific Sunwear, Anaheim, CA
DIRECTOR OF MARKETING: **Carol Apkarian**
WEBSITE: **www.pacsun.com**
ADVERTISING AGENCY: **Doner,** Detroit, Newport Beach, CA
Newport Beach Office:
PRESIDENT: **Tim Blett**
SENIOR VICE PRESIDENT BRAND INTEGRATION/STRATEGY: **Mark Weinfeld**
ACCOUNT MANAGER: **Erik Glassen**
CHIEF CREATIVE OFFICER: **John DeCerchio**
VICE PRESIDENT, CREATIVE DIRECTOR: **Ken Camastro**
ART DIRECTOR: **Sue Chong**

Visible Changes

Business: Brothers Rob and Webster Stone collaborate on books, films and on life adventures, and achieved critical acclaim for their work in publishing, music and film production.

J OSEPH ABBOUD, a highly successful men's designer brand (since 1993, the brand has grown from a $40 million annual business to $125 million), has undertaken some high-profile changes that should take it to a new level.

This month the company is opening its first retail store in a high-powered location—Columbus Circle, site of the new AOL tower, in New York City. "This is extremely exciting for us, because it offers a showcase for our entire brand on a global level in an environment that reflects the aesthetic of the Joseph Abboud brand," said Traci Young, vice president marketing & creative services. "Having our own store also allows us the opportunity to manage and provide a template for future growth concepts."

Retail represents a definite area of expansion for the company. The plan is to open two or three stores a year in key markets around the country over the next three to five years.

Joseph Abboud's advertising also reflects change. For the first time in the history of the brand, the company has developed an advertising campaign that capitalizes on its lifestyle image by featuring notable figures from the worlds of business, music and sports as the models. "The theme of this season's campaign, more than any previous campaign, truly illustrates the message of the Joseph Abboud brand as a lifestyle collection," said Young. "By featuring successful men immersed in their element, working with other men, and living real lives, we have developed a story that our customer can understand and relate to."

Each of the campaign's three executions features either two or three high-profile men to illustrate a fundamental theme: A man is largely defined by his relationships and interaction with other men. "It just seemed right in today's world to transition from featuring models to using 'real' men from real walks of life," Young explained. "Although many campaigns feature real people, the difference for us is that there is a definite message that runs through the campaign—specifically the dynamic relationships and interactions between men. Men tend to have mentors through their lives; they are instinctively competitive with each other whether they are negotiating a business deal or playing a game of basketball, and they traditionally work in teams."

The campaign, which was conceived in-house and executed by the Glover Group, features men of different ages and styles, who work together as teammates, as family, and sometimes even as rivals.

The noted portrait photographer

JOSEPH ABBOUD

"WE'VE GOT A SEASON THAT'S NINE MONTHS LONG. SURE, WE PLAY LIKE A TEAM, BUT WE LIVE LIKE A FAMILY."

FLIP SAUNDERS, COACH, MINNESOTA TIMBERWOLVES
WITH SHOOTING GUARD WALLY SZCZERBIAK

Sports: Flip Saunders and Wally Szczerbiak are, respectively, head coach/general manager and star forward for Minnesota's basketball team, the Timberwolves.

Sometimes the ads ran as a spread with a b/w portrait (above left). The ads also ran as single pages and as multiple pages.

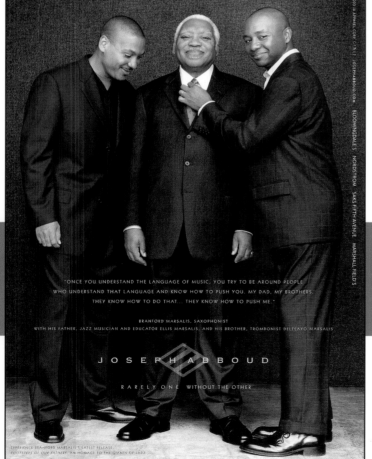

"ONCE YOU UNDERSTAND THE LANGUAGE OF MUSIC, YOU TRY TO BE AROUND PEOPLE WHO UNDERSTAND THAT LANGUAGE AND KNOW HOW TO PUSH YOU. MY DAD, MY BROTHERS, THEY KNOW HOW TO DO THAT... THEY KNOW HOW TO PUSH ME."

BRANFORD MARSALIS, SAXOPHONIST
WITH HIS FATHER, JAZZ MUSICIAN AND EDUCATOR ELLIS MARSALIS, AND HIS BROTHER, TROMBONIST DELFEAYO MARSALIS

JOSEPH ABBOUD

RARELY ONE WITHOUT THE OTHER

EXPERIENCE BRANFORD MARSALIS'S LATEST RELEASE, FOOTSTEPS OF OUR FATHERS, AN HOMAGE TO THE GIANTS OF JAZZ.

Music: Ellis and Branford Marsalis are legendary figures in the jazz world.

Norman Jean Roy, who describes himself as a "documentary portrait" photographer, shot the campaign in New York City.

The ads started running in August and are continuing through this month in *The New York Times Magazine*, *GQ*, *Esquire*, *Gotham* and the *New Yorker*. In the fall there was a billboard at the midtown tunnel on the Long Island Expressway in NYC. The company is also considering more outdoor advertisements, such as bus shelters.

"This campaign has been the most popular and successful for the Joseph Abboud Brand," said Young. "The company has never received so much positive feedback on a campaign from competition, industry people and most importantly consumers! We get constant calls on our 800 number and I personally get calls, emails and letters with comments! It is a huge hit and I would say it is extremely successful—the most visible campaign we've ever done!"

The company's newly relaunched website (www.josephabboud.com) represents yet another change in how the brand is being presented. The interactive site is updated constantly with news about the brand, celebrity wardrobing and up-to-the-minute images of the various collections. "The new website is a continuation of our brand building strategy," said Young. "We believe it is an integral part of building the brand awareness globally."

Joseph Abboud, New York
AGENCY: **In-house**
PRESIDENT & COO: **Robert J. Wichser**
VICE PRESIDENT MARKETING &
CREATIVE SERVICES: **Traci Young**
CREATIVE AGENCY: **Jill Glover - Glover Group**
PHOTOGRAPHER: **Norman Jean Roy**

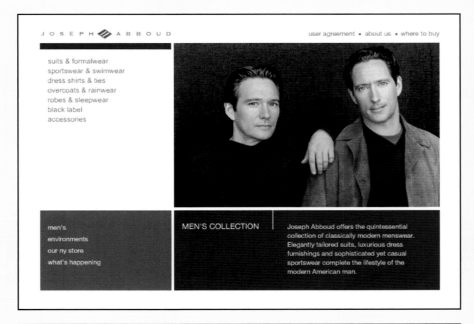

The site directs readers to discover the various offerings from the brand including sportswear, tailored clothing, formal wear, swim, accessories, coats, furnishings and the Environments Collection for the home.

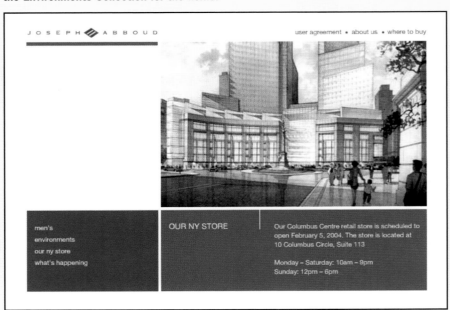

Timberland's Urban Journey
A footwear maker heads into new territory

TIMBERLAND'S typical advertising features majestic mountains, winding trails, nature in all its glory. So the brand's fall campaign, featuring sketch-like paintings of people in the subway signaled that perhaps the brand was setting out for a new destination. "Timberland got adopted by the urban market, and it gave a nice spike to the brand," says Marc Gallucci of the Boston-based Fort Franklin agency, and creative and art director for the cam-

paign. He describes it as the "Tommy Hilfiger Effect." "Hilfiger never advertised to the urban/inner city market, but the brand caught on with that customer, so Tommy Hilfiger began targeting that customer," he says. "Timberland was looking to connect with the metropolitan market—New York and other urban/inner city markets," says Gallucci. The difference, he explains, is that while Timberland wanted to tap into that market and support its retail outlets in inner

city areas, it didn't want to erode its core brand identity.

The challenge, according to Gallucci, was to translate the Timberland lifestyle image and make it relevant to the urban market. "It's difficult to suddenly start marketing to a new customer without looking like you're trying too hard. It has to really be subtle. The danger was that we didn't want to alienate the very customer we were targeting," he explains, pointing out that Timberland's core campaign image is a far cry from the concrete jungle. "It was tricky because we didn't want to come across as 'fake'. You lose them when your customer thinks you're talking down to them or trying to be them."

Timberland's tagline, "For the Journey," was an important element, and ultimately a guide to the direction of the ads. "It represents life—how you experience it and what you see along the way," Gallucci says. "We took it to the urban experience-the great outdoors in an urban environment." In much the same way that Timberland's traditional advertising evokes an attitude and a lifestyle, rather than spotlight specific products, Gallucci's team decided to focus on expressing the mood and buzz of life in the city. "The idea was to capture slices of life, the every day of that market. What you see everyday on your way to work or school, living life in the city."

The result is a pair of illustrations, paintings actually, in earthy tones, depicting an iconic part of city life—the subway. The images have the quality of

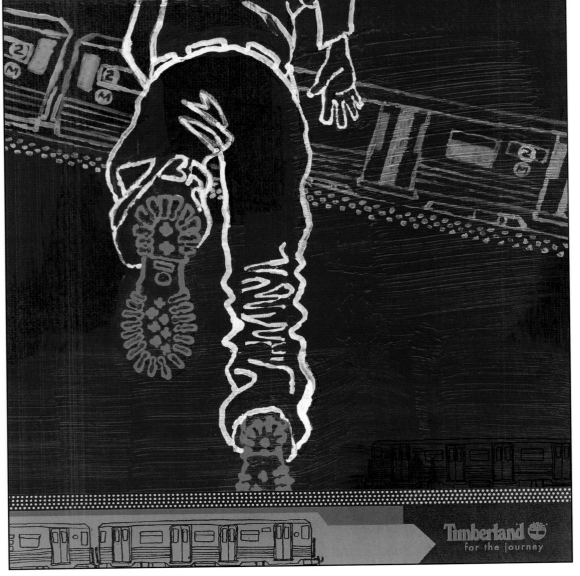

Timberland ®
for the journey

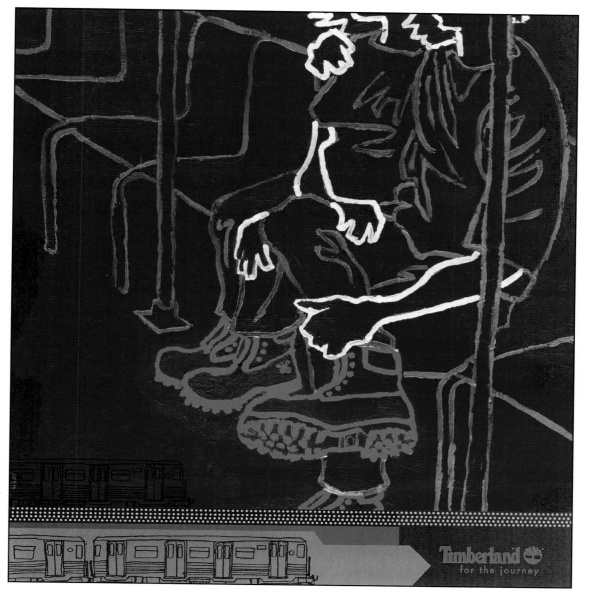

sketchbook impressions, which, Gallucci explains, is because they sent artist Chris Valencius down into the subway to sketch what he saw. He says they chose illustration over photography to avoid being locked in to any particular idea of race or gender. "By going with art, we didn't have to be tied down to specific clothes or a look, allowing someone to say, 'That's not me.' We wanted people to be able to envision themselves in the situations—running for a train, riding the subway—that are a part of life for anyone living in New York, no matter who they are."

A key difference between Timberland's ads featuring, for example, hikers in a panorama of nature, and the ads created by the Fort Franklin agency, is the focus on the product. In the "traditional" Timberland ad, the figures, and the shoes they are wearing, are a small and more or less unidentifiable part of the total image. In the urban campaign, while the figures are similarly nonspecific, the boots are a distinct part of the visual, even though they are simply drawn. Gallucci relates this difference to the strength of the brand name and its identity. While it's easy for the customer to relate Timberland to the outdoor location and situation without actually seeing the boots, the connect had to be more direct, putting the boots in a new environment, while maintaining a lifestyle approach. "If we had gone with photography, we could have gotten the same basic images, but it would have had a completely different feeling; it would have been far less subtle," Gallucci says.

The fall campaign ran all over New York City in outdoor locations, and especially on bus shelters and in the subway. But, Gallucci adds that they were designed to speak to any urban market that has a subway system, and there are plans to take it other metropolitan areas, such as Philadelphia, Chicago and Boston. In addition to the outdoor ads, the campaign included point of sales materials, such as posters and counter cards. "People really loved the posters. They also did T-shirts with the graphic from the ads that did well too."

Ultimately, the striking differences that mark the Fort Franklin ads are what make them work with Timberland's core image. Rather than creating a new brand image, the ads send the message that, whatever the journey, a different path may be just an alternate route to the same destination.

The Timberland Company
AGENCY: **Fort Franklin**, Boston, MA
CREATIVE DIRECTOR/ART DIRECTOR:
Marc Gallucci
ARTIST/DESIGNER: **Chris Valencius**

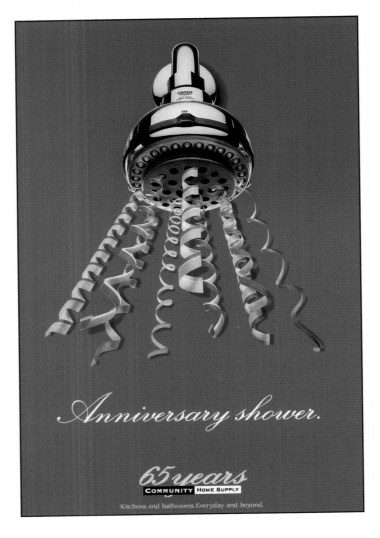

Anniversary shower.

65 years
COMMUNITY HOME SUPPLY
Kitchens and bathrooms. Everyday and beyond.

Still having a bowl.

65 years
COMMUNITY HOME SUPPLY
Kitchens and bathrooms. Everyday and beyond.

A Chicago Institution Strengthens its Brand

COMMUNITY HOME SUPPLY is one of Chicago's leading purveyors of kitchen and bath fixtures. However, like most retailers in that category, despite the boom in home buying, 2002 was a year of flat growth due to post 9/11 consumer spending. However, as 2003 neared and with it, Community Home Supply's 65th anniversary, it was clear that this would afford the retailer an ideal opportunity to strengthen their position.

While it isn't often that we here at RAW are blown away by the ads that we see, (and we do see a lot), we were captivated by the wit and whimsy of this retailer's creative efforts, especially since the products involved included such less-than-exciting items as a shower head and faucet. When was the last time a magazine ad for a bathroom fixture caught your eye? We thought so.

Working hand-in-hand with Wildflower Advertising & Design, Community Home Supply laid the groundwork for an image campaign designed to strengthen the retailer's brand in the minds of consumers, not only as a Chicago institution, but as a prime source for upscale bath and kitchen furnishings.

The agency's marketing strategy centered around the three-week 65th anniversary sales period. The primary objective was to continue to raise awareness of Community Home Supply's range of offerings—from the "ordinary" to the "extraordinary." One goal was to insure that sales rose above YTD for the duration of the three-week event. Another objective was to bring new customers into the doors to build the retailer's database and word of mouth.

The plan included hosting sales events tied to specific vendors, plus a formal anniversary party held for employees, the media and vendors, complete with in-store signage, advertising, and direct mail. Sales events were themed and created around vendor partners who could provide co-op money to help fund the events. One fun "happening" was co-sponsored by *Chicago Magazine* and Armanetti Wine Shoppe who joined with Community Home Supply. This party drew over 150 guests who turned up to

And many more...

65 years
COMMUNITY HOME SUPPLY
Kitchens and bathrooms. Everyday and beyond.

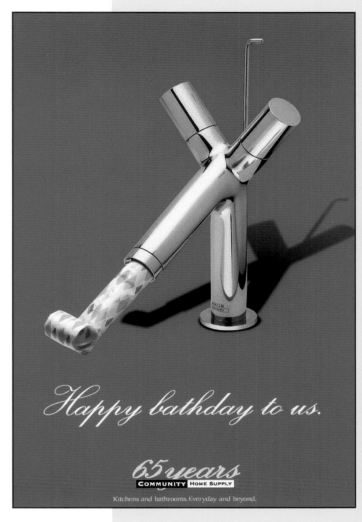

Happy bathday to us.

65 years
COMMUNITY HOME SUPPLY
Kitchens and bathrooms. Everyday and beyond.

mark the 65th anniversary. From 6 to 9 p.m., designers were on hand to help answer questions as the guests mingled in the festive atmosphere And in a savvy move, wine and cheese stations were set up in kitchen displays which provided the perfect setting to showcase Community Home Supply's merchandise.

Chicago Magazine's role in all this? They provided a complimentary one-third page ad in their May issue, 1,500 zip-targeted subscriber labels for invites to the event, and 150 gift bags with copies of the magazine tucked inside.

Other fun events held at the store included "Bathroom Tropics," "Ugliest Bathroom Contest," "Best Customer Party" and "Home Spa Day." Each event featured prize drawings to capture names, free food or drinks (always

a good move), and branded tip-sheets based on the sales event topic.

These efforts certainly paid off as the sales results of the three-week celebration rose significantly above those of the previous year. In addition, over 1,000 names were captured for Community Home Supply's database, while sales associates reported a higher number of new customer visits over this period. We'd certainly give a lot of credit to the eye-catching and humorous creative, especially the dramatic accordion-folded party invite and colorful in-store posters with the humorous copy and bold product shots on the vivid red backgrounds. Happy Anniversary!

Relexa shower head by
GROHE

Let your shower reign.

Join us for exceptional values and specials during our May anniversary celebration.

65 years
COMMUNITY HOME SUPPLY
Kitchens and bathrooms. Everyday and beyond.

Appointments Welcome: 773.281.7010
3924 N. Lincoln Ave. · Chicago IL 60613 | www.comhs.com

Community Home Supply
3924 North Lincoln Avenue
Chicago, Illinois 60613

You're invited to an evening
of wine discovery
and gourmet kitchen design.

Wine Tasting Event

Thursday, May 8
6 PM to 9 PM
Community Home Supply
3924 North Lincoln Ave.

Sip, savor and shop. Len Armanetti of Armanetti Wine Shoppe will be presenting wines from the Friuli region of Northern Italy. Then, stroll and discover Community Home Supply's latest kitchen displays for inspiration. Designers will be available to answer any questions or to get you started planning your dream kitchen.

Space is limited!
RSVP: Chicago magazine, Emily Levenstein @ (312) 832-6765.
Parking available at Corus Bank SW corner of Damen & Irving Park.

Your hosts for the evening:

Chicago | Armanetti

65 years
COMMUNITY HOME SUPPLY

3924 N. Lincoln Ave. | Chicago IL 60613 | Appointments Welcome: 773.281.7010 | www.comhs.com

A wine soirée.
Dreamy kitchens.
Fortunately, this
isn't a fantasy.

Community Home Supply
3924 North Lincoln Avenue
Chicago, Illinois 60613

Join us with chef Judith Dumbar Hines
for an evening of cooking demonstrations
and gourmet kitchens.

Chef's Night Out

Thursday, May 15
6 PM to 9 PM
Community Home Supply
3924 North Lincoln Ave.

Get a taste of the gourmet life as you sample dishes made in our working kitchen. Then, stroll through our showroom and get inspired by our newest kitchen displays featuring Viking Ranges and Schrock cabinetry. Designers will be on hand to answer questions or to get you started planning your gourmet kitchen.

Space is limited!
RSVP: Community Home Supply, Myra Jasenof @ (773) 281-2181, ext. 213.

Your hosts for the evening:

VIKING | Schrock

65 years
COMMUNITY HOME SUPPLY

3924 N. Lincoln Ave. | Chicago IL 60613 | Appointments Welcome: 773.281.7010 | www.comhs.com

Viking ranges.
A professional chef.
Fire up your
taste buds.

How to cook up a gourmet kitchen.

What's the range of your gourmet taste?

48" VGRC Gas Ranges

The flagship of the VIKING Range product line, these 27" deep, ultra-premium ranges set the standard for commercial-type construction and performance. With an unmistakable commercial appearance and outstanding features, like a self-cleaning oven and gentle even simmering.

Like cooking with greens?

Cabinets in Homestead Hickory/Natural/Green Moulding

Good taste manifests itself in many different ways and the tiniest details are often the most important. Design your kitchen with SCHROCK Homestead Hickory cabinets in natural and add color like these green mouldings.

Professional Series Warming Drawer

Full Height Wine Cooler

Warm?

It's your kitchen. You're the cook. And you know precisely where everything should be. How about a couple of strategically placed VIKING warming drawers to keep your ovens free? Versatile temperature settings (90 to 250 degrees); largest drawer available; moisture selector control; drawer removes for easy cleaning.

Or cool?

The VIKING Professional full-height wine cooler provides horizontal storage for up to 150 bottles of your favorite vintages. The exclusive TriTemp™ Storage System features 3 separate temperate zones to preserve different types of wine at their optimum serving temperatures. Full-width shelves pull out for easy access to standard, magnum, and half-size bottles.

Are you traditional or vintage?

Mission door style in maple/natural

Incorporate this SCHROCK wine rack into your kitchen to store those ready-to-open Merlots and Cabernets.

Like cooking side by side?

Professional Series Side-By-Side Refrigerator/Freezers 48" Width

What good is the perfect rack of lamb if it's preceded by a wilted salad? Or accompanied by a weak chardonnay? That's why VIKING felt the need to complete the perfect kitchen with a line of professional quality refrigeration products. With the complete Viking kitchen by your side, you'll have everything you need to host an incredible evening. Just don't forget the corkscrew.

VIKING

Schrock

Choosing a throne

Here's what to consider when choosing a new toilet.

• Round front toilets are compact to fit in small spaces. Elongated toilets have extra room in the front for added comfort.

• A "one-piece" toilet has six to ten individual pieces sculpted into a seamless unit. The result is a sleek toilet with no crevices between the tank and bowl to collect dirt and odors.

• "Two-piece" toilets require a separate tank and bowl which are bolted together.

• Gravity-fed flush toilets use the force of gravity and a siphon "pull-through" action to empty the bowl.

• Pressure-assisted toilets harness pressure from the water supply in the home to create a powerful "push-through" flush. All waste is removed quickly in about four seconds. Pressure-assisted toilets are slightly louder and there is no condensation or "sweating" on the outer tanking.

Big ideas for small bathrooms

Use lighter, cooler colors. Wall paper with a small pattern also helps expand the space. Try some on the ceiling. Or install tile with a subtle pattern that repeats on the floor. Go heavy on the lighting. A skylight, a bay window or a glass block wall could do wonders. Choose reflective surfaces, such as a shiny marble vanity. Try a glass shower enclosure. Put up lots of hooks. Hang baskets.

Go from moldy, oldie, ugly to bathing beauty.

American Standard Town Square Collection

A well-coordinated bath blends performance and style, peace and relaxation. Just like you'll experience in the new American Standard Town Square bathroom. The 20 coordinated pieces in the Town Square Collection all work together, making the design process virtually stress-free. Plus, every element performs as good as it looks, so that peaceful relaxing feeling will last a long time.

American Standard

Bertch

Choosing a sink

Drop-in sinks fit into a vanity or countertop and offer the most simple installation. They also maintain undercounter storage space. Pedestal sinks feature sophisticated styling and large bowl areas. Many can enlarge a room visually and create a luxurious setting. A pedestal sink does not allow for undercounter storage. Undercounter sinks create a clean, distinctive look. Because there is no rim or "lip" above the counter to catch soap and debris, they are the easiest to cleanup. The faucet is mounted directly to the countertop. Above counter lavatories rise above the countertop or furniture to create a decorative focal point in any bath or powder room.

Bertch Legend bath vanity

Value the most used room in the house

When determining your bathroom budget, keep in mind that cabinets account for 34% of costs, on average. But an investment in quality cabinets, such as BERTCH vanities and cabinetry have lasting appeal. Next, fixtures and fittings account for a high cost percentage in the bathroom. Installation accounts for nearly a quarter of the total cost because installation work in a bathroom tends to be intricate (eg, tile setting). If you're looking to cut corners, this is probably not the place to do it.

Party hand-outs.

Front and back of accordion-folded invitation.

Community Home Supply, Chicago, IL
OWNERS: **Ralph and Marla Richardson**
AGENCY: **Wildflower Advertising & Design,** Chicago IL
PRINCIPAL CREATIVE DIRECTOR: **Michelle Merritt Johns**
CREATIVE DIRECTOR: **Robert Jasenof**
PHOTOGRAPHER: **John McCallum Photography**
ACCOUNT SUPERVISOR: **Crystal Roberts**

A New Day

A. TESTONI is a company entrenched in tradition and renown for its craftsmanship. Three generations after its founding, by master shoemaker Amedeo Testoni in 1929, all footwear and leather goods are still handmade in Italy. This utmost attention to detail takes time—12 hours is required for the production of just one shoe.

"Our customers have a definite sense of style. They're affluent, professional, appreciate design and quality and look at A. Testoni for high-end products that meet the demands of their busy lifestyles, ranging from business meetings to evening parties, to holidays in the Riviera," said Flavio Buratto, president of Testoni USA. "In looking at our ads, the customer is looking for the product itself (our photography usually emphasizes it as much as possible), as well as the lifestyle behind it."

The company's creative process starts with the product: its design, what it represents, and how it blends with the current trends. Every decision is made in-house, spearheaded by Michela Frangilli, press and advertising manager, and Barbara Fini, marketing director, and then fleshed out with the aid of their agency, Ago Bologna—all in Italy. "There's no difference between the American and European campaigns," said Buratto. "There is no reason to do two, the world is getting very small."

Three or four years ago, the company made a decision to embrace a more modern persona. "We wanted to evolve toward a more contemporary look," stated Buratto. That meant increasing its ladies' product line, updating classic products, widening the casual and sports line and opening up more markets in Europe and America—all without neglecting their core business, which is men's shoes.

The focus of each season's advertising is different, although luxury and quality are always emphasized.

The photography for the spring/summer 2002 campaign

featured an ethnic tone. Models were adorned with bodypaint that echoed the rugs, bamboo fetishes and colored powders used as props. "The "ethnic" campaign had a strong visual impact, bringing forth the product while setting it in a very specific environment," said Buratto.

The next campaign, for fall/winter 2002, was photographed by Peter Lindbergh and captured a more modern, contemporary mood. Attention was drawn to the merchandise by posing the models against stark cubes. This campaign also included close-up shots of the newly updated product details.

"We're now in a transitional period," said Buratto. "We're in the midst of creating a business plan for development over the next five years." Rather than focusing on the models as a frame of reference for the product Testoni plans to emphasize tigher shots of merchandise in future campaigns.

Testoni tends to use print when adver-

tising, usually running in a mix of fashion and lifestyle books and newspapers. "In the general conservative spending mood in retail advertising, we decided to focus on widely read media with bigger circulation (*The New York Times*) and at the same time on a more niche, affluent audience (*Departures*)," said Buratto.

Images from the campaigns are used to produce customer catalogs as well as seasonal press books for journalists. The company also uses the advertising images on posters for its store windows and on its website (www.testoni.com). The site was launched three years ago and is used primarily to offer a brand presence on the Internet.

In addition, A. Testoni often organizes in-store events in collaboration with magazines, to bring customers, old and new, to the store and to make the whole advertising experience more interactive. A recent event, for instance, paired A. Testoni with *Departures* magazine where clients from both organizations met for a cocktail hour to view the New York store and its products. They also increase traffic with mailers.

"Printed advertising, website and in-store events usually gener-

ate a lot of responses," said Buratto. "Some customers even come to our store carrying our advertising page and asking for the product displayed."

"The ultimate objective of our advertising," said Buratto, "is to increase brand awareness, which ultimately translates into increasing store traffic, sales and distribution,"—a goal the company intends

to keep meeting, as it reworks and refines its image, advertising campaigns and website over the next few years.

A. Testoni, Bologna, Italy
CEO: **Carlo Fini**
PRESIDENT OF TESTONI USA: **Flavio Burrato**
PRESS AND ADVERTISING MANAGER:
Michela Frangilli
MARKETING DIRECTOR: **Barbara Fini**
AGENCY: **Ago Bologna**

Break Through Branding

As in other disciplines, having a breakthrough means having a new or sudden advance in knowledge or technique or breaking through a defensive obstruction. That is what BrandPower is all about—inventing new approaches and taking innovative strides to change the strategies and tactics of making the brand and the brand promise: Going beyond the customer's expectations to deliver differences.

More than ever, retailers need to use **Break Through Branding** to create believable and desirable differences between their brands and their competition. The brand's unique value propositions, attributes, benefits and satisfactions need to be communicated so that they are fully understood by the customer. Our model for **Break Through Branding** is a *"DISCUS"*—which the retailer has to throw farther than his competitors:

Differentiation
Information / Interest
Self-Image
Commitment
Understanding
Satisfaction

In the new competitive retailing arena, here's how the DISCUS needs to be thrown: Difference is the primary necessity, but even that is not enough. The **differentiation** in store, product, shopping experience and services must communicate **information** and arouse **interest** to the customer that are relevant to their own management of lifestyle and **self-image**. The customer must see evidence of the brand's **commitment** to earning her loyalty, based on her **understanding** of the brand's performance and the brand's understanding of her.

The second "S" in DISCUS is saved for last because it has to be a value perception that lasts beyond the initial purchase. A brand might *break through* the communication clutter with one-time sales promotions, bonuses or rewards, but **Brand-Power** should be *earned* through a consistent program of pro-

viding customers with genuine value, service and **satisfaction** over the long term.

Here are retailers who have thrown the **"brandiscus"** for a competitive breakthrough:

• **A & P Canada** realized that competing between the discount grocer and the supercenter *"could be difficult if we didn't bring some **new meaning**"* to the supermarket. Its *"We're fresh obsessed"* concept strategy becomes a breakthrough in differentiation, as well as internal branding that refreshed everything inside and outside their stores. See page 150.

• **Nordstrom's** opening in Las Vegas was "challenged with how do we announce this opening and get attention" of people and visitors who may be more information-advantaged amid "all that glitz and glitter." Its breakthrough was to provide 40 of its leading vendors with ads, billboards and total taxi and vehicle wraps that moved with and through the people. See page 156.

• **I.N.C. International Concepts** of Federated Stores does a **self-image** breakthrough by moving the brand "away from being associated with super models to a model of another kind—this time a *super **role model***, humanitarian Heather Mills. Her international concept of inspiration added to the U.N.'s **commitment** to resolving the global landmine crisis. Heather really represents what the brand I.N.C. is all about—an awareness of importance for what is international and what is important on an international scale. See page 158.

- **The Mall at Millenia** has a different way of making a breakthrough in mall-shopping **satisfactions**. "Imagine shopping in your local mall and being able to watch the latest shows from Milan and Paris!" The mall's BrandPower is built on satisfying customers with experiences that have "never before been done in a retail setting." Its **Preferred Shopper Program** was a first for shopping centers. Customers can pay to become a "*Preferred Shopper* member" who gets pampered with satisfaction, from Millenia valet parking to membership-only invitations to special mall events, designer appearances, trunk shows and special sales. See page 161.

- **Water & Fire's** brand mission breaks through by blending the uniqueness of the European kitchen with American savvy. The brand gets power from the stories of the custom kitchens as told by the customers who **understand** how Water & Fire can improve their home, "regardless of style preferences with a custom kitchen for them." The brand communication strategy is to connect prospective customers with satisfied customers who can help them understand what inspired their "story of a kitchen." See page 168.

These are retailers who are determined that their brands should break through the retail brand clutter with differences that their target customer segments can perceive. Today's retail formats are indeed a blur. The question of who is in what business is no longer easily answered. What can't you buy in a super Wal-Mart?

The DISCUS breakthrough model recognizes the emotional appeal of attributes and benefits as a benchmark for BrandPower. More than ever, consumers choose a brand for emotional reasons that are strictly individual. A brand builds power by appealing to these emotions through an understanding of how to personalize relationships. And by promoting a two-way communication system, by providing *original retail experiences* (O.R.E.), by being conscious of lifestyle and time-saving needs, and by generating trust through long-run commitments to customized service.

Break Through Branding strategies can and should consider how to add to the rational attributes of a brand, a whole new set of emotional benefits that increase the power of the brand's personality.

Fresh Obsessed

IN CANADA, where supermarkets are called grocery stores and grocers are regionalized, The Great Atlantic and Pacific Company of Canada (A&P Canada) is going all out to differentiate itself from its competitors in the minds of its customers.

"The grocery industry has gone through an evolution in the last few years," said Doug Brummer, senior VP marketing and advertising. "We've seen the emergence of three formats—the discount format, conventional traditional format and the creation of supercenters."

According to Brummer, the discount grocer is all about price-focused utilitarian products with limited selection. The supercenters on the other hand offer a vast selection at good prices and no-frills service. "We realized that to be in the middle could be difficult if we didn't bring some new meaning to it," Brummer said. "We really needed to look at what was meaningful to

our customers and how we could differentiate ourselves versus the price segment."

The vehicle is "We're Fresh Obsessed" —an aggressive, all-encompassing merchandising, marketing and advertising effort built around the concept of product freshness. "We completely overhauled our business model to recognize that this traditional segment was going the way of the dinosaurs," said Brummer. Warehousing, distribution, store design—virtually every aspect of the operation was changed to ensure and promote product freshness.

In some sense as good as the concept of fresh is, it's a no-brainer. As Chris Staples, creative director at Rethink Advertising, A&P Canada's agency put it, "a can of beans is a can of beans, a box of Tide is a box of Tide, but you can differentiate on fresh."

When fresh became the strategy, it also became a way of life inside and outside the

store. Everything was redone. "'We're Fresh Obsessed' was always more than just an ad campaign," Staples said. "We tried to create a religion the staff would buy into and customers would respond to, including areas ad agencies don't get involved in such as uniform design.

That was only the beginning. "We stripped them of every sign from the washrooms to signs on the shelves right down to aisle directories," said Staples. Name tags, corporate communications materials, even trucks were redesigned. "All the cylinders work together." said Staples. Think of it as an eight-cylinder car. Too often in retail advertising only one or two cylinders are going at once. Typically most ad agencies just focus on one or two cylinders—the advertising." He explained that while a retailer might be doing really interesting TV advertising, but then when people go into the store, the store doesn't look like that.

IT'S FRESH OR IT'S FREE.

If you find any spoiled item in our store, just bring it to the Customer Service desk and we'll give you a fresh replacement free of charge.*

*See instore for details.

The unique guarantee is communicated in store, on billboards, in flyers and a series of TV spots.

The freshest fruit, cut daily.

A&P

The Cut Fruit Mosaic was used in store and in flyers to support the retailer's popular cut fruit program.

Billboards.

Our produce manager, on vacation.
We're fresh obsessed.

The brand advertising campaign has evolved over time. The basic elements are TV spots, point-of-sale materials, flyers and billboards. According to Blummer, the flyers play a particularly important part in driving day-to-day business. "When we were looking at our new strategy, we were looking for a strong call to action. What we did was restructure, reformat and redesign our flyer (circular) to support fresh obsessed on a weekly basis." The 16-page flyers are done in house, where product photos are treated with care in settings that supports the fresh message. "The pictures aren't too fancy, because we don't want to come across as being expensive," said Brummer. "The idea is to help customers put together their shopping list." A&P produces some six million flyers each week. Distribution is via direct mail, newspaper inserts and in-store.

"TV is important too," said Staples.

Our deli manager, on a picnic.
We're fresh obsessed.

Our bakery manager, at the beach.
We're fresh obsessed.

It's fresh or it's free.
Some exclusions apply
A&P   Ultra food&drug
We're fresh obsessed.

It's fresh or it's free.
Some exclusions apply
A&P   Ultra food&drug
We're fresh obsessed.

In-store banners are elements in a strong storewide point of sale program.

We bake 27 kinds of bread. Every day.

The Exhausted Baker poster supports the 27 varieties of bread program—an added value service that further differentiates the company from discount grocers and supercenters.

Apple Search

Open on a customer sorting through a pile of apples, bag in hand… other customers and A&P staff populate the background.

She picks up an apple, looks disappointed, puts it back. Picks up another. Puts it back…

She picks up anther one…frowns, puts it back….

SUPER/ANNCR: Find a bad apple

She picks up another one, puts it back…

SUPER/ANNCR: and we'll give you a fresh one free.

LEGAL: See store for details.

The woman keeps looking, looking, looking….

EMPLOYEE: (FRIENDLY) Hi!

She responds with a cold smile.

SUPER/ANNCR: It's fresh or it's free

LOGO: Dominion.

ANNCR: Dominion. We're fresh obsessed.

Checking Dates

Open on a guy digging through the dairy case at an A&P/Dominion store,

…other customers and A&P staff populate the background.

The guy is checking the expiry dates on the milk cartons… he looks disappointed…

pushing cartons aside, looking for a 'good'

date, piling cartons on the floor.

He digs and digs and digs, reaching waaaaaay into the back….frowning…

SUPER/ANNCR: Find an expired product

He keeps on digging…

SUPER/ANNCR: And we'll give you a fresh one free.

LEGAL: See store for details.

EMPLOYEE: Can I help you?

CUSTOMER: (SHOCKED) No! Uh… no. I'm …fine.

He starts to reshelve the milk… once employee leaves, he keeps on digging …

SUPER/ANNCR: It's fresh or it's free

LOGO: Dominion.

ANNCR: Dominion. We're fresh obsessed.

Squeeze Test

Open on a young woman in the bread section of A&P/Dominion…. other customers and staff in the background….

She's testing the loaves of bread by giving them the universal "gentle squeeze" test…. she's unsatisfied.

She squeezes another… and another….

frowning…

SUPER/ANNCR: Find a stale loaf.

she squeezes another…

SUPER/ANNCR: And we'll give you a fresh one free.

LEGAL: See store for details.

BAKERY EMPLOYEE: (HANDING HER A LOAF) This one's still warm!

CUSTOMER: (NOT MEANING IT) Thanks!

She tosses the fresh loaf on the shelf, walks away.

SUPER/ANNCR: It's fresh or it's free

LOGO: Dominion.

ANNCR: Dominion. We're fresh obsessed.

Special Announcement

Inside a grocery store, an employee in an A&P uniform picks up a PA handset...

PA ANNOUNCEMENT: Attention shoppers, have you heard of A&P's Fresh or Free Guarantee? It's a simple policy. If you find any spoiled item in our store, we'll give you a replacement, free of charge. Only at A&P!

Two large stockboys from Superfoods approach behind him, angry. He notices them.

PA ANNOUNCEMENT: (FAST) A&P A&P A&P A&P A&P A&P! We're fresh obsessed! (HE RUNS OFF)

Cut to exterior shot of Superfoods, swish pan to A&P across the street. Cut to exterior of A&P.

ANNCR: It's fresh, or it's free. Only at...

ANNCR/SUPER: (OVER SHOT OF STORE) A&P. We're fresh obsessed.

Honest Fish Guy

A woman in the fish department of a grocery store stops a man in an A&P uniform...

WOMAN: Excuse me, is this fish fresh?

EMPLOYEE: (SMILEY) Oh...no.

SHE'S AMAZED

EMPLOYEE: See all these fillets on ice? (SHAKING HIS HEAD) That affects flavor and texture. If I were them, I'd store them in humidity controlled cases.

PULLS A BROCHURE FROM HIS POCKET

EMPLOYEE: (OVER SHOT OF FISH CASE BROCHURE) Look at that beauty.

A stern Superfoods manager and two large bag boys apear.

MANAGER: What are you doing?

Thinking fast, employee tosses ice at manager, grabs customer by the shoulders, looking panicked.

EMPLOYEE: I'll hold them off! Run, don't look

back, *run!*

MANAGER: Chase him!

cut to exterior shot of superfoods, employee bursts from front door. swish pan to the A&P store across the street.

ANNCR.: Temperature and humidity controlled fish cases, at...

ANNCR/SUPER: (OVER SHOT OF STORE) A&P. We're fresh obsessed.

"Because so much of grocery advertising is price, you really need to have that emotional component, and the best way to have that is television."

The spots underwent a major change last year when A&P raised the bar with a unique guarantee— "it's fresh or it's free." As a result, the three TV spots that ran last spring and summer went from simply promoting freshness to proving it. Customers were shown in the act of squeezing items, checking dates on milk, looking

for that one bad apple. The commercials were gutsy in a humorous way, because they show customers trying to take advantage of the guarantee.

This season four new spots are running. They take a more competitive stance. A&P employees are shown going into competitors' stores. "Last year was proving we're fresh obsessed," said Staples. "This year takes it to a whole new level, saying we're fresh obsessed and a lot of our competitors aren't."

Billboards are also utilized. "We look at our trucks as traveling billboards," said Brummer. "We have at least 300 trucks traveling around with various Fresh Obsessed messages. Beyond that we buy stationary billboards in key markets sometimes five or six, sometimes as many as 200 or 300 depending on what we're promoting at the time." A&P also maintains a board outside of its head office, where three creative executions have been rotated for the last year and a half.

A&P CANADA

Manager Complaint

A man in a manager's uniform stands in a grocery aisle, checking items off his clipboard

CUSTOMER: Excuse me, are you a manager?

MANAGER: Yes I am.

CUSTOMER: This lettuce is all wilted.

MANAGER: (HAPPY) Wow, I know!

The customer doesn't quite know how to respond.

CUSTOMER: Don't you have a store policy or…

MANAGER: Well, I could give you a fresh replacement free of charge…

CUSTOMER: (HAPPY) oh!

MANAGER: …If this were my A&P store.

PA ANNOUNCEMENT: Two large bag boys to aisle 6. Two large bag boys.

Manager looks at her, scared. they look up. we

see he's in aisle 6. customer looks down…manager has vanished.

cut to exterior of superfoods. A&P manager bursts from the front door. Swish pan to A&P store across the street.

ANNCR.: It's fresh, or it's free, only at…

ANNCR/SUPER: (OVER SHOT OF STORE) A&P. We're fresh obsessed.

Fresh Cut Sample

An A&P employee stands at an ice-filled fresh cut fruit display.

EMPLOYEE: (TO MALE CUSTOMER) Would you like to try some freshly cut fruit?

CUSTOMER: Sure!

EMPLOYEE: Too bad.

SHE DROPS THE SAMPLE DISH

EMPLOYEE: See, some places just ship this stuff in, pre-cut. In buckets. (SHIVERS)

THE CUSTOMER LOOKS MORE STUNNED.

A "staff only" door opens, out walks the real superfoods employee. the A&P employee realizes the gig is nearly up…thinking fast…

EMPLOYEE: Cover me!

SHE GOES IN FOR THE OL' FAKE KISS…

Kissing…kissing…she shuffles themselves into the next aisle, safe.

CUSTOMER: (BREATHLESS, IN AWE) Who are you?

EMPLOYEE: I work at the A&P store across

the street. (CHECKS HER WATCH, ALL BUSINESS) Oh, lunch break's over. (SHE BOLTS)

CUSTOMER: (STUNNED) Can I call you?

Exterior of superfoods. A&P employee runs from the store, swish pan to A&P store across the street.

ANNCR: Freshly cut fruit, from our own perfect produce, at…

ANNCR/SUPER: (OVER SHOT OF STORE) A&P. We're fresh obsessed.

The fresh obsessed campaign has helped A&P build and maintain customer loyalty across Ontario. If imitation is the sincerest form of flattery, then it can be said that A&P Canada has been feted with compliments. According to Staples, a lot of other grocery retailers have attempted some version of "fresh." "But we staked out that ground first," he said. "Awareness of the slogan now is over 90%.

"We're fresh obsessed has been very

powerful for us with our sales increase and our market share increase behind it," said Brummer. "When we ask customers why they shop here, we're getting all the answers that tell us all the elements are working. We're changing people's perception. It's also been very motivating for employees."

The campaign has worked so well in fact, A&P Canada has experienced two years of record sales and profits.

Now, *that's* delicious.

A&P Canada, Toronto
SR. VP MARKETING AND ADVERTISING: **Doug Brummer**
AGENCY (flyers): **In-house**
ADVERTISING AGENCY **Rethink Advertising**, Vancouver
CREATIVE DIRECTOR: **Chris Staples**
ART DIRECTOR: **Mark Hesse**
COPYWRITER: **Rob Tarry**
DIRECTORS: **Tim Hamilton** (2003), **Derek Horn** (2002)
PRODUCTION HOUSE: **Avion Films**
PRODUCER: **Terry Green**

For the flyers, a picture is worth a thousands words.

A new prototype store has a gas station outside.

A car wash is part of the gas station.

Taxi!

WHEN NORDSTROM was scheduled to open a store in Las Vegas, it was clear that advertising the grand opening would be more difficult than usual. With its largely transient population, Las Vegas doesn't have a major newspaper with a strong readership. On top of that, there's all that glitz and glitter competing for attention.

"Things get lost out there, because of all the lights Vegas has," said Milissa Cole, account director at Emergence, Atlanta. "They were challenged with how do we announce this opening and get the attention of people who live there, and find an audience in the people who are there visiting?" Factor in that they needed to do it with limited resources, and this was indeed a challenge.

Intense brainstorming ensued, and the idea of doing something like wrapping a bus came up. "We started talking about it, when Nordstrom VP brand creative director Cheryl Zahniser said 'Let's wrap the cabs because that's what people get in and out of,'" said Cole.

Nordstrom then went to key vendors with a package in which the vendors could participate on three different levels. The first was to have a cab wrap, the second was to buy a cab and mini billboard, or the third option—the cab, a billboard

and an ad in the Las Vegas edition of *USA Today*.

More than 40 vendors signed on. "The technical part was little difficult, because none of us had done anything like that before," said Cole. Each product had to be laid out and photographed, then repeated in Photoshop. Working off a flat template, they had to make sure that for the crossover to the hood, to the side, to the front and to the back of the cab, everything lined up. "We couldn't print in certain areas," said Cole. "Then a blowtorch had to be used to adhere these things to the cabs."

The cabs took to the streets on October 31 for the month of November. Toppers said "Nordstrom – We are Here" Cole who was in Vegas for the opening, said "They looked great on the street. The reaction was incredible. People's heads turned. The cab drivers were even excited about it."

So are we. There's nothing like the power of a good idea.

Nordstrom, Seattle
VP BRAND CREATIVE DIRECTOR: **Cheryl Zahniser**
SOUTHWEST REGIONAL ADVERTISING DIRECTOR: **Denise Bisdorf**
AGENCY: **Emergence,** Atlanta
ACCOUNT DIRECTOR: **Milissa Cole**
CREATIVE DIRECTOR: **Amy Weaver**
STUDIO MANAGER: **Janice Delosky**

Selections from six-page ad that ran in February *Vogue*.

Inspired Branding

STRICTLY SPEAKING, I.N.C. International Concepts, is an in-house private-label brand. Created by Federated Merchandising Group exclusively for Federated Stores (Bloomingdale's, The Bon Marche, Burdine's, Goldsmith's, Lazarus, Macy's and Rich's), the brand has gradually morphed over the years into the status of a national brand.

"We have achieved brand recognition," said Nancy Slavin, group VP marketing and advertising. "Consumers don't seem to see it as a house brand." Much of that perception can be attributed to an advertising campaign that associated the brand with supermodels, the likes of Heidi Klum.

Now the brand has moved away from being associated with supermodels to a model of another kind—this time a super role model, the humanitarian and Nobel Prize nominee, Heather Mills.

The people at I.N.C. had been looking to create a campaign that was cause-related. "We had in our mind to create a campaign about the

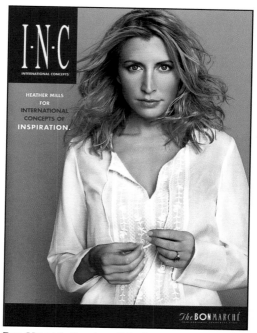

Bon Marché direct mail Spring 2002.

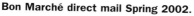

Rich's direct mail Spring 2002.

things that matter most, then to find a woman who would inspire us," said Slavin. The marketing campaign I.N.C. Concepts of Inspiration became the new campaign vision.

Finding the right spokesperson to make that vision a reality turned out to be absolutely serendipitous. I.N.C. wanted someone who was substantive. Coincidentally, on September 10, a Federated executive had attended a luncheon where Mills was being honored for her work on behalf of Adopt-A-Minefield, a program of the United

Nations committed to resolving the global landmine crisis. The Federated executive came back from the luncheon and sent Mills an e-mail that afternoon. The next day, September 11, reinforced the company's desire to do something cause-related. Mills also felt compelled to get involved in something that would bring more awareness to her cause.

The partnering has been a perfect fit. "She represented a cause that hadn't necessarily been promoted tremendously in the U.S.—a cause that now had greater significance than we ever imag-

ined." said Slavin. "Heather really embodies what the brand is all about. Heather is international, the brand is now international." By partnering with Mills as the new face for I.N.C.'s advertising, I.N.C.'s mission then became to raise consumer awareness of the cause.

The I.N.C. campaign marks Mills' return to modeling after a road accident in 1993 that resulted in the loss of her left leg below the knee.

As part of the "International Concepts of Inspiration" campaign, Mills has been making personal appear-

September *Marie-Claire.*

May *Marie-Claire.*

I.N.C. International Concepts, New York
Federated Marketing Services, New York
AGENCY: **In-house**
GROUP VP MARKETING AND ADVERTISING:
Nancy Slavin
MARKETING MANAGER: **Jennifer Kyvig**
CREATIVE DIRECTOR: **Maryellen Needham**
PHOTOGRAPHER: **Walter Chin**

ances at I.N.C.-sponsored events around the country to educate consumers about the global landmine crisis. "In some ways we debuted her to an average American audience, rather than putting on a pedestal," said Slavin. "This worked for her in that she was introduced as a humanitarian." Throughout the spring and fall, Mills made personal appearances at Macy's East, Macy's West, Bloomingdales, Rich's, Burdines and The Bon Marche.

Concurrently, I.N.C. promoted awareness of Mills and the Adopt-A-Minefield program with extensive print advertising and direct mail. Starting in February with a six-page ad in *Vogue*, single-page and double-truck ads ran in *InStyle, Marie Claire* and *Vogue* throughout the year.

There was tremendous direct mail support as well. "All told, we have done six direct mail books distributed nationally to all our best Federated customers in every major DMA to tie in to each store," said Slavin. "We distributed over a million each time."

Additional advertising ran in major newspapers in cities in which there were personal appearances. In addition, outdoor was done in New York, Los Angeles and San Francisco. "We had lots of boards in each market—telephone kiosks, mall kiosks and a Jumbotron in Herald Square when we launched in February," said Slavin.

By partnering with Mills as the first corporate sponsor of Adopt-A-Minefield, I.N.C. was able to raise more than $100,000 as a contribution to Adopt-A-Minefield.

New Center. New Brand.

NOWADAYS, BEING different has never been so desirable. Especially at retail. A new shopping center, The Mall at Millenia, is in certain striking respects not like other malls, even other new ones.

The center is part of Millenia, a new 4.5-million-sq.-ft office, hotel and retail complex in Orlando, FL. Right off the bat, The Mall at Millenia looks different. It has 50-foot vaulted skylights reminiscent of a conservatory, an abundance of natural light, and innovative glass

and water features everywhere.

In center court is a shopping center first—12 LED screens, the first of their kind in the world, perched 30 feet in the air. This 360-degree multimedia theater complete with surround sound airs The Video Fashion Network, the largest venue for fashion footage in the world. What's it like to see it? Imagine shopping in your local mall and being able to watch the latest shows from Milan and Paris. "It's never been done in a retail setting before," said Rocell Melohn, marketing director. "It's incredible to see customers' reactions!"

Management wanted to send out the message that the Mall at Millenia was a thing apart. Together with agency Panzano & Partners, preparation started nearly 18 months prior to the October 16, 2002 grand opening to give Millenia its own long-term signature

brand. The desire for a signature brand that wasn't trend-dependent was predicated on the idea that successful brand building goes beyond an ad campaign that may run only a year or two.

Taking the idea that branding begins with the things people see every day, the agency created a signature series in much the same way that Tiffany has its blue box and Neiman Marcus its butterfly.

Shopping bags, directories, gift-certificate envelopes and other materials with the most extensive visibility were transformed from merely functional products into branding vehicles. Based on the principle that branding and color go hand in hand ("Target Red," "Tiffany Blue," etc.) all the materials were done in "Millenia Blue."

The Signature Series also included elements for another Millenia point of difference—the Preferred Shopper Program—a first for shopping centers. "The program is based on service and privilege, kind of like an airline club where you pay to be a member to make it easier and more convenient," said Melohn. The program ($150 annually) pampers the customer with valet parking, gift wrapping, and other privileges as well as membership-only mailings throughout the year offering exclusive invitations to special events, advance notice of designer appearances, trunk shows, very special sales and more. "We did several focus groups prior

The signature series was designed to help build ongoing brand awareness.

the advertising tagline, "You were meant for this." Unlike many retailers in a resort area, the local consumer was the target. The agency chose an emotional appeal that focused on the benefits to the consumer—of what they were deserving of rather than on the center's features. The campaign included local magazines, TV, posters and the Holiday Fashion Retailer Catalog, which was direct mailed to 100,000 homes in early November.

While the main focus was the local community, Millenia can't ignore the fact that it's located in Orlando—the #1 tourist town in the nation—with 42 million visitors annually. A strong tourism component was part of Millenia's strategy. In place is a comprehensive tourist marketing program, complete with a full-time tourist manager. But here again, Millenia has put its own stamp on tourism materials. A miniature accordion-fold piece designed to fit into just about anything (the size of a business card), provides tourists with a short list of unique shopping opportunities, phone info and directions. Its practicality is no accident. Millenia actually conducted focus groups with concierges from the area's top hotels to determine what materials would work best. "Everything in it is built around the needs of the customer," said Melohn. "It gives them everything, and it's small. When they take it home, it has all the information handy."

Another excellent piece for the tourist market is the signature savings coupon book. Available in many languages and including an international size chart, the coupon book is different from the usual in that the focus isn't on savings. "Retailers at the center aren't the type that like discounts," Melohn explained. "We added offers for some community and arts types things to do. We're not just Disneyworld. We wanted to give people a cultural experience as well."

It's just one more example how in so many ways—from the paid membership loyalty program to the comprehensive signature series branding—Millenia is putting its own special stamp on shopping center marketing today.

to launching the program from key business leaders to very affluent women to a broad spectrum," said Melohn. "People are all about bragging rights and we all get so busy we want things easy." After only one mailing to elicit membership, the program has generated strong enrollment. A second mailing is in the works.

To reinforce the idea that The Mall at Millenia was truly special, the marketing campaign encouraged consumers to dream big dreams, to realize their potential and finally to recognize that indeed they deserved such a place—hence,

you were meant for this.

TASTES OF MILLENIA

THE CHEESECAKE FACTORY
P.F. CHANG'S CHINA BISTRO
BRIO TUSCAN GRILLE
MCCORMICK & SCHMICK'S SEAFOOD RESTAURANT
CALIFORNIA PIZZA KITCHEN
JOHNNY ROCKETS
PANERA BREAD

Plus, the exceptional dining options of the Orangerie Cafés:

Bistro Sensations
Cajun Grill
Chick-fil-A
Chinatown
Fruit 'n' Smoothie
Sensations
Gourmet Grill

Häagen-Dazs
Mrs. Fields Cookies
Nori Sushi & Grill
Sbarro
Southwest Grill
Tango Grill

The photography was envisioned as aspirational as well as approachable, showing people in optimal situations.

The TV spots were shot in an ultra-wide format, giving the imagery a panoramic feel. They included delicately detailed icons and custom music.

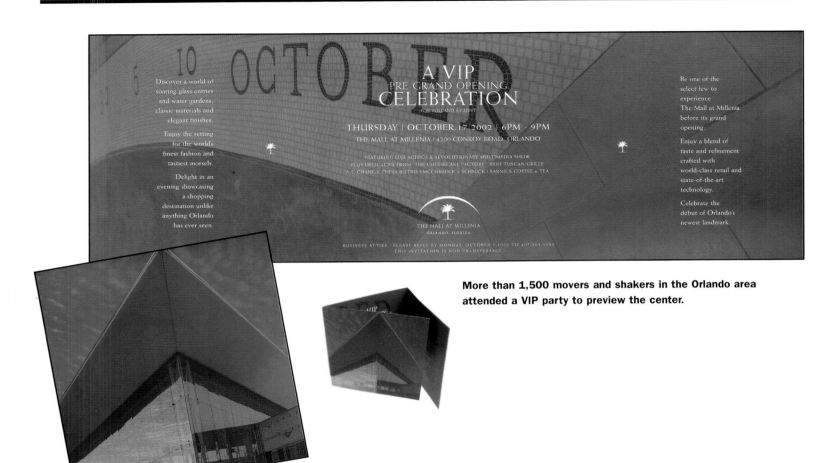

More than 1,500 movers and shakers in the Orlando area attended a VIP party to preview the center.

Embodying stylized, lifestyle photography and an elegant design, ads provided the promise of a unique experience that only The Mall at Millennia could fulfill. Ads ran monthly in _Orlando Magazine_, _Orlando Leisure_, _Where_, _Travel Host_ and _Guest Informant_.

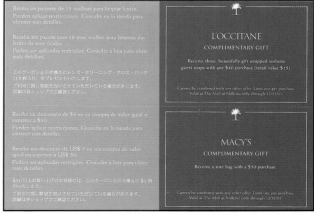

The signature coupon book is about a lot more than savings. An international sizing chart is one of the little extras.

fine lines
an inside look at our hottest
fashions of the season

fine dining
culinary masterpieces
of the mall at millenia

holiday 2002 premiere issue

FINE
designs
the mall at millenia story

Co-developers: The Forbes Company and Taubman Centers, Inc.

"We're creating a story, the story of
man's existence on the planet,"
Mr. Ryan explains. "The story is
conveyed through the themes of
earth, sea, time and universe."

The sunlight touches your face as it streams through a 60-foot-high, semi-circle of glass that forms the sparkling entry rotunda. Beneath your feet, water cascades through a maze of rapids that stretches to a finale of synchronized fountains. Children laugh in delight at the motion of the flowing water and projecting lasers. You stop and smell the tempting aromas of several nearby restaurants.

And so think, this spectacular array of sights, sounds, and smells all takes place even before you reach one of the finest collections of merchandise ever assembled.

From the onset of its creation, The Mall at Millenia's goal was to create a world-class collection of stores and restaurants that was befitting of Orlando's emergence as a world-class city. The stores were carefully selected to bring both luxury merchants that were new to Orlando, as well as the shops that were already familiar favorites of area residents.

And as that dream unfolded, the architecture of the center needed to serve in a worthy canvas for the masterful blend of merchandise encapsulated there. "From the very beginning, our vision was to create a shopping destination that was unsurpassed in its design and architecture," states Nate Forbes of The Forbes Company and managing partner of The Mall at Millenia. "We envisioned a place where every person was able to take away a unique and special experience," he continued.

While the spectacular collection of merchants began to form, the architectural plans for The Mall at Millenia ambitiously soared as well, serving as a worthy backdrop for the stores. The reality is even better than the vision," explains Mr. Forbes. "The architect's traditional blend of classic with contemporary architecture has risen to a new height."

It has been said that truly great work requires enormous passion. If the passionate collaboration of developer Nate Forbes and architect Jim Ryan is any indication, The Mall at Millenia's greatness should be secured for decades to come. When he speaks of his firm's work at The Mall at Millenia, Mr. Ryan, president of JPRA Architects, can review every detail, minute or grand, from the 250 million-year-old Jurassic stone floor tiles imported from a quarry in Germany, to the meandering "S"-shaped skylight running throughout the Center's public areas. Every detail was thoughtfully considered and executed with a grand goal in mind.

"We were creating a story, the story of man's existence on the planet," Mr. Ryan explains. "The story is conveyed through the themes of earth, sea, time and universe." This is a world where

architecture uses the universe as a backdrop, the earth as a palette, and the water to communicate the ongoing flow of life. Each time you visit The Mall at Millenia, you'll find new evidence of this all-encompassing design theme based on man's existence. For instance, after entering at the Water Garden entrance, walk along an 80-foot running river. Watch the water underfoot as you cross the river's glass bridge. Smile as you stroll by the synchronized fountains that dance like a mini version of the water show at Las Vegas Bellagio hotel.

"One of the most important aspects we needed to convey was that this is a changing venue. Every time a person visits, their experience will be different from the last," Mr. Ryan notes. This concept comes alive in the Grand Court, where mere shopping turns into a multi-sensory experience

While on a break from visiting the top fashion stores in the world, you'll be able to enjoy a relaxing moment and experience something you've never seen before. Twelve, curved LED screens are perched like sails atop 30-foot high masts, encircling the Grand Court. Twelve-channel surround sound brings entertaining vignettes alive, alternately creating excitement with 120 seconds of a fast-paced sailing adventure, or quiet scenes of our great country. With dozens of different mini-programs, you'll be fascinated by the refreshing moments this adds to your shopping trip.

As you leave the Grand Court with its swirl of fish and leaves in the striking terrazzo underfoot, follow the 1200-foot-long timeline of the Universe, past tempting merchandise-filled stores. You can actually chart the history of the Universe through this innovative floor design.

As you explore the second level, you'll come upon the "Juliet Balconies," small, semi-circular overhangs that pay homage to the lovesick title character of Shakespeare's romantic play. They allow you to step away from the flow of traffic and enjoy the sights and sounds of The Mall at Millenia.

And that simple moment is the essence of The Mall at Millenia experience: a time when you can take away the exact experience that you desire. You can focus on the dazzling technology and grand features, or you may choose to notice the tiniest details that dot this unique and groundbreaking landscape. This is a world that was created for such moments, and you are invited to savor every second of it.

- Brendan Quinn

The view at dusk through the striking glass prism entry of Orangerie Cafés.

Grand Court LED showing international fashion trends.

The sparkle of Orangerie Cafés, The Mall at Millenia's 12 on-the-go dining options.

[22]   [23]

fine lines

Black is back. That's one thing the designers made clear this season with their Fall/Winter collections. Clean lines and a structured look were prevalent on many runways. And tailored fashions combined with glamorous jewelry and the classic high heel made for a triumphant return to the golden age of Hollywood when grace was considered an art. There's only one place to find all the latest styles in Orlando. The Mall at Millenia. You were meant for this.

this page
jacket **gucci at gucci**
pants **gucci**
black pump **gucci**
wide wrap belt **gucci**

opposite page
sequined halter **bcbg at macy's**
bracelet **cartier at cartier**
rings **cartier**

[32]

FINEdining

culinary masterpieces of the mall at millenia

*Photo: P.F. Chang's, North Miami, Florida.

[46]

"Rosemary, oregano and thyme tickle the tastebuds as they waft gently through the air."

W isps of fragrant spices from all corners of the world drift into the far corners of Orlando's new Mall at Millenia, their aroma so tantalizing, so close that you can almost reach out and touch them. Through glass-bottomed paths over winding rivers and in 60-foot rotundas leading to the sky, they meander, making the mouths of a thousand shoppers water as they make their way through the nation's most exclusive stores. Rosemary, oregano and thyme tickle the tastebuds as they waft gently through the air, and the appetizing aromas of vanilla beans, saffron and honey tempt the palate in a mysterious blend of sweetness and spice.

At The Mall at Millenia, the flavors of the world come to life with dishes evoking the romance of vine-draped Tuscany, the alluring mysteries of old China, the glorious adventures of the white-capped seas and the sun-drenched shores of Southern California. Even before you make your way through the arched doorways that are home to these sweet and savory secrets, your nose sends your imagination on a journey to lands you have never seen but can imagine, if only by the distinctive flavors they have given up to the hands of master chefs.

Inside The Mall at Millenia, central Florida's premiere shopping and dining destination, the foods of the world come together in sweet harmony through a unique combination of restaurants that have never before appeared together in one place. McCormick & Schmick's, one of the nation's favorite seafood restaurants, makes its Florida debut alongside longtime favorites such as The Cheesecake Factory, Brio Tuscan Grille and P.F. Chang's China Bistro. The unique flavors of Southern California tempt the tastebuds at the California Pizza Kitchen; the innocence of another era springs to life at the 1950s inspired burger restaurant Johnny Rockets; and the scents of baking bread and hearty soups come alive at Panera Bread. At this central Florida haven, food is not just for nourishment, it is a passport to the world, a ticket to the far-reaching boundaries of your own imagination. "In this situation, the restaurants are all complimentary," says George Varaldes, the managing partner of the new P.F. Chang's at The Mall at Millenia. "It will be festive and provide choices, and that's what people like."

As you make your way through the fashion capital of central Florida, you follow your nose to McCormick & Schmick's, where dark wood, exquisite glasswork and intimate, draped booths are the setting for exquisite creations from the freshest creatures of the sea, flown in daily. Some of the nation's most creative chefs make magic with black grouper encrusted in a medley of cashews, smothered with savory Jamaican rum butter. As your mouth breaks the surface of salmon stuffed with brie cheese, dungenous crab and dill, you are transported to the chilled waters of the Pacific, where sunsets come with a dazzling glory of evening haze and the fresh salt of the sea. Freshly squeezed juices awaken you on northern California shores, where the magic of the ocean washes over you in enchanting waves.

At Brio Tuscan Grille, wide open spaces and arched architecture mirror the romances of Tuscany's signature cities, Siena and Florence. On plates piled high sautéed shrimp, red peppers and lobster butter mingle in Shrimp Risotto and send you on a journey through the magic of taste sensations to a land of rolling hills covered with sunflowers, olive trees and Chianti vineyards. As veal sautéed with the flavors of Parmesan, lemon and spinach sizzles on the plate before you, you can almost feel the hard earth of a medieval Tuscan city beneath your feet, the crumbling walls of a tiny kingdom still standing strong around you.

Orangerie Cafés
For those who want gourmet tastes on the go, The Orangerie Cafés offer unparalleled flavor and choice. Fulfill your appetite at these scrumptious eateries:

Bistro Sensations	Fruit 'N Smoothie Sensations	Nori Sushi & Grill
Cajun Grill	Gourmet Grill	Sbarro
Chick-Fil-A	Häagen-Dazs	Southwest Grill
Chinatown	Mrs. Fields Cookies	Tango Grill

At P.F. Chang's China Bistro, where pork dumplings, shrimp, green onions and bean sprouts mingle in Pon Rice Noodle Soup, and crispy plates of delectably crisp honey shrimp melt in sweet union with exploding tastebud, you embark on a journey to the mysterious Orient, draped in the mists of time.

And at The Cheesecake Factory, three dozen enormous cheesecakes, some drenched in strawberries, others stuffed full of silky caramel and giant pecans, sparkle in bakery cases, drawing a larger crowd than the windows of Tiffany & Co. just down the way. Like gemstones set in perfect treats of silver and gold, they call your name with sweet promises of perfection that are fulfilled as sweet, soft pieces of heaven melt in your mouth.

Around the Center, through forests of laser lights and dancing fountains, more than a hundred different wines from all corners of the world are ready to dance with the hundreds of dishes they compliment. Even the rich twists and warm loaves of bread that come from ovens at all corners tempt you with their own brand of magic, some mingling with extra virgin olive oil and Italian spices, others holding their own with blends of tomato and basil, rosemary and onion, Asiago and Parmesan, honey and wheat.

The subtle mingling of spices, the sizzle of perfectly grilled meats, the rich gardens of vegetables in all the colors of the rainbow all sing together in a perfect harmony. You are filled with the promise of sensory sensation until you return, ready again to explore the world, to the culinary haven of The Mall at Millenia.

- Kristin Harmel

[47]

TASTES OF MILLENIA
THE MALL AT MILLENIA
DINING GUIDE

P.F. CHANG'S CHINA BISTRO
A unique combination of traditional Chinese cuisine and American hospitality in a contemporary bistro setting.
407-345-2888

McCORMICK & SCHMICK'S SEAFOOD RESTAURANT
Chef creates a seafood menu daily to reflect the freshest seafood possible. Dining rooms for private parties are available.
407-226-6515

BRIO TUSCAN GRILLE
Upscale Italian concept, using authentic Tuscan cooking methods.
407-351-8909

THE CHEESECAKE FACTORY
Famous for generous portions and 40 mouthwatering desserts, this restaurant pleases all palates.
407-226-0333

AND
CALIFORNIA PIZZA KITCHEN
JOHNNY ROCKETS
PANERA BREAD

ORANGERIE CAFÉS

BISTRO SENSATIONS
CAJUN GRILL
CHICK-FIL-A
CHINATOWN
FRUIT 'N' SMOOTHIE SENSATIONS
GOURMET GRILL
HÄAGEN-DAZS
MRS. FIELDS
NORI SUSHI & GRILL
SBARRO
SOUTHWEST GRILL
TANGO GRILL

TASTES OF MILLENIA
SEVEN RESTAURANTS AND TWELVE EXCEPTIONAL CAFÉS

THE MALL AT MILLENIA
I-4 at Conroy Road (Exit 78)
407.363.3555 mallatmillenia.com
Valet parking is available at the main Conroy Road entrance.

European Style, American Savvy

WHEN PAUL HAZILLIADES established Water & Fire in 1999, his vision was to bring the uniqueness of European kitchen, and baths to American homes. Since then, the Newton, MA, business, which both designs and imports European high-end kitchen and bath furniture and accessories, has expanded three-fold.

As often happens with new enterprises, Hazilliades did his own advertising in the early years. Two years ago, with the business growing, he hired a Boston ad agency, The Laidlaw Group, to develop a consumer advertising campaign and collateral materials with a secondary target of architects and interior designers.

Because Water & Fire carries high-end items, an element in the strategy was to make people feel comfortable with the idea of making a major investment in doing their kitchen using European products. "One of the things we have found is that people are somewhat intimidated by the process," said Cindy Laidlaw, agency president. "You might be the president of a company but might not know anything about design."

How this situation was circumvented came about somewhat serendipitously. "We were sitting in an input meeting with the client and he was talking about some of the experiences he had had," said Laidlaw. "It all started with his telling us stories. The more we pressed him, he's say 'oh yeah, there was this person and that person." Those stories turned out to be the perfect solution to the intimidation problem. Letting Water & Fire's customers speak for themselves about their experience in doing their kitchens was a vehicle for demonstrating the diversity of the product line, the different kind of people and age groups and the diversity of styles from traditional to contemporary. "That was important, because we wanted everyone to understand that regardless of their style preference, we had a custom kitchen for them," Laidlaw noted. "We also wanted architects and interior designers who read the same magazines as consumers to know about Water & Fire's kind of business operation."

Those stories and the manner in which they're written are engrossing. Friendly and down-to-earth in tone—and occasionally even tongue-in-cheek— they're definitely reassuring for the home-improvement-bound reader. It's

THE STORY OF A KITCHEN INSPIRED BY A YACHT.

Not long ago, a couple walked into the Water & Fire Design Center and told us they had a vision — and they wanted us to make it a reality.

In loving detail, they described a stunning 56-foot yacht – the kind that immediately grabs your attention. Stately, classic, majestic, as its highly polished teak decks and brass finishings glisten in the sun. Every day, after exploring yet another idyllic deserted Caribbean island, they would find themselves below deck, basking in the luminous glow and comfort of the yacht's hand-polished, high-gloss mahogany interior.

Wouldn't it be nice, they thought, if they could take this beauty home with them? But, because a 56-foot yacht takes up slightly more living space than most people have, they did the next best thing: They turned to Water & Fire and worked with our design team to develop detailed drawings and renderings of the kitchen they had envisioned. Today, the inviting space, with its hand-polished, custom-made quartered mahogany cabinets,

Shingle style home in Manchester By-the-Sea, Massachusetts

is a faithful remembrance of that glorious Caribbean adventure.

Needless to say, a Water & Fire kitchen isn't the kind you pick out of a catalog or find at a typical showroom. There are no limits at Water & Fire. Our highly skilled and talented design staff makes sure you get what your heart desires. No matter what the inspiration — even if it's a 56-foot yacht glistening in the Caribbean sun — we help you realize your dreams.

WATER & FIRE
Inspired European Kitchens and Baths

38 Crafts Street Newton, MA 02458 866.387.6228 www.waterandfire.com

THE STORY OF A KITCHEN INSPIRED BY PROVENCE.

The renovation of this kitchen in a gracious New England townhouse was inspired by a family's love of Provence and fine European craftsmanship. Within the kitchen, carefully turned legs enhance the corners of the maple island. A custom mantle style canopy hood crowns the cooktop and frames a spectacular mosaic imported from Ravenna, Italy. All of these custom details capture a distinctly European feeling.

New England Townhouse in Saugus, Massachusetts

The family worked with our design team to develop detailed drawings and renderings of the kitchen of their dreams. We carefully refined the drawings, selected appliances, and supervised construction. The result? A custom European country kitchen, that reminds them of their beaucolic holiday in Provence.

Needless to say, a Water & Fire kitchen isn't the kind you pick out of a catalog or find at a typical showroom. There are no limits at Water & Fire. Our highly skilled and talented design staff makes sure you get what your heart desires, down to the last detail. No matter what the inspiration we help you realize your dreams.

WATER & FIRE
Inspired European Kitchens and Baths

38 Crafts Street Newton, MA 02458 866.387.6228 www.waterandfire.com

Full-page ads.

Ads communicate the custom capability of the staff and the business in general.

THE STORY OF A KITCHEN INSPIRED BY A COLOR.

The renovation of this loft kitchen was inspired by a couple's love of the color red and clean Italian design. The space is open, inviting and tailored to their personal style. Needless to say, a Water & Fire Kitchen isn't the kind you pick out of a catalog or find in a typical showroom. There are no limits at Water & Fire.

WATER & FIRE
Inspired European Kitchens and Baths

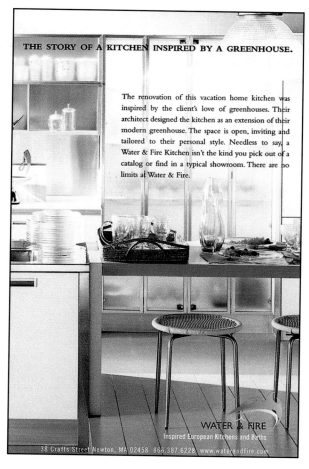

THE STORY OF A KITCHEN INSPIRED BY A GREENHOUSE.

The renovation of this vacation home kitchen was inspired by the client's love of greenhouses. Their architect designed the kitchen as an extension of their modern greenhouse. The space is open, inviting and tailored to their personal style. Needless to say, a Water & Fire Kitchen isn't the kind you pick out of a catalog or find in a typical showroom. There are no limits at Water & Fire.

WATER & FIRE
Inspired European Kitchens and Baths
38 Crafts Street Newton, MA 02458   866.387.6228   www.waterandfire.com

THE STORY OF A KITCHEN INSPIRED BY A FIREPLACE.

Not long ago, a couple visited the Water & Fire Design Center with an idea for their dream kitchen. They knew we could make their dream a reality. She told us about how, on their last trip to France, they had fallen in love.

With a fireplace.

It was a fireplace with a gorgeous carved-lime-stone mantel, its graceful presence the irresistible focal point of their 18th century hotel's suite.

Every day, after a walk through the exotic gardens of the French countryside, they would be lured back to the fireplace's warmth and comforting presence.

Tudor style manor house in Chestnut Hill, Massachusetts.

Wouldn't it be nice, they thought, if they could feel like this everyday? But, since most hotels frown on allowing guests to take home even a towel or two, they decided against asking about the fireplace.

They did, however, do the next best thing: They worked with our design team to develop detailed drawings and renderings of the kitchen of their dreams. We carefully refined the drawings, selected appliances, and supervised construction. The irresistible focal point? A cast-limestone surround for the cooktop, a faithful re-creation of their French countryside fireplace.

Needless to say, a Water & Fire kitchen isn't the kind you pick out of a catalog or find at a typical showroom. There are no limits at Water & Fire. Our highly skilled and talented design staff makes sure you get what your heart desires, down to the last detail. No matter what the inspiration – even if it's a fireplace in an 18th century French hotel – we help you realize your dreams.

WATER & FIRE
Inspired European Kitchens and Baths

38 Crafts Street Newton, MA 02458   866.387.6228   www.waterandfire.com

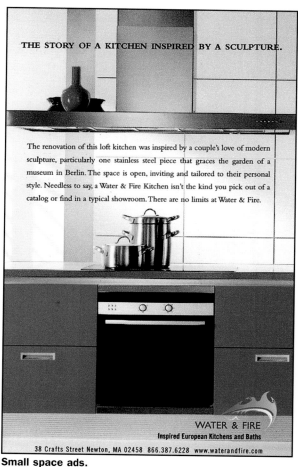

THE STORY OF A KITCHEN INSPIRED BY A SCULPTURE.

The renovation of this loft kitchen was inspired by a couple's love of modern sculpture, particularly one stainless steel piece that graces the garden of a museum in Berlin. The space is open, inviting and tailored to their personal style. Needless to say, a Water & Fire Kitchen isn't the kind you pick out of a catalog or find in a typical showroom. There are no limits at Water & Fire.

WATER & FIRE
Inspired European Kitchens and Baths
38 Crafts Street Newton, MA 02458   866.387.6228   www.waterandfire.com

Small space ads.

WATER & FIRE

The Storybook contains key statistics that help explain the project's cost.

THE STORY OF A KITCHEN INSPIRED

BY A RESTAURANT ON ITALY'S AMALFI COAST

This kitchen is in the home of a family that loves to cook. During a visit to the Water & Fire showroom, they shared the story of a memorable dining experience in Sant'Agata sui Due Golfi, a tiny village at the western tip of the Amalfi Coast. The food was superb and the chef prepared each meal in his well equipped kitchen with the help of what seemed like a cast of thousands. They wanted the same kind of kitchen in the new home they were building — a kitchen that could accommodate many cooks during family gatherings and holidays. They worked with our design team who produced drawings and selected appliances for this Amalfi inspired kitchen. A large island takes center stage. It has plenty of space for food preparation and a dedicated pasta making station. Iridescent glass tile and rope molding gables complete the space which is outfitted with a 48" Viking range. Needless to say, a Water & Fire kitchen isn't the kind you pick out of a catalog or find in a typical showroom. There are no limits at Water & Fire.

The custom backsplash was designed with Iridium glass tiles. It has a beautiful, iridescent quality that illuminates the back wall of the kitchen.

Two large professional sinks (30" x 12" deep) were added to accommodate even the largest pasta pots.

LOCATION
Newton, Massachusetts

HOME STATISTICS
Project: New Construction
Style: Brick Federalist
Size: 6,100 SF

KITCHEN STATISTICS
W&F Designer: Judy Gamble
Size: 17'X10'
Cabinetmaker: Rödl Kitchen Furniture

KITCHEN DETAILS
Solid White Birch Door
Two Custom Stains
Rope Molding Gables
Iridescent Glass Tile

Insert pages slip into this handsome folder.

interesting to see such long copy at a time when "people don't read." In this case, all those words work. And the fact that each ad starts with "The story of…" lets readers know right away that they're in for a "good read." Eight 4C ads—five full-page ads (including one for an event) and three small space ads—have been produced to date. "We have a fairly aggressive monthly schedule," Laidlaw pointed out. The ads have been running for a year and a half. The first six months the full-page ads ran. With the campaign established, it made sense to vary the full-page ads with more

Quotes from actual customers—more reassurance and right on strategy.

economical small space ads, which ran in the second rotation.

The media includes general interest as well as shelter books—*Boston Magazine, Boston Home & Garden, Boston Business Journal, Improper Bostonian, Boston Herald, Boston Globe, Woman's Day Kitchen & Baths, American Homestyle & Gardening* and *Better Homes & Garden.* Ads also run in the *Washington Post.* Asked why, Laidlaw explained that Hazilliades wants to reach some people who have homes in both DC and the Boston area. "It's a bit of a stretch, but he is very anxious to

develop clients outside of the Boston area—people who have homes in Nantucket or Martha's Vineyard."

Besides the ads, Water & Fire has a stunning brochure (referred to as "the storybook"). It contains individual pages that not only show great examples of what can be done, but contain detailed information, including comments from customers, to help demystify the design process. Available in store, the storybook is also distributed to architects and interior designers.

The latest undertaking was a four-day

in-store event, "Wine, Dine, Design" to benefit a local breast cancer initiative. Highlights included cooking demonstrations by local chefs and a silent auction. Orders placed anytime during the 100 days following the event had 10% of the sale going to benefit the fund.

In the works now (we show the first of three) is a series of postcard mailings— the first for the company. On the horizon: there's talk about opening another location.

WATER & FIRE

 Recently, a Montreal couple wanted to design a kitchen to accommodate multiple cooks. To do this they worked with our highly talented design team to develop drawings and renderings of their state-of-the-art kitchen. The space was designed to maximize the work flow of multiple cooks working in separate areas at the same time. White birch cabinets and natural stone surfaces enhance the overall warmth of the space, while wide-framed Euro-style Shaker cabinet doors allow for the easy access to the contents within. Needless to say, a Water & Fire kitchen isn't the kind you pick out of a catalog or find at a typical showroom. There are no limits at Water & Fire.

CALL 866.387.6228
FOR A DESIGN CONSULTATION.

At Water & Fire, we design and install custom built-in furniture for the most demanding and unique cabinetry projects. The knowledge and talent of our design and installation staff, our hands-on approach, the high quality of our products and our finishing process, make us the first choice of New England's finest architects and homebuilders.

WATER & FIRE
Inspired European Kitchens,
Baths & Fitted Rooms
38 Crafts Street
Newton, MA 02458

Telephone: 866.387.6228
Facsimile: 617.559.0522
E-mail: service@waterandfire.com
www.waterandfire.com

A series of direct mail postcards is the newest way to tell the story.

THE STORY OF A KITCHEN INSPIRED
BY 50 POTS AND PANS

WATER & FIRE
Inspired European Kitchens,
Baths & Fitted Rooms

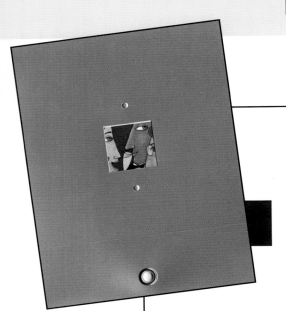

Invitation.

Join Water & Fire and Boston Magazine for

Wine. Dine. Design.

Enter the world of Custom European kitchen design and celebrate an evening of wine tastings and cooking presentations to benefit the Eva Brownman Breast Cancer Fund at the Dana-Farber Cancer Institute.

This festive evening will feature silent auction items, including a private dinner prepared by one of Boston's top chefs and luxury kitchen appliances. For directions, call 617.244.7006 or visit www.waterandfire.com.

Guest Chefs:
Ana Sortun, *Oleana*
Michael Leviton, *Lumiere*

Tuesday, December 3rd, 6:00 PM - 10:00 PM

WATER & FIRE

Water & Fire Showroom
38 Crafts Street, Newton
Complimentary valet parking provided.

RSVP 617.778.5757 or
aburrage@kortenhaus.com

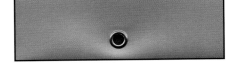

A benefit for the Eva Brownman Breast Cancer Fund at the Dana-Farber Cancer Institute.

Create A Showplace With Water & Fire. Make an appointment to design your kitchen or bath with one of our designers.*

Enjoy Your Own Personal Chef. Place a bid in our silent auction to have one of Boston's top chefs come to your home and prepare dinner for you and your guests!**

Bid On Luxury Kitchen Appliances. Asko washing equipment will be auctioned with the proceeds to benefit the Fund.

Wine. Dine. Design.

Join Water & Fire and Boston Magazine for a weeklong kitchen design and culinary event featuring cooking presentations, wine tastings, and the opportunity to see what Custom European kitchen design is all about.

Meet some of Boston's top chefs, including: Ana Sortun of Oleana, Cambridge; Michael Leviton of Lumiere, Newton; Peter McCarthy of EVOO, Cambridge; Laura Brennan of Café Umbra, South End; and Lee Napoli of Tea Tray in the Sky, Arlington. For more information about this event and directions to our showroom, visit our Web site at www.waterandfire.com.

Thursday, December 5 – Sunday, December 8
Water & Fire Showroom, 38 Crafts Street, Newton

WATER & FIRE   **Boston** Magazine

*10% of all sales go to the Eva Brownman Breast Cancer Fund at the Dana-Farber Cancer Institute
**All proceeds benefit the Eva Brownman Breast Cancer Fund at the Dana-Farber Cancer Institute

38 Crafts Street Newton, MA 02458 866.EUROBATH 866.387.6228 www.waterandfire.com

Full-page ad.

Enter the world of Custom European kitchen design and celebrate 4 days of wine tastings and cooking presentations to benefit the Eva Brownman Breast Cancer Fund at the Dana-Farber Cancer Institute.

Silent Auctions

This festive event will feature silent auction items, including a private dinner prepared by one of Boston's top chefs and luxury kitchen appliances.

Guest Chefs

Our guest chefs will include: Mark Allen, *Le Soir*; Laura Brennan of *Café Umbra*; Michael Leviton of *Lumiere*; Peter McCarthy of *EVOO*; Lee Napoli of *Tea Tray in the Sky*; and Ana Sortun of *Oleana*.

For More Information

For directions to our showroom and a schedule of events, call 617.244.7006 or visit www.waterandfire.com.

Thursday, December 5th through Sunday, December 8th
Water & Fire Showroom, 38 Crafts Street, Newton

Direct mail postcard.

The bottle of wine that was private labeled and given to guests.

POP.

Water & Fire, Newton, MA
MANAGING PARTNER: **Paul Hazilliades**
ADVERTISING AGENCY: **The Laidlaw Group,** Boston, MA
PRESIDENT: **Cindy Laidlaw**
CREATIVE DIRECTOR: **Cindy Laidlaw**
ART DIRECTOR: **Shawn Scott**
DESIGNER: **Cory Fanelli**
COPYWRITER: **Jeff Feingold**

A BrandPower Glossary

The following definitions are derived from the strategic concepts of *retail brand building* that are explored in the *BrandPower* case studies. They may be defined in different terms to describe other marketing concepts.

Added Value – Intangible attributes of a brand that are more than functional.

Appeal – A reason to buy given by the brand designed to motivate the consumer.

Attribute – A tangible feature of a product or a service as perceived by the consumer.

Benefit – A positive outcome perceived by the consumer through the use of a brand product or service.

Brand – A visual or verbal identity (unique name and/or graphic logo, symbol or trademark) used to make a product, person, company or a category stand out from the competition.

Brand Association – Attributes and benefits of a product, service or idea drawn from values and attitudes that already exist in the mind of the consumer. (See the Brandwidth II Model in *How to Use* **The Power of Retail Branding**.)

Brand Awareness – The ability of a consumer to recognize a brand by its attributes and benefits, as well as by its visual or verbal identification. (See the Brandwidth II Model in *How to Use* **The Power of Retail Branding**.)

Brand Building – The design and execution of a strategic plan for creating and communicating an image in the mind of the consumer that is different and "better" than its competition. Also known as **positioning**.

Brand Category – A "membership" in a group of well-known brands that have attributes and benefits with similar values that are relevant to the consumer.

Brand Concept Management – The process of monitoring and advancing everything that affects the equity of a brand.

Brand DNA – The most vital, intrinsic and consistent values of a brand to the consumer and to the company.

Brand Elements – The components of a brand that can be differentiated to create BrandPower: Brand Image, Shopper Image, Brand Channels and Brand Experience. (See the Brandwidth II Model in *How To Use* **The Power of Retail Branding**.)

Brand Equity – The long-time value of a brand's worth and importance to the consumer.

Brand Extension – The use of a known brand to launch a new product in a new category. (See Line Extension).

Brand Health – An evaluation of a brand's strength and fitness based on its value to the consumer over time.

Brand Image Positioning – Brand perception strategy that uses intangible appeals to consumer emotions, associations and values. (See the Brandwidth II Model in *How to Use* **The Power of Retail Branding**.)

Brand Leveraging – Extending a brand and developing co-brands that use and reinforce the brand's identity and integrity.

Brand Meaning – The brand's personality, price/quality/value and experiential connection to each customer. (See the Brandwidth II Model in *How to Use* **The Power of Retail Branding**.)

Brand Media Mix – In the strategic plan, media selected based on the media preferences of the target audience. (See the Brandwidth II Model in *How to Use* **The Power of Retail Branding**.)

BrandPower – The authors' term for an innovative retailer's strategy that dramatically differentiates the value of its store-as-a-brand, its customer-as-a-brand, its products and/or its services from the competition.

BrandPower Checklist – A guide for BrandPower case study that considers the retail marketing plan's situation analysis, brand objective, target audience, creative strategy, media strategy and brand building results evaluation.

Brand Strategy – A plan that describes how a brand will attain a marketing objective.

Brand Tactics – The communication tools and media activities used to implement strategies.

Brandwidth – The authors' term for synergizing strategic elements to create BrandPower. (See the Brandwidth II Model in *How to Use* **The Power of Retail Branding**.)

Brandwidth II Model – A graphic that describes the elements of BrandPower and their relationships to Brand Image, Shopper Image, Brand Channels and Brand Experience. (See the Brandwidth II Model in *How to Use* **The Power of Retail Branding**.)

Break Through Branding – As in other disciplines, having a breakthrough means having a new or sudden advance in knowledge or technique or breaking through a defensive obstruction. That is what BrandPower is all about – inventing new approaches and taking innovative strides to change the strategies and tactics of making the brand and the brand promise. This strategy requires going beyond the customer's expectations to deliver differences.

Channel – A distribution structure that enables goods and services to be delivered. A traditional or non-traditional medium through which communications can be sent.

Channel Branding – Integrating all channels of communications to develop a holistic approach to communicating with customers. From opt-in fashion newsletters to personal shopper PDA services, the range of new tools for building emotional connections with the brand is exploding.

Co-Branding – Retailers are inventing a new era of brand associations and tie-ins between brands and celebrities, musicians, sports stars and teams, charities, artists, and other like-minded brands. Special events retail marketing is now an in-house necessity for the inventive retailer.

Clone Branding – Cloning the brand relies on "brand DNA" analysis to transfer those genes that will impart character, personality and performance to new brands from known brand successes.

Commitment – A brand's promise to deliver the best performance to consumers, their cultures and their communities.

Consumer – A potential customer. The ultimate user of a product or service.

Customer – An individual who is now buying and using a brand. A regular or frequent buyer.

Creative Brief – A checklist to prepare a positioning strategy statement that identifies and describes the market situation analysis, competitive analysis, target audience, brand power strategy, creative execution and results evaluation.

Customer Centric – Strategic planning for marketing and communications where the customer is at the center of all aspects of the planning and execution processes.

Customer Relationship Management (CRM) – The structured effort to create, maintain and monitor relationships with customers through shared values, customized communications and personalized product/service benefits.

Database Marketing — A system that gathers and interprets behavioral data on customers and prospects.

Database Mining – Selecting specific behavioral data to target selected consumers or groups with like interests or other factors.

Destination Branding – Creating a U.S.P. that establishes that *this* is the place to buy, e.g., strategically building the store-as-a-brand desired by consumers.

Differentiation – Distinct elements of superiority or uniqueness for a company, product or service as perceived by the consumer.

Direct Marketing – A non-store distribution system to sell products, services or ideas directly to the consumer.

Direct Response Advertising – Advertising designed to elicit a consumer response or to make a sale.

Emotional Appeal – A reason to buy given by the brand based on the consumer's aspirations and desires.

Events Branding – Sponsorships, tie-ins, expos, co-branding events that leverage the brand meaning. Typically coordinated with consumers' interests in music, sports, charities….

Experiential Branding – Using the consumer's lifestyle and experiences with the brand as the brand's key benefit and connection. (See the Brandwidth II Model in *How to Use* **The Power of Retail Branding**.)

Fitness Branding – How healthy is the brand? The "health" of a brand is its ability to communicate its fitness to offer choice and satisfaction through seamless service, merchandise assortments, personalized size and style information. The fitness workout includes building competitive *BrandPower* based on unique products, value prices and outstanding service.

Global Brand – A brand that has similar appeals and values to consumers in many countries and cultures throughout the world.

In-Store Media – Advertising and promotion media inside of a store with point-of-purchase display, signage, murals, video walls, kiosks.

Integrated Marketing Communications (IMC) – Marketing management that employs a full mix of communication tactics to build Brandwidth.

Internal Branding – The application of marketing and branding strategies **inside** the company is used to encourage customer-focused values. A strong "employee-as-the-brand" culture helps communicate a brand integrity message to customers, building belief and trust.

Line Extension – The strategy of assigning an existing brand name to a different product in the same category. (See Brand Extention.)

LTCV, LifeTime Customer Value – The process of evaluating what the long-term loyalty of an individual customer is worth to the brand.

Market Segmentation – The process of identifying target audiences with similar motivations and predictable responses to appeals.

Marketing Plan – A written statement or program of strategies, creative execution, and evaluation of a campaign to attain a marketing objective.

Marketing Public Relations (MPR) – Strategically planned activities, events and sponsorships designed to make a Brand "stand out" within the target market's community.

Matched Media – Strategically selecting the specific media that matches the target customers' media usage and habits.

Media/Medium – The communications channels through which advertiser's messages can be carried to their intended audiences.

Media Mix Options – The customer's own plan for selecting only those media that fit her needs and lifestyle.

Media Plan – A statement of how media, as well as which media, will be implemented to attain marketing objectives. Includes how the media budget will be spent.

Multi-Channel Retailing – Retailers using Web, catalog, and the physical store to provide "seamless service" to their customers.

PDA, Personal Digital Assistant – Hand held device that enables one to communicate interactively with a database.

Position – The comparative perception of a brand's appeals to a consumer segment.

Positioning – The process of creating perceptions of a brand in the mind of consumers that challenge its competition.

Product – A reference to a brand that describes its function, service and benefits.

Profile – A list of characteristics or descriptions identifying prospective customer types, including interests, preferences, lifestyles, buying habits, … to better serve customers with a brand's offer.

Promotion – The mix of communication activities used to get response from a target audience. Also an abbreviation for Sales Promotion. Sometimes used to describe special offers to increase traffic and sales.

Promotional Mix – Advertising, direct mar-keting, sales promotion, publicity/public relations, special events, visual merchandising, and personal selling.

Rational Appeal – A reason to buy given by the brand based on information for the functional and utilitarian needs of the consumer.

Repositioning – Creating and communicating new perceptions of an existing brand for new or changing target audiences.

Role Branding – Communicating the image of the target consumer featuring her own lifestyle and persona. The strategy's focus is consumer centric with the **customer-as-a-brand**. Incorporating the way the customer brands herself – for example: aspirational *"id"* or perhaps the way the company brands itself through positional *"ID,"* identification with the customer.

Sales Promotion – Activities that provide extra incentives to encourage the consumer to come to a point of sale and to buy.

Spiral Branding – The development of a program to *surround* the consumer with a synergy of communications, especially in new and unexpected places. Also known as Surround Branding. (See the Brandwidth II Model in *How to Use* **The Power of Retail Branding**.)

Sponsorship – When an advertiser is responsible for producing or funding a program in exchange for the exclusive or co-branding right to air commercials during that program or present their advertising at an event.

Strategy – A statement of how an objective will be attained.

Tactic – A specific action that is directed by an objective and its strategy.

Target Audience – A common segment of people that has the right profiles for the brand. The profiled group for whom the *brand is right*.

U.S.P., Unique Selling Proposition – An attribute, benefit or commitment of a brand that is uniquely different and more appealing than its competition. U.S.P. can also stand for: Unique Styling Persona, Unique Service Personality, and Unique Strategic Positioning.

Viral Branding – A program designed to encourage customers to communicate (spread) the brand's value to others. Before it was "programmed" into the marketing plan, it was known as "word-of-mouth advertising." Internet chat rooms, planned special events and one-to-one promotions are often employed. (See the Brandwidth II Model in *How to Use* **The Power of Retail Branding**.)